FAMILY *Blood*

The True Story of the Yom Kippur Murders: One Family's Greed, Love, and Rage

MARVIN J. WOLF *and* LARRY ATTEBERY

HarperCollins*Publishers*

HarperCollins books may be purchased for educational, business, or sales promotional use. For information please write: Special Markets Department, HarperCollins Publishers, Inc., 10 East 53rd Street, New York, NY 10022.

FIRST EDITION

Designed by George J. McKeon

Library of Congress Cataloging-in-Publication Data

Wolf, Marvin J.
    Family blood : the true story of the Yom Kippur murders : one family's greed, love and rage / Marvin J. Wolf and Larry Attebery — 1st ed.
      p.   cm.
    ISBN 0-06-016569-3
    1. Murder—California—Los Angeles—Case studies. 2. Woodman, Gerald, d. 1985. I. Attebery, Larry. II. Title. III. Ninja Murders.
HV6534.L7W65   1993
364.1'523'0979494—dc20   92-56228

93 94 95 96 97 ❖ / RRD 10 9 8 7 6 5 4 3 2 1

For Carol and for Victoria

Contents

1 Last Supper 1

2 Seven-foot Ninjas 22

3 Sins of the Fathers 36

4 Suspects 44

5 Family Business 49

6 Alibis 63

7 Plastics 76

8 Gut Feelings 88

9 Manchester 95

10 Showtime 107

11 Glory Days 115

12 The Big O 130

13 Family Drama 138

14 The Homicks 157

15 A Fish in the Desert   170

16 Leads, Dead Ends, Blind Alleys   184

17 Clan Clash   193

18 Cutthroats, Swindlers, and RICO   209

19 Pledges   219

20 Conversations   226

21 Riding a Tiger   234

22 Endgames   251

23 Arrests   265

24 Trials   282

25 Confessions   299

Epilogue   316

Acknowledgments   319

"I just want to say one word to you. Just one word: Plastics."
"Exactly how do you mean that?"
"There's a great future in plastics."
    —MR. MCGUIRE (Walter Brooke) to Ben Braddock (Dustin Hoffman), *The Graduate*, Embassy Films, 1967

"I'd guess a thousand guys came up to me and said, 'Plastics,' like they thought they were the only one who saw the movie. Shit, maybe it was ten thousand guys."
    —STEWART WOODMAN, 1992

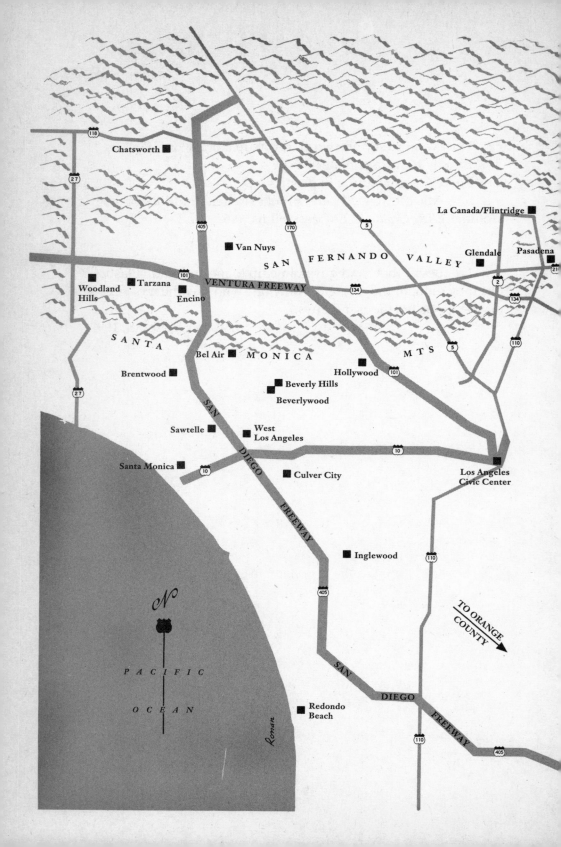

Last Supper

SEPTEMBER 25, 1985

More exclusive even than adjacent Beverly Hills, Bel Air's rolling, landscaped, perpetually green lawns define an expansive yet tightly defended enclave where spectacular homes with breathtaking views nestle along canyons shaded by towering eucalypti. Here live the most bankable movie stars, big-league sports superstars, heavyweight studio executives, power-broker agents, oil magnates, moguls of all manner, and more than a few flush with inherited or married money. Five-million-dollar châteaus are not the least unusual in Bel Air, where garages are often bigger than an ordinary Los Angeles tract home and driveways are casually littered with Jaguars, Mercedes-Benzes, Porsches, and Rolls-Royces. The occasional Toyotas, Chevrolets, and Volkswagens on the streets belong mostly to hired help.

From the west, Bel Air is accessible via Sepulveda Boulevard, Los Angeles County's longest street, where it snakes through the Santa Monica Mountains in the shadow of the San Diego Freeway's ten frenetic lanes. A mile beyond Sunset Boulevard, well below Sepulveda Pass, twists Moraga Drive. A block east of Sepulveda, Moraga becomes a private road guarded by iron gates and armed security officers in a glassed-in booth.

About a half mile beyond the gates is a gracious, two-story

Tudor mansion, the home of Muriel and Louis Jackson. And on this particular September 25th, as late afternoon's golden sunlight melted into slanting rays of amber, as pools of mountain shadows gathered in the hollows to herald the end of Yom Kippur, the Jewish Day of Atonement, the Jacksons' sumptuous home began to fill with friends and relatives. When the sun had set, all would celebrate the end of this solemn day with a hearty meal shared with virtually their entire family—sisters and their spouses, children, grandchildren, cousins, and a handful of close friends.

The Jacksons' kitchen was enormous, three times the size of an ordinary one. Equipped with restaurant-sized refrigerators, mammoth stoves and ovens, oversized sinks, industrial-capacity dishwashers, and virtually every culinary appliance available, it reflected Muriel Jackson's lifelong passion for cooking and her resources to feed, on occasion, a small army.

Muriel employed several servants and had hired two extra kitchen helpers for this family gathering, but she preferred to do most of the actual cooking herself, leaving only the cleanup for hired hands. As the day faded, the doorbell chimed endlessly. Muriel dispatched her butler to greet arriving guests. As her expansive house began to fill with family, Muriel and two of her three sisters, Vera and Sybil, retired to the kitchen to make final preparations for the traditional break-the-fast dinner.

More than fifty people were expected, virtually all of whom had obeyed the commandment to fast since the previous sundown. In order that the holiest day of the Jewish year be devoted entirely to prayer and introspection, work and eating are forbidden on Yom Kippur. So, the food Muriel's ravenous guests would consume to break their fasts had all been prepared a day earlier. Muriel and her sisters had chopped, sliced, peeled, simmered, basted, boiled, steamed, fried, baked, and roasted Himalayas of comestibles, including vegetable, potato, macaroni, and Waldorf salads, traditional fare such as chopped liver, gefilte fish, blintzes, creamed herring, and salmon loaf, cauldrons of mashed, fried, and boiled potatoes, hearty entrees of roast turkey and beef brisket, and, as always, Muriel's chicken matzoh ball soup.

All four sisters—Vera (at 63 the oldest), Muriel, Sybil, and the baby, the now-tardy Gloria, forty-five—had toiled for hours preparing the feast.

Thin-boned and delicately feminine, her oval face still smooth-skinned in old age, Vera was a petite, elfin figure beneath a cloud of white, silken hair. A galaxy of sparkling diamonds—pendant, bracelet, earrings, and rings—beamed back the rays of a crystal chandelier. Vera tied on a lacy apron to protect her ruffled silk blouse and dark skirt, but she seemed distracted as she bent over a huge crystal serving bowl heaped with chopped herring. Scattering a final pinch of salt over the bowl, Vera straightened up, wiped her hands, then pulled a tissue from an apron pocket.

"This is ready," she said. "Now what about the soup?"

Muriel and Sybil, engrossed in their own tasks, did not look up to notice the tears Vera dabbed from her eyes. She pushed the thoughts of her son away. There was work to do, and Vera could share her good news later, at the table.

In the den, three husbands—Vera's Gerald, Sybil's Sidney, and Muriel's Louis—"call me Lou"—watched the ABC news on Channel Seven. Gerald Woodman craved a drink. A splash of Cutty on the rocks would do, but he wouldn't ask, not with Lou Jackson, Mr. Religious, right there, fasting. Gerald would wait just a little longer, until sundown.

Gerald—Gerry to everyone—was sixty-seven, a short, powerfully built man with a British accent, not the kind usually heard in movies. "Did I tell you I'm lifting weights now?" barked Gerry to the room at large. "I'll be the next Schwarzenegger. Imagine, an *alte kocker* [old fart] like me, with muscles. My doctor suggested it. Helps to strengthen my heart."

Gerry rolled up the short sleeve of his shirt to expose his upper arm. He squeezed his fist, made the biceps jump. "Not so bad, eh, Lou," he bellowed to the quiet, stooped man relaxing in a La-Z-Boy rocker. "Might do you good, too, going to the gym. Or have one built here, you've got room."

"Gerry, you never fail to amaze me," said Lou, turning back to watch the news.

As the house filled with people, the living room became the center of chaotic juvenile gravity, filled with children of all ages. The teenagers talked excitedly, gesturing expressively with their hands, their faces animated and lively. Younger children squealed with excitement, chasing and dodging each other across the thick carpets and between floral sofas and Queen Anne chairs, stopping only to argue the rules of the game. A magnificent cherrywood coffee table served as home base, its surface already covered with sticky fingerprints as a few toddlers, too young to fast, nibbled on thick slices of bread or purloined sweets from the overflowing bowls Muriel had scattered everywhere.

The older generations—attractive and confident professionals ranging from their twenties to their sixties—lounged on couches and exchanged family gossip, oblivious to the clamorous chatter, raucous laughter, and piercing shrieks. They were a sleek, well-fed, exceptionally well-dressed group, success—defined by these Southern Californians as wealth and influence—radiating from every pore.

As the condor soars, it's about four miles from the Jacksons' luxurious Bel Air home to the corner of Butler and Santa Monica Boulevard in Sawtelle, a trip, in light traffic, of perhaps eight minutes via surface streets. Measured in economic terms, however, there is an astronomical distance between the lavish opulence of Bel Air's great wealth and Sawtelle's comfortable middle-class life.

Santa Monica Boulevard runs east and west beneath the San Diego Freeway. With traffic signals on almost every corner, it's the slowest-flowing street in the entire county. From the freeway to the ocean, Santa Monica is a succession of small specialty shops, minimalls, smallish, low-slung office buildings, homey restaurants and cafes, gas stations, supermarkets, art film theatres, and local government offices. Side streets, running north and south from Santa Monica Boulevard, are a jumble of flimsy, stuccoed apartment buildings, none over three stories, and a few private residences, most of them single-story frame structures built just before or just after World War II.

Even to its own residents, Sawtelle is an almost invisible community; most prefer to think of themselves as living in West Los Angeles. But the pocket between upscale Brentwood in the foothills to the north and the city of Santa Monica to the west is officially Sawtelle, named for an early merchant. Sawtelle Boulevard, a north-south thoroughfare adjacent to the freeway, is overwhelmingly a street of small Japanese restaurants and grocers, Japanese-American–owned real estate and insurance agencies and specialty shops offering assorted Japonica.

Despite a slightly run-down appearance, the streets of Sawtelle are mostly clean. The owners of apartment buildings are likely to invest in flowering shrubs or plant fragrant blooms in interior atriums and along walkways. Automobiles parked at curbside are, more often than not, late models in good condition. This is one of Southern California's safer middle-class neighborhoods, a haven for white-collar employees of the sprawling University of California, Los Angeles (UCLA) campus, the nearby Veteran's Administration Hospital, the vast, multi-agency Federal Building, or one of the myriad advertising and public relations agencies or television production companies that dot Los Angeles's West Side.

Concealed from passersby on Santa Monica Boulevard is one of the city's almost forgotten cultural icons. On narrow, black-topped, residential Butler Avenue, a few yards south of the boulevard, on the south-facing brick wall of a two-story building next to the post office, is the faded remnant of *The Isle of California*, a 1972 mural by the Los Angeles Fine Arts Squad.

The enormous painting depicts a furiously wave-wracked stretch of rocky coastline beneath an azure, cloud-dotted sky. In the foreground, offshore, atop a sheer, massive pile of fractured brown rock, is the shattered remains of a familiarly mysterious structure. Only when the viewer's eye works its way to the top of the painting is a recognizable object discerned: an overhead sign from the San Diego Freeway. Suddenly the painting's scale is revealed. The shattered structure emerges as a ruined section of freeway. One is confronted with an apocalyptic vision of Los Angeles after The Big One, the massive, mystically inevitable temblor that many imagine will one day shake most of the state into the sea.

There is no evidence that any of the men gathered at dusk—just past six-thirty P.M.—at the corner of Butler and Santa Monica had ever gazed on the mural, much less understood it, but it would be astonishing if at least one, who lived nearby and often used pay phones on this corner, hadn't pondered the irony of the painting's message of sudden, violent transformation from dynamic civilization to abandoned ruin.

The leader of the group on the corner was Steven Homick, forty-five, who concealed a thirst for violence beneath a facade of facile charm. Steve sometimes earned his living as a Las Vegas roofing contractor and cabinetmaker. At other times he was an airline and jewelry store security consultant, and occasionally did fieldwork to discourage union activity among hotel employees. He also sold guns and cocaine. Steve was a failed minor league baseball player, a fired casino dealer—and a former Los Angeles police officer.

Steve's brother, Robert, was ten years younger. Robert, who preferred to be called Jesse, was an ursine creature. He sported a full black beard, in contrast to Steve's brown hair and clean-shaven cheeks. Except for his bulk and blue eyes, Robert bore only a vague resemblance to Steve. An unemployed lawyer and welfare cheat, he eked out a living as a part-time collection agent and as a monumentally successful shoplifter and book thief. Jesse lived in an apartment two blocks away.

The Homicks were big men. Steve, six feet one inch tall and 205 pounds, was taller, but Jesse, six feet even, was much heavier. Both towered over Tony "Sonny" Majoy. But forty-seven-year-old Sonny, all of five nine, stood out in a crowd because of his bushy snow-white hair. Sonny's arrest record included busts for sodomy, sex with minors, and aggravated assault and battery. Now he was a video salesman in the San Fernando Valley.

"You fucking moron!" hissed Steve, impaling Jesse with a look calculated to freeze mercury. "I broke my ass sending you to law school—and you're *still* a fucking moron. Shit, you're not even a moron. What's worse than a moron, an idiot?"

"Keep it down," said Jesse, glancing around nervously. A steady stream of pedestrians meandered along Santa Monica Boulevard, and just a block south on Butler was a police station. Every few minutes a black-and-white cruised by. "Calm down," said Jesse. Unlike his companions, who were in slacks and sport shirts, Jesse was dressed, as usual, in dark, baggy trousers and a T-shirt, none too clean, with a picture of a white-topped ocean breaker cascading across his massive chest. "It was just a little accident. A fender-bender. Nobody got hurt."

Barely able to restrain himself, Steve grabbed Jesse's shirt and pulled his brother's head until their faces were almost touching.

"An accident-on-purpose? Nineteen years of school and you don't have the brains of a small dog. I swear, Pepper—that mutt—is smarter than you," Steve hissed, the massive cords in his neck standing out. "You have shit for brains. I'll tell you what your fucking problem is, you've had too much education. Sometimes I can't believe we're brothers."

Steve shoved Jesse away. It was true: he often wondered if Jesse had been left on the doorstep. Certainly, few brothers could be less alike. Steve moved with the grace of an athlete, and when he built furniture, the wood seemed almost alive in his hands. Around a construction site or working on something special for the mobbed-up thugs he hung around, Steve had earned a reputation as a problem solver, a man who made things happen. He reveled in the fast-paced life that Las Vegas offered to those with money.

Steve thought about Jesse, letting his rage feed on disgust. Jesse held degrees in psychology and law, but six years after passing the tough California bar exam, he dressed like a homeless bum, rented a room in a tiny apartment from some greasy foreigner, and couldn't even hold down a bank teller's job, much less find a position in a law firm. All Jesse wanted to do was go surfing, listen to rock and roll, work out at the gym, and hole up in his room with his books and magazines. Reads everything and knows nothing, thought Steve.

But Jesse, after all, was still his baby brother. Steve trusted him, and there were few people whom Steve totally trusted. When this job came up—Jesse, of course, had known all about it, and, as always, needed money—against his first inclinations, Steve had brought his brother in to help.

And now the idiot had gone and run into some joker's car coming out of the very alley where Steve and Sonny would be working in a few hours.

Steve willed himself to let go of anger, to focus on the job at hand. What would Jason Bourne, superhero of Robert Ludlum's fictional epics, do here? he asked himself, and he felt the madness recede, control returning.

"So the cops came?" said Steve, his voice calm.

"Nah. But the guy took off, so that makes it a hit-and-run.

Otherwise they won't even take a report, not unless someone's injured," said Jesse.

"What the fuck could possibly be on your mind?" spat Steve, angry all over again. "Ramming a guy's car in that alley. You must be the stupidest shit in the whole world. Right, Sonny?"

Sonny Majoy had been hanging back, over by the pay phones, listening. He saw no point in responding to a question like that: Sonny knew the Homicks well enough to know that only Steve was allowed to pick on Jesse. He just shrugged at Steve.

Suddenly hungry, Steve glanced at his watch. Almost seven. It would be completely dark soon, and there was much to do.

"Come on," said Steve. "Let's get going. Someplace around here to eat, Jesse? Someplace quick?"

Jesse pointed down the street, and the three men crossed at the light, then trooped a short block east to Delores', a fifties landmark with carpets and waitresses both colorful and worn out. The menu was a mixture of deli and hash house, nothing fancy or expensive, everything edible. They ordered New York strip steaks, french fries, and milk shakes, food, Steve thought, that would stick to their ribs. It was going to be a long, hard night, and he didn't want anyone pooping out from hunger.

It almost broke her heart, but Vera Woodman had to admit that the table her sister Muriel set was magnificent. Muriel's imported, lead-crystal serving bowls were heaped with all the delectable home-made treats the sisters had labored over. The wine goblets, glass-ware, and fine bone china were elegantly framed by an immaculate Irish linen tablecloth. Muriel's heavy sterling silverware reflected the warm light of the dining room's crystal chandelier.

Vera sighed, remembering better days.

For more than twenty years it had been Vera's home at which the clan gathered at Yom Kippur and Passover. And what a home! A sprawling trilevel, half hidden among a grove of eucalypti, with a huge, free-form swimming pool sparkling in the dappled sunlight of the back yard. How she had loved hosting the family, working with the housekeeper, the maids, and the other servants for days before to ensure that the whole house practically shivered with cleanliness, grandly welcoming her sisters and their children—the whole *mishpocha*, or clan. It was lovely, the house echoing to the shouts of grandchildren. It made her whole life, all her suffering and disappointments, seem worthwhile.

But that was then, thought Vera, and this is now. A year earlier she and Gerry, her husband of forty-five years, had been forced into bankruptcy. The house and most of its fabulous furnishings went to creditors.

And now the family gathered at Muriel's.

Vera loved her sister, cared about her deeply, but she felt robbed every time she realized that the role of clan matriarch had shifted. Muriel was now queen bee. Muriel was more reserved, more decorous. Vera thought that the parties and get-togethers at her own home were really a lot more fun. Gerry was in his prime back then, before all the trouble. He was outrageously funny, raucous as a gymnasium full of monkeys, cracking awful jokes that had people rolling out of their chairs with hysterical laughter.

Muriel's husband, Lou, was a fine man, thought Vera, but he just wasn't as lively as her own Gerry. Nobody was, really. He was a star, one of a kind, the center of a universe that he pulled around with him, enveloping people in his aura, having everything his own way, no matter what.

Before the coronary and the family heartbreak that followed. Vera bit her lip and reminded herself: the past is past. It was better to live in the present, to enjoy the grandchildren climbing into their seats around Muriel's massive oak table. If only all her own grandchildren could be here!

Vera brought herself back to the moment. She reminded herself to be grateful for what she did have. Gerry could never be his old self, she knew, but that was probably for the best. In the meantime, whatever time they had left together was getting more pleasant every day. Lately Gerry seemed solicitous, even, if a little tentatively, romantic.

Vera recalled a recent afternoon they spent together in Palisades Park, a narrow strip of grass and trees along the lip of the towering palisades that bar the sea from downtown Santa Monica. She had packed a picnic lunch, and they ate on a bench, basking in the mild afternoon sunshine. On the way back to the car, Gerry had given her hand a squeeze.

Smiling, Vera slipped into the chair next to her husband. Mothers shushed children, and around the table there was a moment, a bare instant, when the hush was almost palpable.

"*Baruch atoh adonai, eluhainu melech ha'olom, ha motzi lechem min ha-auretz,*" chanted Lou Jackson, and the others joined in: "Blessed art thou, O Lord our God, King of the Universe, who has brought forth bread from the earth."

Lou reached for an enormous challah and tore off a piece of the chewy, pale yellow egg bread. He picked up a sterling silver shaker and sprinkled a few grains of salt on the bread, then bit off a piece and chewed. Around the table hungry men, women, and children tore into the challah with gusto. The fast of Yom Kippur was over, and it was time to eat.

Vera, like her husband, had been born in England, and although both had lived in America for nearly half a century, neither were citizens of their adopted country. That suited Gerry; he always said that when the Internal Revenue Service came after him, he would just get on a plane and go back home to Manchester. It suited Vera in a different way: she thought of herself as an Old Country wife, a woman whose life was defined by her family, and chiefly her husband.

"What do you want, Gerry?" asked Vera, lifting his plate.

"Everything," said Gerry.

Vera began ladling food onto his plate.

"Don't be stingy with the chopped herring! God knows Muriel made enough."

After gobbling his steak, Jesse, who ate at Delores' often, wanted cherry pie, baked fresh daily. All three men ordered a piece. Jesse bolted his piece down in four bites, scarlet juice dribbling out of his mouth to stain his beard. Because there was work to do, Steve had forbidden even a single beer, so the trio washed the tart-sweet pie down with cups of coffee. As he had several times during the meal, Steve glanced at his watch.

Seven-thirty. Time to rock and roll.

While Sonny and Jesse went to urinate, Steve tossed three singles on the table for a tip, nodded to the waitress, then strolled to the cashier and paid the bill. Sweeping everything into his pocket, he scarcely noticed if the change was correct, his mind racing nervously through his plan for the night.

Steve wished he had better radios. Those damned walkie-talkies the Professor had loaned him were next to worthless. Maybe he'd better try them one more time before the job. They might work better at night.

Mike Dominguez was at the motel, a few blocks away. Steve decided to pick him up about eight-thirty.

Dominguez, sometimes known by his prison handle, "Baby A," was a fleshy, olive-skinned, dark-haired man of average height who appeared younger than his twenty-six years. He was a burglar, but occasionally worked as a roofer.

Steve decided to go over things with Dominguez one more time, just to make sure he had it right. Mike was a good man, within his limitations, but he didn't always understand things the first time.

Dominguez didn't do a lot of deep thinking. He hid his shallow intellect behind a wall of silence, earning a reputation as an enigma. Unlike Steve, who rarely missed a chance to expound upon his many adventures, Mike did not boast about his night work. In fact, he said very little about anything.

Steve liked that. Dominguez's silent quality gave Steve confidence that no matter what dirty little job Mike was asked to do, if the cops ever nailed him for it, Mike would never roll over and snitch on Steve, not even to save himself. Steve seldom bet, but he would put his life on that.

On the other hand, Steve knew that Mike wasn't up to handling a real big job on his own. He'd fucked up the hit on that broad in Vegas, put five into her boyfriend and the guy just ran away to call the cops. Mike was lucky to have gotten away with that, but he had cost Steve a fat fee. So Mike's punishment was to be demoted to lookout for this one.

Before picking up Mike, Steve decided, he'd have to deal with Jesse. Now that he'd gone and rammed that car, Jesse was out for the actual hit. No way he could let him be near the condo when it went down—Jesse had to stay away. That meant Steve and Sonny would be in the underground garage with nobody close by to give warning. They'd have to risk it.

Finally, he reminded himself to double-check the guns.

After a brief huddle in the restaurant's narrow parking lot, Sonny, following Steve's orders, went across the street to Steve's rented gold Camaro, took one of the Professor's radios from the trunk, and handed the other two to Steve. Steve climbed into the passenger seat of Jesse's battered blue-green 1960 Buick, shoving empty cardboard boxes into the backseat with the others.

"How the fuck can you live like this?" growled Steve, angry again at how his brother managed to screw up everything he touched. "When are you gonna get rid of this damn trash," he raged, indicating the boxes piled high in the backseat.

Jesse mumbled something about recycling, then wisely shut up.

Majoy, driving the Camaro, pulled up behind the Buick, ending the conversation, and Jesse made a right out of the parking lot onto Purdue, then stopped at the corner of Santa Monica to wait for the light. The boulevard was jammed, as usual, and it took them almost five minutes to reach Sepulveda, less than half a mile away. Threading their way through the heavy traffic near the Federal Building, they drove steadily north alongside a freeway still choked with traffic headed for the Valley.

With the Camaro following, the Buick turned right on Moraga Drive, then swept up the long, curving street until they reached a set of massive wrought-iron gates some twenty feet high. A uniformed security guard, a revolver in his polished leather holster, was visible inside the booth.

Jesse drove almost to the booth. Without stopping, he pulled the car into a U-turn. Majoy followed. At the bottom of the street, Steve told Jesse to turn left into the parking lot of the Chevron station next to a restaurant on the southeast corner of Sepulveda and Moraga. Jesse parked the Buick while Majoy got out of the Camaro, walked around, and eased into its passenger seat.

Jesse got out of the Buick and Steve handed him a walkie-talkie. He ran Jesse through the routine again: when he saw the beige Mercedes turn south on Sepulveda, he was to call Mike on the radio.

Steve slid behind the Camaro's wheel. In his mirror he watched Jesse standing in the parking lot, the radio crammed into the pocket of his shorts, with only the plastic-coated antenna sticking out. It looked like a cellular telephone. Jesse looked like a bull kicked out of a china shop.

Steve pulled into traffic as a well-dressed, middle-aged couple in a big new car pulled off Sepulveda and into the lot. The woman riding in the front passenger seat glanced at Jesse curiously, then at the battered Buick with the Nevada plates. Jesse ignored her.

Steve drove a half mile down Sepulveda to Church Lane, where he turned right and went under the freeway, then curved around and drove to Sunset Boulevard, where he turned right. Sunset here is a four-lane blacktop meandering toward the Pacific Ocean, following the contours of foothill canyons in broad, sweeping curves. This is Brentwood, a genteel community extending from the canyons down to Sawtelle and filled with expensive single-family homes, pricey condominiums, and high-security apartment buildings.

At Barrington Avenue, Steve turned left through Brentwood Village, a series of low, rambling brick buildings housing a post office, specialty shops, and restaurants. Passing a Little League field and tennis courts, he drove carefully through the heavy traffic. At the stop sign guarding San Vicente Boulevard he halted. He eyed the bus shelter across the street.

After waiting for traffic to clear, Steve turned right—west—on San Vicente Boulevard and drove two short blocks to Bundy. Sonny's car was inconspicuous in the parking lot in front of Vicente Foods, a local supermarket. Steve pulled into the lot to let Sonny out.

"Nine o'clock, Westgate and the alley. Got it?"

"I'll be there," said Sonny.

"Gonna leave your car in the lot, or put it on the street?"

"Nobody will notice it in the lot."

"Sure you can find your way back here on foot?"

"No sweat," said Majoy. "Walked it once, drove it twice. See you in the alley at nine."

Two blocks below San Vicente, the old creek bed now called Bundy Drive takes a hairpin turn, twisting from due east to southwest. In the middle of this arc, on the left, is the mouth of Gorham Avenue, which leads back two blocks to San Vicente. In the Buick, Steve turned left from Bundy onto Gorham, coasting to a stop three buildings from the corner, in front of an ostentatious, three-story, twenty-seven-unit condominium. Brentwood Place is at 11939, on the north side of Gorham. Steve held the walkie-talkie to his lips, pressing a button. "I'm here, can you hear me?"

"I hear. You hear me okay?" Jesse's voice crackled through the tinny speaker. It wasn't clear like the TV cop shows, but Steve could understand what Jesse was saying.

Steve found a place to park and walked up Gorham, turning to climb a few steps to the front door of 11939. The glass door opens into a spacious vestibule; access to the interior is controlled by an electrically activated inner door that can be buzzed open by residents. The vestibule wall is lined with twenty-seven doorbell buttons, one for each unit.

Squinting in the dim light, Steve peered at the rows of names, looking for "Woodman." Finding the right button, he pressed it and waited.

Nothing happened. Waiting a few minutes, he pressed again. Still there was no answer. The Woodmans were gone, just as they were supposed to be.

Satisfied, Steve walked back to the Camaro, cranked the engine, and headed a mile east to the Westwood Inn, on Wilshire, to pick up Mike Dominguez. Majoy would stay out of sight until just before show time. He was from the old school, a real pro, and saw no reason for anyone except Steve and Jesse, whom he knew anyway, to know he was involved. Humoring him, Steve kept Dominguez away from Sonny. Unless Mike had seen Sonny in Jesse's car after that fender-bender earlier in the evening, he wouldn't even know what Sonny looked like.

Although he had never voted in an American election, Gerry Woodman was a great admirer of Ronald Reagan. Somewhere between the challah and dessert, Gerry launched into a nonstop monologue, praising Reagan to everyone at the table.

"A brilliant man," said Gerry. "The public doesn't know how brilliant. Look what he's done. Look how proud the country was after Grenada. He really showed Castro. Right there, he let everyone in the world know that they can't push us around anymore. And now he's getting those lazy good-for-nothings off welfare. If they won't work, they shouldn't eat. This is America! Anyone can find work. And if you work hard—very hard—well, anyone can get rich. Look at me, I came to this country with nothing, just a boy, a young *pisher*. And no one gave me a damn thing."

Vera had heard it all before, but still she listened, just to show respect for her husband. It was true that Gerry Woodman had come to America just before World War II, all but penniless, and he had built several successful businesses.

For the moment it was convenient to forget exactly how Gerry had made his fortune, and that he had lost everything, every last cent, not once but twice, that in thirty years he had recklessly gambled away literally millions of dollars, and that they now lived in comfort only through the generosity of their daughter and son-in-law.

But let him feel good about himself, thought Vera. It's been a long time since he's been this outgoing, it hurts nothing. And anyway, politics weren't her concern. Let the men worry about such things. But it would be all right, too, if Gerry wasn't quite so argumentative.

Not all her children shared their father's fondness for Reagan. The youngest, Hilary, couldn't find one good thing to say about Reagan. She had voted for Walter Mondale, an exercise in suffrage that enraged Gerry.

"These Democrats! What good are they," he proclaimed, wolfing down a second cup of Vera's caramel custard. "All they know is 'raise taxes, cut defense.' If it wasn't for Ronald Reagan all of Europe would belong to the Russians. All of South America would be run by Soviet puppets, and the Communists would be dictating terms in Mexico."

"That's ridiculous, Dad," said Hilary, but not very loud. It was dangerous to argue with Gerry about anything. His temper had mellowed a little since the heart attack five years earlier, but it remained awesome, an inexorable force of nature. Hilary knew she could never outshout her father, and in the interest of preserving the holiday mood, she cast around for a way to change the subject.

Only her oldest brother, Neil, had ever tried to shout Gerry down. But only Wayne was present. Her older brothers, Neil and Stewart, were conspicuously absent. This was the third consecutive

year they had boycotted the semiannual holiday family get-togethers.

In an effort to get off Ronald Reagan, Hilary asked if anyone
had heard from Neil or Stewart recently.

The table suddenly went silent. Vera, who knew what was coming, studied the folds of the napkin in her lap.

"As a matter of fact, Stewart called to wish me *boker tov* [happy
holiday]," sighed Sybil Michelson.

Vera's face lit up, but she said nothing.

"What else did he say?" asked Hilary.

"Just that he misses his mother. He wishes he could be with us
again, and he sends his love," said Sybil.

Gerry was instantly transformed. His face twisted with rage.
People around the table recoiled even before he spoke.

"MISSES US! He said that he MISSES US," thundered Gerry.
"He wants to come crawling back, to lick my bloody boots and beg
me to forgive him for everything? IS THAT WHAT HE SAID?"

"Gerry, your heart. Calm yourself," said Vera, worried. She
knew how he could work himself into a frenzy.

"My heart. My heart will still be going strong when that
mumser—bastard—is in his grave. I'll tell you why he misses us. He
misses us because he and his *verstunkinah* [stinking] brother have
run that company into the ground. It's all going in the toilet, just as
I said, and he wants me to come back and save him.

"Well, I'll never do it. Those sons of bitches, they deserve to
lose their business. They deserve to lose everything, just like I did.
I hope they lose every cent they own, that they lose their houses
and their cars and their clothes. I hope they have to live on the
street, them and their too-good-for-us wives and their whining little kids. And I hope I live to see it. I want to look at their faces
when they come crawling back to me and I tell them to get out."

"Gerry, how can you wish that on your own grandchildren?"
asked Muriel in her soft, cultured voice.

"Grandchildren? These are my grandchildren," screamed Gerry,
gesturing at the adjacent room where the children were gathered.
"These are my only grandchildren. Neil is no son of mine. Stewart
is no son of mine. I only hope I live long enough to see their sons do
to them what they did to me!"

Gerry stood up, his face a mottled purple, and strode from the room. He felt strong and wonderfully young again.

It was almost nine when Mike Dominguez got to the bus bench near the corner of San Vicente and Gorham and sat down. While it was a mild evening, Mike was glad for the Plexiglas shelter around the bench. A huge poster advertising a new movie screened Mike from the view of most passersby. In ritzy, lily-white Brentwood, a Latino man waiting for a bus might attract attention.

Mike's dark eyes swept the broad vista of San Vicente Boulevard, a six-lane street divided by a wide grassy median. Now and then he rose to stretch his legs, but always he remained alert. He had heard about the old man, that he always drove as if the devil himself was on his rear bumper, and Mike was not about to miss a good payday because he took his mind off the job for two minutes. His left hand clutched a rumpled brown paper bag. The walkie-talkie was concealed inside.

After letting Mike off near the bus stop, Steve had found a parking spot up the street, on the south side of San Vicente. Pulling the tool bag out of the trunk, he walked two blocks through alleys to find Majoy waiting near Westgate. After pulling on black, hooded sweatshirts, the two men made their way carefully down the broad, paved alley running northeast to southwest between Gorham and Montana avenues. It dead-ended at Bundy, blocked by an apartment building. That made Steve nervous; if anything went wrong, the only way out of the alley was the way they'd come.

Getting to the gate Steve had selected as an entry point required either boldly walking up Gorham's brightly illuminated sidewalk or sneaking unobserved down a walkway connecting the alley with Gorham. Steve chose the alley approach, though it meant walking past the door of several ground-level apartments. If anyone saw them, all they could do was run.

Silent as the grave, the two men inched down the alley toward the rear of Brentwood Place. Window lights provided intermittent illumination; had anyone glanced into the alley they might easily have seen the dark-clad duo. Majoy felt naked, glad for the dark sweatshirt with the hood pulled up to conceal his telltale white hair.

The easiest way to the garage, which was partly below ground, was through street-level steel doors on either side of the main entrance—but these required the same key used for the front entrance on Gorham. On the west side of the building, however, was a narrow concrete path through a large planter filled with ferns and ficus trees. Iron gates, too high to crawl over inconspicuously, barred either end. Each gate was secured by a chain wrapped around a gate bar and the iron gatepost and fastened by a massive padlock.

The building immediately west of Brentwood Place is 11959. Unlike the huge, dark-brick-facaded faux château of the luxury condominium, 11959 is merely a three-story apartment building. Each unit's front door faces east, toward the walkway between Gorham and the alley and toward Brentwood Place.

Going down that walkway was the riskiest part of the whole approach. Steve motioned to Majoy in the darkness, then moved forward noiselessly on the balls of his feet, never looking back. It was just after nine o'clock in the evening. The two men stalking down the white walkway could hear the theme music from "Dynasty" through the thin apartment doors as they tiptoed toward their date with death.

Vera was hooked on "Dynasty." At nine o'clock, when most of Muriel's guests had left, she happily huddled before the Jacksons' huge television screen and let herself escape to Denver, to the glamour and intrigues of the cutthroat Carrington clan. It was "Dynasty's" season premiere, and Vera was anxious to find out who had survived the wedding massacre that had provided the cliffhanger for the previous season.

During a commercial, Vera's oldest daughter, Maxine, sat down with her mother. They chatted about inconsequential things until Maxine's husband, Mickey, appeared at the doorway, Maxine's coat folded across his arm.

"We're going now, Momma," said Maxine. "Wait, I almost forgot." Maxine fished in her purse and retrieved a long white envelope, which she put on the sofa next to her mother. "A little extra this time, for the holidays," she said.

Vera stood to embrace her daughter, smiled warmly at her son-in-law, and discreetly tucked the envelope away in her purse. She had mixed feelings. Maxine and Mickey were millionaires many times over. They could easily afford what they gave her and Gerry each week. But it offended her sense of propriety, to say nothing of her pride, to be reminded that she was so dependent on anyone except Gerry. And she knew that as little as Gerry said about the money, he was not happy taking it. He would far rather still be in business, making his own money with his wits, as he had done for almost fifty years.

At a quarter past ten, ready for sleep, Vera said good-bye to her sisters. Even with fifty-three hungry guests, the sisters had prepared so much food that a lot remained. Muriel insisted that Vera take some of the chopped herring, Gerry's favorite, and some of Sybil's home-grown tomatoes. Muriel helped Vera carry the food to her Mercedes. She hugged her brother-in-law before he slid behind the wheel.

Gerry drove away very fast, as always.

Although the padlock on the side gate was almost invulnerable to anything less than an acetylene torch, the chain it secured was Brentwood Place's weak link. It was a mere bicycle chain, covered with a sheaf of plastic tubing. With his penknife, Steve Homick cut off a three-inch section of tubing, then extracted a pair of insulated cutters from a small leather bag. With a single, almost silent cut he was through the small chain. The severed link fell to the sidewalk, the smaller half bouncing into the ivy. Steve ignored the remnants as he dropped the lock and chain into the bag, along with the cutters. He reached through the bars, lifted the catch, and cautiously pushed open the wrought-iron gate that led to the path through the planter and to the garage.

Motioning for Sonny to go first, Steve stepped through the fence. To his left, a four-foot cinderblock wall shielded both men from the walkway of the next building. No one could see them, unless they were on an upstairs balcony and happened to look straight down. The two men stepped through a narrow planter, filled with ivy, and knelt at another iron gate, one of several on either side of the subterranean garage. Steve took out the cutter and snipped yet another bicycle chain, dropping it and the lock into the bag.

They pulled the gate open, then lowered themselves about three feet to the concrete floor of the garage.

Sonny gripped Steve's arm, pointing to a video camera on a pedestal near the ceiling. It was aimed right at them.

"You're the video expert," whispered Steve. He grinned to himself in the dark. "Disable it. That's why I brought you along."

Majoy froze. "I just sell tapes, and like that," he began.

"Relax," whispered Steve. "It's been handled. Nothing to worry about."

The garage was full of expensive cars—Cadillacs, Mercedeses, BMWs. Majoy put one sneaker-clad foot on the bumper of a Jaguar and tied his shoelace. Then Steve led Majoy over to a dark blue Toyota Cressida parked near the entrance to the garage. It was dark near the wall behind the Cressida, and when they crouched down they were all but invisible to anyone else in the garage.

"You remember the plan?" asked Steve.

"Sure. Do the old man first. Head shot. No problems."

"Damn right, no problems. We're just taking a couple of Jews out for Yom Kippur. Nothing to it."

The two men in dark sweatshirts shifted around behind the Cressida, trying to get comfortable. In a few minutes the only sounds they could hear in the darkness were the pounding of their hearts and the rhythmic rush of their own breathing.

Gerry was anxious to get home. Their dog was home alone all day, and if it hadn't already left a big one on the balcony, Gerry would walk it for half an hour before he went to bed. So he drove toward Brentwood, as always, as though he was pursued by the hounds of hell. Four minutes later he rolled the little Mercedes through the STOP sign on the corner of Gorham and San Vicente, then gunned the engine to cross the divided street before Mike Dominguez, half-hidden in the bus shelter, could pull the radio from the paper bag.

"He's on the way, he's coming," said Mike into the radio.

In the shadows of the underground garage, Sonny and Steve stood, pulled up the hoods of their black sweatshirts to cover their hair, stretched backs and legs, then hunkered down. Steve cocked his .357 Magnum and looked at Sonny.

Halfway down the block, Gerry took his foot off the gas, slipped the automatic door opener from the sun visor, and as the building came into view, pushed the switch hard, once.

The portcullis-like gate rumbled upward. Gerry made a sharp right turn, touching the brakes as the car shot down the driveway. A light came on, and the security camera swiveled on its base, its lens pointing at Gerry as he flashed by.

Tires squealing, the car slowed, then turned into a parking space.

Time slowed to a crawl as Steve and Sonny, peering from the darkness, watched Gerry push the door open, then glance impatiently at Vera, who had opened her door but was struggling with a seat belt.

Gerry took his glasses off, rubbing the bridge of his nose.

Sonny rose to a crouch, his .38 up, and Steve touched his arm to whisper, "Wait for her to get out."

But Sonny was already moving, and Steve had no choice but to follow.

"You coming?" asked Gerry, but Vera's answer was drowned out by shots.

Sonny fired from eight feet away through the open passenger door. A bullet smashed Vera's hip. A second grazed her midriff. Sonny fired twice more, one round shattering Vera's shoulder and the last blowing an enormous hole in her abdomen, piercing her heart, stomach, liver, and lungs. Blood sprayed everywhere as Vera slumped toward her open door.

Steve, who had further to go, was about ten feet from Gerry when Sonny's gun boomed. Steve stopped and took aim.

"Who the fuck are you?" roared Gerry, turning to Steve.

The first shot took the elderly man square in the neck. Gerry twisted as he fell backward, his left arm flinging the glasses high. He lay half out of the car.

Glad he had brought such a powerful gun, Steve carefully aimed at Gerry's head. Chunks of bone and flesh flew as the .357 bellowed again.

A cloud of bluish cordite hung in the still air.

"Let's get the fuck out of here," shouted Sonny, deafened by the gunfire.

Two blocks away at the bus stop, Mike heard the shots clearly. He jogged across San Vicente, then walked briskly east toward his pickup point.

Seven-foot Ninjas

SEPTEMBER 26, 1985

It was past ten by the time Detective-Two Jack Holder had done his crime scene workup at the airport. For Major Crimes, it was almost routine: a traffic officer was chasing a suspect at high speed until the suspect stopped, leapt from his car, and started shooting. The officer was seriously wounded, making it attempted murder of a peace officer, and so Holder and his partner had taken the call.

Holder lived near the sea in Orange County, a long drive from Los Angeles International. It was after midnight by the time he crawled into bed, trying not to wake June.

Although June was Jack's second wife, she was all too well acquainted with the often unreasonable demands of her husband's job. When Jack had called at four to say he was headed to the airport and not to count on him for dinner, she had eaten alone and gone to bed at her usual time.

When the phone rang about one in the morning, Holder never stirred. June took the call on the third ring. Her sleepy "Hello" made no impression on Jack at all.

So she shook him awake, a process that took a few minutes.

"Guess what—the police department is on the phone," she said, sarcasm absent as always, handing Jack the instrument.

Holder was on call for the whole week, so he already knew who was on the other end of the line.

Every month there are hundreds of murders in the city of Los Angeles. Most are gang-related. These are investigated by a special Los Angeles Police Department (LAPD) unit, its computer bulging with gang intelligence data, its officers trained to recognize thousands of gangbangers, up to date with ever-shifting hierarchies, long-running blood feuds, and fiefdoms of illicit enterprise.

Other murders result from robberies, domestic quarrels, or sexual assaults. Most of these are handled by industrious, well-trained but deplorably overburdened detectives working out of suburban police stations near the crime scene. These officers clear most of their cases, but many murders go unsolved, mostly because there are too many cases and not enough hours in the day to follow up every lead.

Murders remaining unsolved tend to be those where there are few obvious suspects or when the motives remain unclear after substantial investigation. A murder intended as vengeance but cleverly disguised as the consequence of a simple robbery, for example, might well remain unsolved.

Murders involving police officers or prominent citizens, murders with suspected links to organized crime, those involving multiple or serial victims—anything unusual, anything requiring more investigation and effort than the limited resources available to detectives in outlying police stations—are turned over to Major Crimes.

Rousing Holder from well-deserved rest was his boss, Lieutenant Ed Henderson, head of Major Crimes/Homicide.

"Got a double in West L.A.," said Henderson. "The suspects are seven-foot-tall Ninja warriors. They were barefoot." Holder's three stepchildren—June's, from her previous marriage—were grown and living on their own or with their respective spouses. Jack was a new grandfather and the Teenage Mutant Ninja Turtles had not yet burst upon the adolescent scene. Nevertheless, he held a few vague notions about Ninjas: Oriental martial-arts types, night-blooming assassins who dressed in black and who were experts in all manner of nasty, sticking, and slicing weapons. Jack seemed to recall that there hadn't been any real Ninjas for several hundred years.

"Oh fuck," muttered Holder to himself. "I'm just too tired. I don't want to do this. Let someone else go."

But to his lieutenant, Jack said, "I'm on my way."

He pulled on a robe, and went into the kitchen so as not to further disturb June. There he dialed the home of his partner, Detective-One Richard Crotsley.

"Richie, you're not going to believe this," said Holder. "We've got two down. The suspects are barefoot Ninja warriors."

Holder and Crotsley had known each other, in a casual way, for several years. But they had become partners only the previous day. This was their first homicide together.

Crotsley said, "Jack, what the fuck is a Ninja?"

"I'm not exactly sure. Some kind of martial-arts type," said Holder. "See you down at Parker."

Crotsley also lived in Orange County, though somewhat closer to Los Angeles than Holder. Rather than wake Mary, his wife, he wrote her a note, which he propped on the nightstand. Then he threw on his clothes and went out the door.

Since LAPD regulations forbid officers, including homicide detectives, to use their own cars on official business, Holder and Crotsley each headed for LAPD headquarters at Parker Center, next to City Hall in downtown Los Angeles.

They found the freeways empty at this time of night. Holder and Crotsley picked up their unmarked sedan at a little after two-thirty, then headed west a dozen miles on the Santa Monica Freeway. They rolled up to 11939 Gorham Avenue, Brentwood, a few minutes after three in the morning.

It was easy to find the right building. Red and blue lights blinked from a black-and-white parked across the driveway. A clutch of news media types, some toting minicams and lights, were kept back by uniformed officers. In front of the iron-bar portcullis and steel side doors were plastic ribbons of yellow-and-black crime-scene tape. Two detectives from West Los Angeles Station on Butler Avenue, a block south of Santa Monica Boulevard, were waiting, along with a crime-scene photographer, a fingerprint specialist, and Officers Sean Kane and Daniel Horan, the patrolmen who had responded to the initial call just after ten-thirty.

"What do we have?" asked Holder, nodding at Detective Richard De Anda, senior man from West L.A. Homicide.

"Gerald and Vera Woodman. Rent on the second floor. Vera is age sixty-three, Gerald sixty-seven. Female dead at scene, three hits, large-caliber weapon, maybe a three-five-seven, but at least a thirty-eight. Male, hit twice, same type of weapon, alive when paramedics came. Took him to UCLA Medical Center, too late.

"Woman's wearing diamonds, her purse is still on the seat, never opened. Male was carrying a roll, about two thousand bucks, nobody took it."

"No robbery then," said Holder.

"Neighbors say he's a gambler," said De Anda. "Big time in Vegas. Goes to the track, like every day. Goes to England to buy racehorses and all like that."

"How does it play to you?" asked Crotsley, looking at De Anda.

"They drive in, get out, then wham, bam, thank you ma'am—a hit. Pro job."

"What else we got?" asked Crotsley.

"Let's walk through it," said De Anda.

The detectives entered the garage through a steel door at ground level. Holder immediately spotted the security camera.

"Whoa," he said. "Does that make a tape?"

De Anda and a uniformed officer exchanged wry grins. "You think the guy is on there, but he's not. When the gate opens, the light comes on and the camera starts to swivel. But it's a dummy. Doesn't have any film in it. Might be the body of a real camera, but I think it's a complete fake."

The garage was partly subterranean, its ceiling perhaps five feet above ground level. On the east and west, about two thirds of the space between the ceiling and ground level was blocked by inward-swinging gates of wrought-iron bars. Most of the gates were chained and padlocked; a pair on the west side was open, with no chain or lock. On the concrete floor, muddy footprints led from these gates to the center aisle, then north a few steps to the death scene, then back again to the west wall.

The footprints were indistinct, but clearly not made by shoes. They were huge; judging by the spaces between them, they'd been made by a man as much as seven feet tall.

"Looks like he was barefoot," said De Anda.

Crotsley and Holder nodded. It did look that way.

Maybe all these Ninja guys run around barefooted, thought Holder. Who knows?

Just outside of the garage was a planter running the length of the structure and filled with ferns. Holder reached out and touched the soil. It was damp. "So the guy came through the planter," said Crotsley, mostly to himself.

"How do we know it was a Ninja?" said Holder, looking at De Anda.

"Witness. Roger Backman, age twenty, white male, student, lives next door, third floor, with his mother, saw them go out through the planter, hop that wall and run down the walkway to the alley."

"Them?"

"Two men. Black clothing, heads covered with black hoods."

"We'll want to talk to that guy in a bit," said Holder.

"Probably asleep now. He'll be there tomorrow," said De Anda. "He ran after them, but they got away. More guts than brains, that kid."

All four officers walked back to the death scene.

In parking stall twenty-one was a 1982 Mercedes-Benz model SL450, tan, with California license plates 1EGN842. The driver's door was open, and the window was down. From the door a trail of blood led in a southerly direction, toward the main entrance, to the next parking stall. At stall twenty, Holder and Crotsley saw a large pool of blood, now beginning to congeal, and an assortment of paramedics' emergency paraphernalia—a discarded syringe, protective paper wrappings from large-wound bandages, snippets of gauzy thread—the detritus of sudden terror. Near the blood was a white button-up sweater and a short-sleeved white shirt. Both were bloodstained, and had been cut in front from top to bottom with something very sharp. In the left breast pocket of the short-sleeved shirt was a small black plastic comb.

Careful not to step in the blood or to touch anything, Crotsley and Holder approached the Mercedes. The automatic transmission was still in "drive." A set of keys rested on the console between the bucket seats. On the driver's sun visor was a push-button pager, the sort used to activate an automatic garage door. A beige leather purse, unopened, rested on the front passenger seat. On the floorboard below was a plate containing a plastic-wrapped piece of broiled salmon.

Crotsley observed the blood smeared on the driver's seat and running board. The passenger door was also open, and blood droplets, shivering in the dim fluorescent lighting, dotted the armrest and running board. The top of the passenger's seat was torn, and a round hole penetrated the passenger door near the bottom, toward the front of the car.

In the car, in a supine position, her feet protruding into the driver's area, was the corpse of Vera Woodman. There were wounds in her left hip, waist, and left shoulder. A graze wound, where a bullet had skimmed by her abdomen without entering her body, was just above the middle gunshot wound.

Vera's face and hair were covered with blood, and her blouse had been cut open, exposing her chest. On her chest were tiny adhesive patches, the type used to get readings for electrocardiography.

"Paramedics?" said Crotsley, straightening up and indicating the cut blouse.

"Yeah," said De Anda.

Crotsley looked carefully at Vera's body. There was a gold bracelet on her left wrist, a big diamond ring on the third finger of her left hand, a constellation of diamonds glittering on a necklace around her neck. Diamond earrings hung from her lobes. On the floor next to Vera's foot was a check drawn on the account of Stern, Brenner—apparently a business—for two thousand dollars, and made out to Vera Woodman.

"Anything else?" asked Crotsley, grim and self-contained.

"Over here," replied De Anda. He led the detectives over to stall sixty-three, where a four-door Jaguar was parked. Just in front of the car, on the floor, was a pair of eyeglasses. The right lens was missing. About two feet away, laying against the west wall, was the lens. It was intact.

Holder pointed to the black rubberized bumper on the Jaguar. A muddy footprint, apparently left by some kind of sneaker, was obvious on the otherwise pristine bumper. It was considerably smaller than the muddy footprints running the length of the garage.

"You want to do the scene, I'll take the photographer and the print guy?" asked Holder. "Then I'll get the witnesses."

Crotsley nodded.

"Let's get a picture of that," said Holder, pointing at the bumper. "And before you release that car to its owner, I want to find out what we can do to enhance it."

For more than two hours, the detectives went through the weary routine of sudden death, Crotsley collecting careful notes about everything in the crime scene, outside and in, taking measurements and diagramming the scene, inventorying the automobile and its contents, then the body for clothing and jewelry. He was deliberate, carefully never touching the victims' possessions.

Holder directed the photographer and fingerprint specialist to shoot here, dust there. There were few fingerprint locations, but Holder checked every parked car carefully. He saw a palm print spanning a spot on the hood where it dipped into the bumper, and told the print man not to miss it.

Holder is a careful man, a bit over average height with a crew cut and a big gut straining at his shirt front that causes some people to ignore the graceful way he moves, his hulking shoulders, and well-muscled arms. The gut is a legacy of Holder's love of fine food. But Jack has, since adolescence, surfed Southern California's big-wave beaches year-round. He's also a deep-powder skier, with legs and reflexes to match.

Jack Holder was born in December 1942. He grew up in the San Gabriel Valley, ten miles east of downtown Los Angeles, graduated from San Gabriel High in 1960, then did two years as a Navy electrician's mate. After discharge he worked as a cabinetmaker until he was accepted by the LAPD Academy, graduating in May 1965.

Following the usual pattern, Holder served two years as a uniformed patrolman in what is now called Southwest Division, the largely black community surrounding the University of Southern California and the venerable Coliseum. Three months after graduation, in August 1965, the Watts riots broke out after a highway patrolman arrested a young black motorist for drunk driving. The savagery of racial violence—days of rioting, arson, sniping at fire-fighters and police—was a unique baptism of fire that Holder would forever refer to as "a real eye-opener."

After two years in Southwest, Holder transferred to Central Division, where he spent another eighteen months on patrol. Then he was transferred to Metro, the LAPD's elite central command. In Metro, Holder found himself assigned to a wide variety of police chores. One day he might work at directing traffic; the next he could be detailed to assist detectives in a homicide investigation. After about five years in Metro, Holder earned a post in Robbery/Homicide.

One of his early cases was as part of the so-called West Side Rapist Task Force. He was one of dozens of officers looking for a serial rapist who was killing elderly women. After several months, during which time the West Side Rapist seemed to have stopped killing, the task force was dissolved. Holder went back to Metro. Soon after, the rapist struck again. Another task force was formed; Holder was again tapped for duty. When the unit accomplished its mission, Holder went back to Robbery/Homicide.

His education on the depths to which Los Angeles's kinkiest killers could sink was expanded with work on the Sunset Slayer case. "He'd pick up prostitutes on Sunset Boulevard, take them to a motel, and get them to give him head," recalled Holder. "And then, just as he was getting his nut, he'd shoot them in the head. Because they'd vibrate. A real charmer."

Holder was back to Metro in 1978 when the Hillside Strangler murders started. For months, Los Angeles shuddered with fear as the nude bodies of young women, one after another, were discovered in hilly areas near downtown. Then they stopped, and Holder was called back to Robbery/Homicide. After Angelo Buono and Kenneth Bianchi were arrested and eventually convicted of the Hillside Strangler murders, Holder remained with Robbery/Homicide.

By 1982 he was a Detective-Two, a supervisory grade. Admired by his colleagues for his dogged persistence and attention to detail, Holder was often assigned to work cases involving police officers as victims, including the murders of Officer Paul Vernor and, later, Officer Danny Pratt, machine-gunned while picking up his toddler from a San Fernando Valley day-care center.

Holder also handled many rape-homicide cases, earning a record as an investigator whose work usually lead to solid convictions.

Yet nothing in his background or experience had prepared him for a case as complex as the one he had just been handed. Before Holder wrapped up the Ninja murders, his patience and persistence would be thoroughly challenged.

A bit under six feet tall, Richard Crotsley was a muscular 220-pounder. He was born in Buffalo, New York, in April 1943 and came to California as a toddler. Crotsley grew up in the bohemian Venice area and after high school enrolled at San Fernando Valley College. But he dropped out to join the Marines, and went to Vietnam in 1966.

Crotsley finished college after his discharge, then applied to the LAPD Academy, graduating in June 1968. After two years as a patrolman in the tough Watts area, Crotsley was seen as a hard-charging, no-nonsense type and recruited to Special Weapons And Tactics (SWAT), the LAPD's paramilitary elite. After a few years, he was reassigned to work out of Metro and Robbery/Homicide. After he became a detective in 1980, Crotsley was detailed to the Hillside Strangler Task Force. His work there impressed Lieutenant Ed Henderson, the task force commander, who in 1984 brought him to Major Crimes.

Aside from the bullets, later removed from the victims' bodies, the only physical evidence at the scene was half of a bicycle chain link, found on the sidewalk near the southwest corner of the building. Holder watched as Crotsley used a pencil to nudge the half link into a clear plastic bag. He wrote the date and his name on a tag, then sealed the bag.

About six-thirty, as the sun was working its way through the usual early-autumn morning coastal fog draping Brentwood, deputy coroners arrived to take charge of Vera's body. Holder decided it was time to question Roger Backman, the witness who had seen the "Ninjas" escape after the shooting.

"Little early, isn't it?" objected one of the West L.A. detectives.

"Maybe—but he's had six or seven hours more than me or Richie," said Holder. "Wake him up."

Ten minutes later, Holder and Crotsley were shaking hands with Roger Backman. Roger was a slender six-foot-five or -six, earnest and a little shy. He said he had been in the bathroom getting ready for bed about ten-thirty P.M. when he heard several shots, one after another. He opened a sliding window and looked down in time to see two black-clad shapes swinging over the cinderblock wall separating 11939 from 11959. Roger yelled, "Hey, what are you guys doing?" and one of the black-clad figures looked up.

Roger ran downstairs and chased one of the men down the alley toward the northeast, but the dark-clad killer had too big a head start. After a few blocks, Roger gave up. He came back to 11959, vaulted the cinderblock wall, and went through the planter and then the yawning gate to the garage. When Roger saw Gerald Woodman's bleeding body on the concrete floor, he ran back to his mother's apartment, where he called 911, the emergency response number.

As Roger was describing what he'd seen, Holder's mind was racing ahead, thinking about the footprints in the garage. They were humongous—and now, looking at Roger, a little light bulb strobed in his mind. He said, "Listen, did you have your shoes on when you ran after those guys?"

"No," said Roger. "My feet were all muddy when I got back upstairs, so I washed them off and put on my socks and shoes and went to talk to the police when they got here."

And just like that, Holder had solved the problem with the footprints. "We don't have a barefooted murderer," he said.

Roger explained that when the patrol officers arrived, only minutes ahead of the first reporters, he'd described the dark clothing and hooded heads as similar to martial-arts gear.

"Like a Ninja?" asked one reporter, shamelessly eavesdropping.

"Something like that," said Roger.

The reporter used the word "Ninja" in his story—and the other media echoed it.

"Policemen always give their cases slang names," said Holder. "What else we would have named this I don't know, but from then on it was known as the 'Ninja Murders' case," said Holder. "Always has been and always will be. You mention the murders in Brentwood and people don't know it, but you say the Ninja Murders and they all say, 'Oh, yeah, I know that.' "

When he had finished interviewing Roger Backman, Holder got out his notebook and wrote down the license number of every car in the garage, and every one parked on the street in front. While he was doing that, Crotsley sketched the building, diagramming the entrances and the points where it seemed likely the killers had entered the premises.

There are two basic types of handguns, revolvers and autoloaders. The latter automatically eject a spent cartridge after each shot. Ejected onto a concrete surface, the spinning brass could bounce and roll for several yards.

In their careful examination of the crime scene, however, neither Holder nor Crotsley, nor any other officer, had found even one expended cartridge. Since Roger Backman's account of events placed the fleeing gunmen at the wall outside the garage only "a few seconds" after the shots, there would have been no time to gather up empty cartridges. From this, Holder concluded that the murder weapons were revolvers.

It was now past eight A.M., and the neighborhood hummed with the routine of its workday. A river of cars squealed through the asphalt curves of Bundy Drive. Holder was beat—but he knew it would be hours before he was permitted the luxury of sleep.

Holder and Crotsley, accompanied by the building manager, took the elevator to the Woodmans' second-floor apartment. The manager opened the front door and stepped aside.

As Holder stepped into the living room he heard a strange noise. A shadow flitted across the balcony.

Someone was out there.

Heart in mouth, Holder reached behind his coat jacket and withdrew his revolver. Crotsley, gun drawn, moved to the wall nearest the sliding door that opened on to the balcony. He took up a shooting stance.

In movies homicide cops are always shooting someone. But in the real world, police detectives like Holder and Crotsley rarely even so much as unlimber their weapons—and when they do, it's usually to satisfy the LAPD's mandatory target practice regulation. After the Watts riots in 1965, in twenty years behind a badge

Holder had rarely heard a shot fired in anger. Nor, since leaving SWAT, had Crotsley.

So when the strange noise came again, a sort of snuffling sound through the thick curtains of the sliding door, these two officers of the law could feel the adrenaline coursing through their bodies. Their heartbeats accelerated, perspiration moistened their gun hands, their guts contracted, they experienced the primal feeling called fear.

Holder, flattened against the other wall, cautiously reached out and slid the door lock open.

The noise came again.

Holder giggled in relief, straightening up. He pushed the door open and a tiny Yorkshire terrier bounded into the room, tail wagging furiously.

With a sigh and a weak grin, Holder put his gun away.

The two officers walked around, noting the expensive furnishings. It was apparent that Gerald and Vera had good taste and the means by which to indulge it. Holder decided there was too much in the apartment; probably the Woodmans had moved into this place from a much larger home.

There were no signs of forced entry, nothing disturbed. Holder decided that going through the apartment an inch at a time would have to wait until he could get a crew in to do the job right. For now, however, they took all the papers they could find in drawers—bills, letters, receipts, insurance paperwork, several paper grocery sacks full of evidence.

Leaving the apartment, they carefully pulled the door shut behind them and put yellow crime-scene tape across the door.

Just as Holder and Crotsley got in their car, a large Mercedes sedan pulled up in front of Brentwood Place. Two couples, one in their forties, the other much older, got out.

"You're with the police," said the woman. It came out flat, more a statement of fact than a question.

"Detective Holder. My partner, Detective Crotsley."

"Vera Woodman is my sister."

"I'm truly sorry," said Holder, unable to meet her gaze.

"I'm Muriel Jackson," said the woman, who appeared to be in her fifties. Her accent was faintly British, and her clothes expensive and well tailored. "This is my husband, Louis, my niece, Maxine—Vera's daughter—and Maxine's husband, Milford Stern."

Maxine was composed, but Holder could tell she'd been crying. Her eyes were red and her face, bereft of makeup but for a trace of lipstick, was puffy. Stern, announcing that "everyone calls me Mickey," wore a stone face, his lips pursed.

"We need to speak with you," said Muriel Jackson. "It's very important. Perhaps we might all sit down . . . "

This was the part that Holder hated. He had learned long ago that while some people reacted with bitterness and anger, others with tears, and a few with stoic silence, they were all suffering. There was no easy way to deal with this.

Holder and Crotsley retraced their steps, returning with the four visitors to the apartment upstairs. When everyone was seated comfortably, Holder looked at Crotsley, who nodded, as if to say, better you than me, buddy boy.

"I'm really sorry you folks have to go through this," said Holder, knowing how trite it sounded, wishing he could be eloquent enough to help them through their pain.

"What we know right now is that somebody shot Mr. and Mrs. Woodman," said Holder. "She died instantly. Mr. Woodman was taken to UCLA Medical Center, but he died on the way over."

Holder looked up and saw heavy tears of grief rolling silently down four faces.

"Nobody should ever have to deal with a tragedy like this," continued Holder. "But now that it has happened, it's our job to find out who killed Mr. and Mrs. Woodman."

The four mourners sat silent, immobile.

Holder gave them a few minutes. When they started sniffling and dabbing at their eyes, he took out his notebook and thumbed down the business end of his ballpoint.

"From our preliminary investigation, it appears that nothing was taken. This wasn't a robbery, it was . . . an assassination. It would be a big help if you could tell us anything you know about who might have wanted to kill Mr. and Mrs. Woodman."

Holder looked at Lou Jackson expectantly, but it was his wife who spoke. "We *know* who did this," said Muriel. "Neil and Stewart. Their sons. Gerald and Vera's oldest sons."

"You have evidence of this, Mrs. Jackson?" asked Holder.

"Well, it's just so obvious. The whole family knows. It has to be Neil and Stewart. No one else would do such a thing. It has to be them."

"Why would two sons kill their parents?" asked Crotsley.

"Money. And hatred, of course. Neil and Stewart were their parents' enemies—especially their father."

"Putting the hatred aside for a moment—they stand to inherit Gerald's money?" said Holder.

"Not a penny. Gerry changed his will three years ago, when they forced him out of the business. Anyway, he was broke. Lost everything, took bankruptcy. But Vera had insurance—half a million dollars—payable to them—really, payable to the company they stole from their father. Vera tried and tried, but they wouldn't cancel it. So you see . . ."

Another fat tear slid down Muriel's cheek.

Holder held up his hand. "Better start from the beginning," he said.

CHAPTER Three

Sins of the Fathers

Just east of the San Diego Freeway, in the Fox Hills section of Culver City, is Hillside Memorial Park, a Jewish cemetery. Visible from the freeway, the cemetery is gentle slopes of green, dotted with dark, weathered gravestones set nearly flush into trimmed lawns. Near the center, well below the summit of the low hill, is a circular fountain cascading well water down broad blue tile steps into a rectangular pool. A little higher on the knoll are white columns and a dome shading the enormous marble tomb of Asa Yoelson. Better known as Al Jolson, he starred in the first full-length talkie, *The Jazz Singer*, the 1927 film that changed the film industry as no other movie has before or since.

After Jolson's death in 1950, Hillside became the cemetery of choice for Southern California's leading Jewish families, and especially those involved in the film industry. So it was appropriate that Jack Covel's daughters—Vera, Muriel, Sybil, and Gloria—chose Hillside as his final resting place: for decades, Covel was an itinerant seller of films. Representing American film studios and the J. Arthur Rank Organisation, he roamed Europe selling distribution rights to British and American films. Along the way he acquired the rights to many of the films of Buster Keaton and Marlene Dietrich, an investment that would bring in money long after Covel's death in April 1974.

Covel was buried in a corner of the cemetery near the housing tracts that surround its south side. A frequent visitor to his grave is Lynda Beaumont. Every few weeks, and whenever she has to pick up or drop off a friend at nearby Los Angeles International Airport, Beaumont, now past seventy but still comely, stops to pay homage to the great love of her life.

Covel died as he had lived, strong of mind and concerned for others' feelings to the very end.

Lynda remembers the first time she visited the grave, a few weeks after the funeral, looking up from the greensward to notice a huge billboard across the freeway. "It was for Cutty Sark, Jack's favorite Scotch," recalled Beaumont. "I thought that was a riot, and I sat there and laughed and cried at the same time, talking to him. And it made me happier to know that he would have thought the view was great.

"I went again, several months later, and the ground seemed so uneven, like a little hill was pushing up around his grave. So I told him, 'You'll have to quit trying to get out of there.' This was the way we talked to each other. We laughed all the time."

Jack Covel was born in 1898 in Manchester, England. He was a charming, virile, handsome man. While presenting a dignified appearance, he loved to laugh and didn't much mind if it was at his own expense. Although he was a Jew from a working-class family in class-conscious England, Covel learned his fine manners traveling Europe between the world wars; in maturity he impressed people with his worldly sophistication. Not tall, Covel dressed with expensive good taste and fastidious grooming. He habitually wore tortoiseshell glasses. Women thought him a marvelous dancer. Perhaps recalling his humble origins, he tipped lavishly: few bellmen, bartenders, parking attendants, or porters failed to remember his generosity.

"He met people so well," recalled Beaumont. "He was a consummate salesman. He remembered everybody's name. He entertained them and seemed to be able to get on their beam."

In 1970, Lynda Beaumont, along with her married daughter, Anne, and her three sons, took a week-long Princess cruise to the Mexican Riviera. The boys usually went off on their own; one afternoon, "Anne and I walked into one of the lounge areas and I looked over and saw Maxine and Neil Woodman—he married a

girl with the same first name as his sister, but this was his wife—
who appeared to be about my daughter's age," recalled Lynda.

"I said, 'Let's go over and speak to that young couple. They're
very attractive—maybe they'll be fun to be with.' There was a sofa;
on each end of it was a chair. Neil and Maxine were sitting on the
sofa and I said, 'Are these seats taken?'

"Maxine did the cutest thing—she got up and went over to the
vacant chair as though she were embracing someone seated in it
and she said, 'We're saving this space for Gramps.' I thought that
was so cute and loving and darling and amusing. I knew I was going
to like her immediately when she said that, because I like to do
things like that myself. In a little while here came Covel, so that's
how we met.

"After we got back to Los Angeles, Maxine called to invite us to
her little child's second birthday party."

Jack Covel was at the party as well; before long Beaumont and
Covel were steady companions. Covel, a widower, then lived with
his daughter Muriel and her husband, Louis Jackson. The Jacksons,
who observed the tenets of their religion quite strictly, were somewhat uncomfortable with Lynda Beaumont. Not only was she
young enough to be Covel's daughter—younger than Vera and
Muriel—she was a *shiksa*, a female gentile.

Jack Covel, widely admired for his generosity, rarely arrived
empty-handed. While dating Lynda Beaumont, Covel often played
Santa Claus, filling his Cadillac with bags of groceries and carry-
out food from Nate 'n' Al's, the premier delicatessen of Beverly
Hills. Beyond that, he showered Lynda and her four children with
thoughtful gifts.

Jack loved a Scotch or two "when the sun was past the
yardarm," and on Sundays, visiting Beaumont's home on a canyon
ridge in upscale Flintridge, he and Lynda often shared a bottle of
champagne on the terrace. He'd tease open the cork until it flew
into the air and landed on the roof. Beaumont sold that house in
1973; she heard later that the first time the new owners went on
the roof they were amazed; they'd never seen so many champagne
corks.

Covel spoke with an (almost) upper-class British accent, acquired in early adulthood. He routinely used all sorts of dandified

Britishisms, such as "bloody," "which absolutely knocked out" not only Lynda Beaumont but many Americans, who may have unconsciously associated the accent with the sort of rich, mannered Englishmen they saw in movies.

Covel made his life in England until after World War II. By then, three of his four daughters were married to Americans, and Jack decided his future lay closer to Hollywood. Even before he left the film business, Covel acted to ensure his daughters' futures by helping their husbands start businesses. In this, as in everything else he did, Jack Covel had a peculiar outlook which reflected both his salesman's instincts and his Jewish origins in Manchester, England.

England's first Jews arrived in the wake of the Norman conquest in 1066. They were not widely welcomed. In 1190, an army of Crusaders herded the Jews of York—all of them—into a castle, where, facing an assortment of cruel tortures leading to the most horrifying of deaths, all committed suicide. Soon afterward all of England's Jews became the King's chattels, protected slaves taxed exclusively by the royal family, and forced to wear distinctive dress. In 1290, all of England's five thousand Jews were expelled, leaving their property behind for the benefit of their Christian neighbors. Not until the middle of the seventeenth century, at the invitation of Oliver Cromwell, did Jews return to England.

For centuries after Cromwell, a steady trickle of Eastern European Jews arrived in England with little but the clothes on their backs and the name of some distant kinsman, sure that their relative would offer food and shelter and help them find a livelihood. Despite the painful price of penury, few were turned away. These immigrants and their descendants, for generations forced to render unto caesars, kaisers, and czars—and even petty princes and kings—nearly all they produced, felt little allegiance to king or country. Only family could be trusted, and therefore these English Jews did whatever was necessary to make sure their families survived.

Over several generations, some of His British Majesty's Jewish subjects, operating various small businesses, developed elaborate strategies to protect their profits from Inland Revenue, which levies taxes on practically everything in England. If these businessmen had difficulties reconciling their business tactics with their religious beliefs, which demanded that they deal fairly with everyone, including gentiles, they did so by rationalizing their tax evasion by agreeing that the Crown's constant taxation was oppressive and threatening. In that case, as the sages of old had written, it was permissible to violate a few Biblical commandments in the name of a more fundamental issue: survival. So they cheated the taxman in good conscience, believing that otherwise they and their families would not survive.

This knowledge of survival even in the face of oppressive taxation was passed from each generation to the next. Succeeding generations sought ways to adapt their family's legacy of secret wisdom to the changing world.

One of those Manchester families was named Covel. By the time Jack Covel and his four daughters came to America, he knew much about keeping business profits in the family.

By 1937, Hitler had held power for four years; England's Jews had more than an inkling of what awaited their Continental brethren. Many in Western Europe saw war clouds dotting the horizon; it was plain that great struggle was in store for France, England—every country that stood against fascism.

Gerald Woodman wanted no part of that struggle—he wanted to make money, to enjoy the sort of life he had so far admired only from a distance. Gerry was one of three children of Isadore Woodman, but the only son. He grew up in an old house that shared a wall with Strangeways Prison, where some of England's most incorrigible felons are kept, in the Prestwitch district of Manchester.

Gerry completed his education at the age of sixteen, graduating from Manchester Grammar School, one of the city's best. He knocked around Manchester—with neighboring Liverpool, one of the world's great centers for manufacturing, shipping, and mercantile commerce—and worked in the family garment-making business. Slowly, he came to feel he could never realize his grand dreams in England, where his Jewishness barred many doors. By his nineteenth year, he had decided there was little to hold him in Manchester.

Certainly not his family: Gerry's father, Isadore, a hard-drinking, womanizing, sly but not always wise businessman whose fortunes fluctuated wildly between poverty and opulence, was usually preoccupied with his own affairs. Constantly feuding with his wife, Nell, Izzy was always in debt to one relative or another. He did little to encourage his son Gerry to remain in England.

So Gerry said good-bye to family and friends. Among them was Vera Covel, a petite beauty whom he had known since she was thirteen. With a friend, Bernie Lazar, Gerry sailed for America in 1937.

They went first to Chicago, where Bernie had relatives. The Depression was almost over in America; already there was far more work available than in England.

When war came to Europe in 1939, Jack Covel, fearing for the safety of his wife and daughters, sent them to America, where friends in the motion picture industry helped get them settled.

Vera Covel, Jack's oldest daughter, left Britain with mixed feelings. She was glad to be away from the dive bombers and buzz bombs that Hitler unleashed at British cities, but she had an understanding, of a sort, with a wealthy and titled English gentleman. It wasn't exactly an engagement, but Vera had supposed it might lead to one. When she left England, the young man, angry, had said some hurtful things.

Vera was seventeen and lonely. She had stayed in touch with Gerald Woodman by writing him in care of Bernie Lazar's family in Chicago. When Gerald called her, long distance, Vera was impressed enough to take a train to Chicago. They were married on June 22, 1940.

The newlyweds moved to Brooklyn, New York, and set up housekeeping on Beach Thirty-Ninth Street in the Seagate section of Coney Island. Gerry found good wages at Todd Shipyards, which ran round-the-clock shifts to meet the wartime demand for Navy and merchant marine vessels. The shipyard was a noisy place, however, and Gerry would lose some of his hearing before he moved on to quieter realms.

About the time Gerry and Vera married, the U.S. Congress, eyeing the situation in Europe, voted authority to the Selective Service to draft young men between the ages of eighteen and forty-five. Draft boards were set up all over the country to decide which men were to go into uniform, and when.

Local draft boards much preferred to dragoon every immigrant in their communities before calling up the sons of their friends and neighbors, so Gerry, as a resident alien, was particularly vulnerable to the draft.

For the rest of his life, Gerry Woodman would complain of anti-Semitism. He would label any gentile—and even a few Jews—who opposed him in anything a Jew-hater. He would complain that Jews never got an even break, not even in America.

In 1941, he had a chance to do something about the worst anti-Semite of all time. He could join the army, learn how to use a gun, and go off to Europe to kill Nazi anti-Semites.

Gerry wanted no part of it.

Instead he asked around about ways to avoid the draft. At the public library he read the Selective Service exemption regulations. He found an obscure rule that exempted from the draft certain farmers whose production supported the war effort. Gerry read that law hastily; he thought it said that anyone who kept a flock of five *thousand* chickens was exempt.

Gerry and Vera moved to the eastern tip of Long Island, where they leased a few acres of farmland and bought thousands of baby chicks. He spent the entire war there, enduring the stench and flies associated with chicken "ranching" but making good wages with plenty of overtime in the booming, labor-hungry wartime economy. Not until the war's end did Gerry learn that the flock that kept him safe from having to fight Nazis could have been as small as five *hundred* chickens.

But when Gerry made up his mind, when he'd decided that anything was a certain way, no one and nothing could change his mind. He could not bear to be shown to be wrong, even in the least important matters. Instead he chose to defend his opinions with his fists. Gerry was a small, wiry man but a very tough presence among his shipfitter colleagues. He accepted no insults, real or imagined, and delighted in his ability to whip much larger men in fistfights. He had an awesome, frightening temper, which he displayed not only at work but also to Vera and their children. When Gerry Woodman came home from work every night to his chicken ranch and family, he was in every sense ruler of his roost.

As Gerry's hearing worsened, he began to shout more often

than speak. When he learned that raising his voice made most people cower before him, Gerry shouted at everyone.

A few years after the war ended, Jack Covel was reunited with his wife and children in Los Angeles. After several years with Gerry, the children, and thousands of chickens, Vera yearned to be with her family again. She telephoned her father, who was pleased to offer financial help to Gerry, Vera, and their children. If Gerry would come to California, promised Jack Covel, he would set him up in business.

Gerry usually rejected Vera's ideas and suggestions, reminding her, none too gently, that he was the boss of their family. But this time, to Vera's surprise, he readily agreed. Not for many years would she realize that Gerry had, all by himself, decided that Southern California was where the big money was, that Los Angeles was where he would make his fortune.

Gerry sold the chickens, and with Vera and their three children, Maxine, Neil, and the infant, Hilary, headed for Southern California. Hundreds of thousands of ex-servicemen and their families were moving to the area, and to meet their needs an enormous number of new homes would be required. A real estate and home-building boom was about to begin.

CHAPTER Four

Suspects

SEPTEMBER 1985

Detectives Jack Holder and Richard Crotsley sat in the overfurnished apartment of the late Gerry and Vera Woodman and listened to Muriel Jackson, tacitly but obviously the leader of the well-dressed family foursome, explain why her nephews Neil and Stewart Woodman had to be responsible for the murder of their parents.

There had been a bitter family feud, explained Muriel, spanning several years and including several lawsuits. The sons had won, forcing their father, Gerry, out of the company he had built. But the rest of the family had sided against Neil and Stewart and backed their parents. After losing his company, Gerry hadn't been able to accept defeat. He had retaliated by starting another company to compete with his sons. Instead he had gone bust himself.

So, said Muriel Jackson, everyone in the family knew that Neil and Stewart would love to see their father dead. Everyone had heard both brothers say, many times, how much they hated him.

Holder was thinking, Wow, I didn't know you could do that, take a business away from your own father. If *my* father had owned a business and I'd tried to take it away from him, he'd have killed me, for sure.

And he thought, But the sons won, they got the company, their father went broke—so why would they want him dead?

Then Muriel said there was insurance. Upon Vera's death, Jackson explained, a half million dollars was payable to the company Gerry and his sons had founded and operated. But Manchester Products now belonged to Neil and Stewart, and the company remained the sole beneficiary. After Gerry was forced out of Manchester, Muriel explained, she had tried to get Neil and Stewart to cancel this insurance, but they refused. They'd taunted her, saying it was "a good investment."

That got the detectives' attention. Family hatred is not often enough motive for the kind of professional hit that snuffed Gerry and Vera, thought Jack Holder. But money—that might be plenty of motive.

"Tell us about this company," said Holder. "What do they make?"

"Plastic panels," said Lou Jackson. "The sort of thing you see in kitchen ceilings, with fluorescent lights behind them, or in office buildings. And on walls."

"Big outfit?" asked Crotsley.

"Not so big. Maybe fifty or sixty employees. But there are only a couple of companies in that industry. Manchester was right up there."

"How much of this plastic panel stuff did they sell?" asked Crotsley. "Million dollars a year? Two million?"

Lou exchanged glances with his wife and Mickey. There was something going on here, definitely, thought Holder. Something they don't want to say in front of strangers. Or police.

That didn't especially bother Holder. He had learned, long, long ago, that most people lie when they speak to the police. Maybe only a lie of omission, like leaving something out of a story—but about the time people stop believing in Santa Claus, Holder believed, they learned not to tell the police everything they knew. So Lou Jackson's little glance at his wife and Stern told Holder something, and it made him even more careful about writing down what they would say next.

"Before Gerry was forced out of the company, they were doing maybe three million a year, or a little more," said Mickey Stern.

"And now?" asked Holder.

"Hard to say . . . we don't talk to them much. But they bought a new building, put in more machinery . . . I'd guess . . . probably two or three times as much . . ."

Maybe nine million a year, say at fifteen percent profit, or more, thought Holder. Call it one and a half million dollars a year, split two ways. And of course, they're paying themselves nice salaries, and there's bound to be a company car, some nice perks. So maybe a half-million-dollar life insurance payout isn't such a big deal to these guys.

But still, he thought, maybe. Maybe the company was in trouble and a half million would save it. At this point in the investigation, Holder had few names but many suspects. The Woodmans were gunned down at ten-thirty the night before. Holder knew that he and Crotsley were out at the airport at ten-thirty, so that eliminated them as suspects in the Woodman murders. The cop who got shot was also ruled out.

Everyone else in the world, including the four pale, worn-out relatives sitting in front of him, remained suspects until they could be cleared of any possible involvement.

"Excuse me, Mrs. Jackson," said Holder. "I know you're very upset right now, but I've been wondering where *you* were at ten-thirty last night, and how is it that the four of you happened to come down here this morning? I mean, the victims' names haven't been in the media yet."

Muriel Jackson, her skin pale with no makeup on, colored slightly.

"A perfectly proper question," she replied. "Last night about fifty people came to my home to celebrate the breaking of the Yom Kippur fast. We're Jewish," she said, unnecessarily. "Several of them, and my kitchen help, were still at my home last night at ten-thirty, and they will tell you that I was there, too."

Crotsley looked at Mickey Stern and cocked an eyebrow.

"We were at Muriel's. We live just down the street, so we walked. We were home by a little after ten," said Stern. "You can check."

"Thank you, Mr. Stern," said Holder. "We will. So, who told you that your sister and her husband were dead?" he asked, looking at Muriel again.

"My baby sister, Gloria, called me. Woke me up to say that Gerry and Vera had been shot, murdered."

"Do you have any idea how she found out?" asked Crotsley.

"She said that Michael, Michael—I can't remember his last name. Somebody she's dating. Maybe they *used* to date. Well, Michael lives here in the building, and he called Gloria, and she called me, and I woke up my husband and called Maxine, who is Vera's—*was* Vera's oldest daughter."

Crotsley wrote it all down in his notebook. Two more names to be checked out, Gloria and Michael.

"And what's Gloria's last name?" asked Crotsley.

"Karns, K-A-R-N-S," said Muriel. "Here are her numbers," she added, extending a small address book.

It was midmorning by the time Holder and Crotsley made it to their desks at Parker Center. Their phones had been ringing nonstop since early morning, and some anonymous office wit had taped the yellow paper slips with callback messages end to end and suspended them from the ceiling. A ribbon of messages reached down to each desk: calls from the press, citizens offering leads and clues, the usual percentage of kooks and cranks, and members of the victims' families.

A murder investigation is a marathon, not a sprint. Long accustomed to the pace of such events, Holder and Crotsley began methodically organizing their material and following a routine birthed by departmental fiat and long personal experience. They summarized the known facts of the killings: the use of handguns, which they had learned were either .38 or .357 caliber; two victims, both elderly and Jewish; two gunmen; the Ninja getups; the fact that the killers broke into an underground garage—all the minutiae of the preliminary investigation. They notified the Firearms lab to do a full forensic workup on the Woodmans' Mercedes. The results of their study would be useful in reconstructing the crime, because Firearms would test surfaces inside and out for gunshot residue, among other things. With this information, Holder and Crotsley would be able to say with certainty from where the fatal shots were fired.

Then they put the summary out on an interagency teletype network that went to law enforcement agencies throughout California. A copy also went into a national crime database maintained by the

FBI. Any agency seeing the report that had experienced a similar crime within its jurisdiction could be expected to contact Holder or Crotsley at LAPD Major Crimes and share this information.

Shortly after lunch—spent at their desks, writing up the preliminary reports, including a draft press release—Holder's phone rang. Muriel Jackson was on the line. She had asked her family—all those who lived in Southern California—to come to her home for dinner that night. She wanted Holder and Crotsley to come over, to meet everyone, to hear more details about the vendetta involving Neil and Stewart Woodman and their murdered parents. Tired as they were, Holder and Crotsley agreed to attend.

Just as the detectives were leaving the office, Holder took a call from Don Riggio, a detective who worked burglary out of the Hollywood station. About eighteen months earlier, Riggio said, he'd busted two young men on robbery charges. They'd broken into the home of one of television's best-known actresses and held her hostage. And, said Riggio, they had both been wearing black Ninja garb.

CHAPTER Five

Family Business

The name Beverlywood rarely appears on city maps; officially it is part of Rancho Park. But to those who live in this leafy, prosperous, upper-middle-class neighborhood on the low, gentle slopes south of Beverly Hills, it is a distinct and well-defined community adjacent to Hillcrest, the first—for many years, the only—Jewish country club in Los Angeles.

In 1948, Jack Covel and his wife, Rachel ("Lakey" to her family), bought four lots on the 2200 block of Beverlywood's Duxbury Circle and built custom homes for themselves and their three oldest daughters. Jack's youngest and favorite daughter, Gloria, lived at home with her parents. Duxbury Circle was home to the Covels, the Vera and Gerry Woodmans, the Muriel and Louis Jacksons, and the Sybil and Sidney Michelsons. To neighbors and family friends, the notion of all these close kinfolk living cheek-by-jowl on the same block often seemed strange, as though the family had herded together like musk oxen threatened by wolves.

Covel saw it another way. Like his Manchester forebears, he valued nothing more than family. Keeping them close was, to Jack—known familiarly as J. C. or Gramps—a means of enjoying them all the more, of being on hand to help when needed. It was also a constant reminder of who was in charge, who was the font of familial powers. For years, every Sunday morning Jack made the rounds of his progeny's homes, distributing bulky newspapers, mounds of exquisitely thin slices of smoked Nova Scotia salmon, tubs of whipped cream cheese, and bags of freshly baked bagels, stopping in each kitchen for a cup of coffee and a few words with his children and grandchildren. His daughters and their children were in and out of each other's homes daily, never bothering to knock or ring doorbells. His grandchildren played together, cousins closer than most siblings. It was, on the smallest scale, very much like the Eastern European *shtetl* and Manchester's Jewish ghetto from which his ancestors had escaped, though, of course, the Beverlywood homes were far nicer.

Covel owned rights to many Buster Keaton films, and had started a company called Lancaster Productions. A stream of cash gushed through his pockets; some of it he generously used to help his sons-in-law start their own businesses and steadily, quietly, get rich.

His son-in-law Gerry Woodman had a gift for spotting trends and market niches. As Gerry's sons would later say, you could lock Gerry in a phone booth and he would still find a way to start a company. His first enterprise, launched—partly with capital borrowed from Covel—in the early fifties, cashed in on Southern California's seemingly endless real estate boom and America's newest infatuation: television. Sited on industrial San Fernando Road in Glendale, at the eastern rim of the San Fernando Valley, Central Industries made cheap aluminum television antennas.

When that business tapered off, in 1954, Gerry sold out and started a new Glendale company, Fullview Industries, riding the post–Korean War home-building boom by manufacturing sliding aluminum windows and patio doors.

Meanwhile, the Woodman family grew to five children: Maxine and Neil, who had been born during the war, were joined by Hilary in 1947, Stewart in 1949, and finally, six years later, by Wayne.

As Fullview grew into a cash cow, Gerry became ingenious at finding ways to skim off cream. For example, manufacturing patio doors required the sawing, grinding, boring, turning, and chopping of aluminum alloys. As the business boomed, it generated tons of scrap aluminum, worth thousands of dollars a month. But while he turned his paychecks over to Vera, the scrap proceeds were his private funds, secretly used to indulge his growing vices: gambling, drinking, and seducing women.

Gerry Woodman had met Sid Michelson while living in New York during the war. When he moved out to California, he encouraged Sid to come along. Gerry introduced his good friend to his wife's pretty younger sister; after a brief courtship, Sid and Sybil were married. But while the Woodmans were flying high with Fullview, the younger couple struggled with their own business, Paper Fibres, which bought and sold scrap paper—and scrap metal.

"The Michelsons at that time were the poor ones," recalled Stewart Woodman. "They lived on our street but they never had two pennies to rub together. They drove older cars, their house was a mess. But rather than give Sid the scrap business, my father gave it to a man who lived across the street, a stranger, who became a millionaire off my father, Ralph Pearlstein."

Despite Vera's nagging, Gerry refused to give his brother-in-law the opportunity to make some badly needed money—and with it, acquire knowledge of how much cash Gerry was pocketing for his own amusement. When Vera challenged her husband to come up with a single reason why the Michelsons shouldn't, at least, *share* in the scrap sales, Gerry attacked, screaming vicious obscenities. It was his business, he said, and how he ran it was none of her affair.

Vera exploded, ransacking an ornate china hutch to fling gold-rimmed plates at Gerry. With each porcelain missile launched, Vera reminded her husband of his lies, his broken promises, his drinking and wenching and rotten behavior.

Retreating to the kitchen, Gerry counterattacked with pots, pans, serving bowls, small appliances, serving utensils, handfuls of knives, forks, and spoons—anything that came to hand. For a quarter of an hour, as Neil, Stewart, and their siblings cowered in uncomprehending fear, virtually everything in the house not fastened down went flying as husband and wife, neither willing to concede an inch, called each other the most obscene names they could conjure.

Finally Vera, choking out great sobs, threw Gerry's clothes on the lawn and said that she would never again share his bed.

Gerry stormed off in a huff.

The next night, Vera packed a bag and left as well, vowing never to return to any house where Gerry lived. The five Woodman children, shocked and frightened, were left in care of their nanny.

Gerry took a suite at the Beverly Wilshire Hotel, where he stayed for weeks, until Vera's sisters brokered a reconciliation and both parents returned to their home.

This was not the first of Gerry and Vera's quarrels, but it had lasting results: for more than twenty years afterward, even through his worst financial straits, Gerry kept that suite. It became his refuge from a tumultuous marriage—and a place to entertain a series of girlfriends and mistresses. At least one out-of-wedlock child was conceived there.

Growing up in the Woodman household, Gerry's children experienced a peculiar jumble of privilege and abuse. They learned to fear their father, but worshiped him for what he could provide.

As Fullview prospered, Gerry, rolling in money, became more and more enamored of gambling. It drove Vera up the wall.

"They were fighting over everything," recalled Stewart. "When I say he was gambling, you just can't imagine what he did in the late fifties and early sixties. He would bet anywhere from fifty dollars to one hundred and fifty thousand dollars on a game. Once my father and Sid Michelson were watching a Dodger game on television, and Dad locked Sid in the closet because he thought he was bad luck. For three hours, he wouldn't let him out."

In 1957, jockey Willie Shoemaker, riding Gallant Man, stood in the stirrups a heartbeat before he would have won the Kentucky Derby—and lost to Bill Hartack on Iron Liege. Gerry, who had bet heavily on Gallant Man, put his foot through Duxbury Circle's first color television set.

"When I was about ten years old, our house was raided by the police because of a poker game. Everybody ran into the backyard and climbed over the fence," said Stewart.

Not long after that, recalled Stewart, Neil, then sixteen, went to a bookmaker's office to collect Gerry's winnings. Police on stakeout watched Neil leave, followed him home, and arrested him with over a hundred thousand dollars in cash. Charges were dropped when Neil refused to claim the money.

Hilary and Stewart were raised by Sue Nelson, a live-in nanny. When they were twelve and ten, respectively, Nelson quit to marry a doctor. Stewart was shattered. "At that age, she was my whole life," he recalled. Soon after her marriage, Nelson brought her husband to visit the Woodman house. Stewart became furious, screaming at her husband, "You can't take her away from me!"

Wayne, who was four when Sue Nelson left the Woodman home, was raised by another nanny, a black woman from Norway. Young Stewart developed an early crush on her, too. "Gracie was wonderful," he recalled.

Deprived of a nanny's affections, Stewart became increasingly close to his mother. While attending the pricey, exclusive California Military Academy in the Baldwin Hills, a scholastic interlude Stewart remembers fondly, his mother often came to watch Friday parades. "She'd walk down the hall and I would think, 'She's the most gorgeous thing in the whole world,'" he recalled. Beyond his adolescent crush on Vera, Stewart came to think of himself as his mother's favorite child, her best friend. She confided in him, sharing her dismay over her often tumultuous life with Gerry. "She was miserable," said Stewart. "She used to always say to me, 'I could have married a prince or a lord, and I had to go marry your father.'"

Vera also railed against Gerry's father, Isadore, who had drank and gambled away a family and a fortune, leaving Gerry's mother to live with a notorious *shiksa*. "Like father, like son," sobbed Vera. Stewart, who had met his paternal grandfather but once, didn't know what to think.

Stewart left military school when he was thirteen and started seventh grade at a public school, Palms Junior High. He picked up a semester in the process, skipping the last half of the sixth grade.

The biggest reason for Stewart's change of schools in 1962 was that Gerry, who had made millions in the aluminum window and door business, was all but flat broke.

In 1960, for reasons Gerry never shared with anyone—his family always suspected it was because he had gambled away much of his operating capital and needed more—he took as a full partner in Fullview Jack Salzburg, who had previously prospered in the retail clothing business. In less than a year Salzburg was frantically unhappy with the way Gerry ran roughshod over him—and just about everyone else. He was also suspicious of Gerry's accounting methods: Fullview was taking in $20 million a year—equivalent to almost $100 million today—but somehow the company never returned much profit. Infuriated at Gerry's arrogant refusals to cooperate, driven almost mad by his temper tantrums and stubbornness, Salzburg filed suit to dissolve the company.

"He was so mad at my father that he said, 'We'll go down together,'" recalled Stewart. "And they did go down together."

After hearing the suit, a court ordered Fullview liquidated, its assets sold off. The partners got nothing for their trained work force, nothing for the hundreds of accounts salesmen had worked years to build up. The inventory, fixtures, office furnishings, and plant machinery yielded $2.4 million; Gerry came away with half. He was bitter; if the company had been sold as a going concern, with its goodwill and healthy customer base, his share would have been five times as much.

Gerry made a photostat of the check, framed it, and hung it in his study.

He then announced that, at age forty-four, he was now retired from business and would make his living by playing the stock market, an occupation he was sure couldn't be nearly as difficult as starting a manufacturing concern.

A neighbor, Lou Goodman, was a serious investor. He and Gerry were acquainted because Neil, Gerry's oldest son, went to Hamilton High with Lou's son, Larry.

Lou Goodman, being neighborly, offered Gerry some investment advice: "There's this new issue coming out," said Goodman. "You've got to go big into this because you'll make a fortune. It's a new issue from a small company called Fairchild Camera & Instrument. They've just developed the first integrated circut, a little chip that replaces vacuum tubes. And you ought to go in right now, before the market drives up the price." Gerry Woodman knew little about the stock market and nothing at all of Fairchild. But it was vitally important to his huge but fragile ego to appear before all the world as master of everything he attempted. To that end, he spent rivers of money on appearances—over forty thousand dollars on his sons' bar mitzvah parties—and reveled in playing the role of rich man.

So when a neighbor, the father of his sons' friend, told him what he *ought* to do with his money, Gerry reacted quite predictably.

He refused to listen to Lou Goodman. Worse, he was insulted at the advice.

He worked himself into a frenzy, deciding that he, Gerry, would decide where and how to invest his money, and nobody, but nobody, could tell him what he should do. Besides, thought Gerry, who does this stupid pipsqueak think he is? What the hell gives him the right to tell me how to spend money I've sweated blood for?

Gerry put almost every cent he'd received from the liquidation of Fullview into the common stock of Certainteed Products, then selling at about seventy-seven dollars a share. He bought on margin, paying a large fraction of the sales price and owing the balance to the brokerage, convinced beyond certainty that the stock would rise and he would make a big killing.

But a few months later the stock began to drift downward. Stubbornly Gerry held on, riding Certainteed down until it bottomed out at under eight dollars a share. It recovered to a little over nine dollars, then fell back.

Gerry was forced to sell all of it to cover margin calls.

When the dust settled he was all but wiped out, down to his last few thousand dollars. It was hardly enough to buy groceries, let alone support the Woodmans' luxurious lifestyle, which included a nanny, live-in maid, part-time cook, and a gardener. While Gerry ran Fullview, all of Vera's domestic servants were carried on the company payroll, enabling Gerry to take additional tax deductions. After liquidating Fullview, Gerry had paid the help from his own pocket, but now, with no income and little cash, he had to let them all go.

For years, no one in the family dared remind Gerry that if he had invested even a tenth of his money in Fairchild he would have reaped millions.

Devastated, Gerry had to endure Vera's carping for months. He was too proud to ask his father-in-law for a loan, too vain even to allow Vera to mention their need.

He called his sisters in Manchester, England. In 1958, when Fullview was going full blast and Gerry had more money than he knew what to do with, he had loaned one of them, Anna Hymanson, and her husband, Don, about a half million dollars. Don Hymanson wound up losing it all in a business. Now Gerry needed help, but the Hymansons had no cash.

Gerry knew a lot of people. He started asking around, but no one seemed ready to ante up. Gerry couldn't, of course, ask his brother-in-law Sid Michelson, even though the scrap company was beginning to prosper.

It was strange being broke, but ironically, Stewart remembers this time as the happiest period of his childhood, a time when he and Gerry grew close, when they spent days frolicking in the water in front of Santa Monica Beach Lifeguard Station Seven—and not just on weekends.

"We used to go the beach all the time. We always had five dollars, and that had to last us all day. Parking cost two bucks. We'd have hot dogs for lunch and on the way home we'd stop at Foster's Freeze on Pico and have a cone, and that would be the last of the money," recalled Stewart.

In these tender years, both Stewart and Neil looked up to their father as an almost godlike being. The unconditional love of a young child, however, was constantly tested by a father who could not stand to relinquish control of his children, even when they were at play. When Stewart was learning to surf as a teenager, Gerry, who never hung ten in his life, would stand at water's edge, bellowing, "You're not going into the waves right. You're not bodysurfing right."

Even in team sports, Gerry would not let up. At age eleven, Stewart pitched for the Rancho Park White Sox, a Little League team coached by his uncle, Lou Jackson. "My father used to get out there and shout at the top of his lungs, 'You fucking idiot, you're not supposed to do it that way, your fucking arm's too high,'" recalled Stewart. "I remember the umpire came up to me and said, 'Don't listen to that guy who's screaming at you.' I said, 'That's my father.' And he said, 'Oh, I am so sorry.' Finally they wouldn't let Dad in the park anymore during games."

Gerry never saw limits on the world he attempted to control. He had strong opinions on almost any subject, and once they were voiced he could never allow himself to change his mind. "There was always something," said Stewart. "My father could talk about politics and end up having the whole neighborhood hate him. When neighbors were outside their houses and saw him walking down the street, they'd hurry back inside. He could be the nicest guy in the world and one minute later he'd be screaming. He'd kick a neighbor kid in the tush—just the way he did to his own kids, and really, just to express affection—and the kid would cry and Dad would say, 'How can that be?'"

One of the Woodmans' neighbors was Louise Fox, who objected to the way Gerry spoke to her five-year-old daughter, whom he addressed as "Ugly."

"She runs and hides from you," said Fox. "She's afraid of you."

"I wouldn't say it if it wasn't true," returned Gerry.

Gerry held strong views on political issues and rarely missed an opportunity to air them. His brother-in-law Lou Jackson had a very different outlook. "They argued a lot over politics," recalled Stewart. "Dad was a staunch, staunch Republican and the Jacksons were 'liberals,' as long as no blacks moved in next door to them."

Vera, whose political beliefs paralleled those of her sisters, usually avoided the subject when speaking to her husband. When she did speak her mind, "Dad would just rip her apart," said Stewart. "I remember my mother always listening, taking all the arguing and never saying anything. But once my father said, 'Women shouldn't be allowed in sports. They can't run.' Mom said, '*I* can outrun *you*.' And the two of them changed clothes and went up the street, then raced down the sidewalk." Vera won easily.

But if Gerry Woodman was something of a Neanderthal, there is little doubt that in his strange, convoluted way, he loved his family. He provided them with the best food, stylish clothing, a clean, spacious home—every physical comfort—and even when he had little money to spare, lavished cars and expensive gifts on his children.

There was, however, an element of braggadocio in all this: appearances were extremely important to Gerry. He wanted people to think he had it all, loads of money and a close, loving family. Thus birthdays and other family celebrations were almost invariably extravagant events, attended by the whole neighborhood. Gerry made such a big point of reminding his family how lucky they were that he was their breadwinner that Stewart, as an adolescent, astonished his neighbors by bragging about how rich his father was.

Unfortunately, Gerry could never find the inner resources to risk telling his family of the love he felt for them. "He couldn't use the word 'love,' not ever. I never heard him ever use it, not once," recalled Stewart.

Gerry was so anxious for his sons to excel in everything that if Stewart or Neil botched a homework assignment, his rage knew no bounds. "The only time I remember really getting whacked around by Dad was during homework, and then I really got belted," said Stewart. "He'd hit me right in the face. My mother used to come in and try to get him out of the room, and then they'd get into another fight."

As a teenager, Neil worked part-time for his father at Fullview. They went to the racetrack and to weekend football games together, just the two of them. And just as Stewart admired his father, despite his abusive ways, Neil idolized Gerry. He tried to emulate his every mannerism. Physically, Neil most resembled his mother, with Vera's oval face, delicate bone structure, and fine features. But in every other way, Neil tried to be his father's little double. He aped Gerry's rolling walk, his British brand of profanity, his drive to prove himself the superior of everyone else he met. After trying but failing to emulate Gerry's British accent, Neil came up with a pseudo-Brooklyn Yiddish accent that sounded oddly like Gerry conversing with the older generation at the Orthodox synagogue. It was markedly incongruous coming from a Southern California teenager who spoke little Yiddish.

Neil also imitated some of his father's worst behaviors. He threw furious tantrums, screaming filthy epithets, throwing furniture, punching walls, slamming doors. These tantrums were not confined to home and family; he threw them in school or while out with friends, and they continued, whenever he felt stymied or embarrassed, into adulthood.

"I lived around the corner from Neil," recalled Susan Rosen, who went to Hamilton High a few years behind Neil. "So I saw him around the neighborhood, and in school. When I was about fifteen he had a friend of mine ask me if I'd go out with him. But he was known in the neighborhood as a very weird kid, strange and scary. I just couldn't stand the idea of being alone with him."

Neil was just out of high school when Gerry lost all his money. Suddenly, he had a different perspective on his father. "That was when Neil lost his respect for Dad," said Stewart. "I think Neil was hurt over the whole thing."

As boys, Neil and Stewart had little in common. Nevertheless,

Gerry seemed to delight in pitting one against the other, a tactic he would employ until almost the end of his life.

"Neil and I had very different relationships with Dad. We were always fighting, but of course Neil was six years older so there was no point in me punching him. But, finally, it did get to the point where it was always a physical fight, not just screaming and yelling," said Stewart.

Part of what they fought over was pool—billiards. When Stewart was barely out of diapers, Gerry had a special room added on to the house to accommodate a full-size pool table. Almost every night, unless the family went out, Stewart was required to spend two hours practicing billiards while Gerry watched, screaming and yelling criticism.

"We played fourteen, one-pocket billiards. Continuous. You go for the fourteen balls, leave one ball up and your cue ball and keep racking them. Each ball is one point; you play to fifty, a hundred, whatever. I had to call everything—there were no luck shots. If it was going to kiss another ball first, go off a bank, whatever, you have to call it. That's how the championships are played," said Stewart.

Egged on by his father, "Neil would say, 'I can always beat you. You want to play?'" Or Gerry and Neil would play, Gerry pointing out his own successful shots and berating Neil for his occasional failures. In spite of himself, Stewart became an excellent pool player.

"I got to the point where Neil couldn't beat me in pool. But I hated it. I hated to play it. I didn't play any of the games for fun, I played them because I had to be perfect at them," he said.

"It was just a game," continued Stewart. "But as far as my dad was concerned, if you played a game you had to become perfect in it. When we went bowling, he used to scream at us in the bowling alley. He required perfection in everything we did. People would stare, and he'd curse them out for not minding their own business."

When Stewart was about twelve and Neil about to graduate high school, Neil often came home in the afternoon and challenged Stewart to play pool. And at such times, with their father off at work, Stewart recalls that Neil often said, "Dad's teaching you all wrong. . . . He's nothing but a fucking asshole."

"Neil used to say that for hours on end," said Stewart. "At that time my father stood on a pedestal. I looked up to him. So one day I recorded everything Neil said, and I told him, 'The next time you say it I'm going to play it back for Dad.' After that, we didn't speak for a long time. Then Neil started up again and I gave my father the tape. Dad said, 'You think I don't know that he says this?' They hated each other, all those years growing up. But still, my father liked to pit us against each other."

One thing the brothers did share, as children, was suffering together from Gerry's fondness for public humiliation. He seemed to take special pleasure at having an audience—family, neighbors, friends, or even total strangers—to hear him scream about their stupidity and ineptitude.

After losing his fortune in the stock market, Gerry was desperate but unwilling to let his father-in-law have the satisfaction of seeing him beg for money. With nowhere else to go, Gerry took a mortgage on his home. He used some of the money to live on; the rest he loaned, at high interest, to a man named Milton Siegel, secured by a chattel mortgage on an elaborate piece of machinery called a vacuum former. When Siegel defaulted on the loan, Gerry took over the machine, which became the basis for a company called, at first, First Columbia Sales, on 104th Street in Los Angeles.

A vacuum forming machine is used to fill molds with fiberglass. Siegel's company had used the machine to make small boats for use in home swimming pools. Gerry had the idea to make bigger boats, up to fourteen feet long, that could be sailed from the new marinas budding along Southern California's glittering coastline.

Gerry's forte was building, not sales. Within days of starting production, Columbia was pumping out one boat hull every seventeen seconds. Gerry filled the factory yard, he filled every available storage area, he leased buildings. He built hundreds, then thousands of boats.

And almost nobody was buying them.

The day Neil Woodman graduated from high school, Gerry put him on a plane to Hamburg, West Germany. His job was to sell boats, first in Germany and then in other European countries.

Neil was given a one-way ticket and a few hundred dollars. He knew absolutely no one in Hamburg, and except for a few words of

Yiddish, which is related to German, could make himself understood in no language but English.

He slept in a closet-sized room in a boarding house, venturing out daily to sell his father's boats. For a year he endured Gerry's telephonic ravings, his fury over his eldest son's failures.

"Neil did what he thought was the best he could do, but my father was always on the phone to Germany, screaming and yelling at him," recalled Stewart. "You're stupid!" and "You can't do this right!" and "You're lazy!" bellowed Gerry, a man desperate to move the merchandise needed to keep his company intact, angry words from a man more than familiar with the tools of scorn, contempt, and derision.

There were few buyers for injection-molded fiberglass boats in Europe. Fewer still were willing to buy the larger sizes, which had an unfortunate tendency to crack in half without warning. After a year of bearing the unbearable, Neil returned in disgrace. He quit his job at Columbia Boats and took a position working for his big sister Maxine's husband, Milford "Mickey" Stern. Brother-in-law Stern taught him how to sell municipal bonds, and within months Neil was proving that he could make money by working a few hours a day on the telephone. Well before his twenty-first birthday, Neil Woodman was earning almost two hundred thousand dollars a year, and enjoying the sort of relaxed, bountiful life his father had lived before he lost his fortune in the stock market.

Neil married Maxine Shepard, a tall, pretty, big-boned, chesty woman whom many in Neil's family saw as too assertive for their tastes. The couple bought a house in Encino, the San Fernando Valley's "Golden Ghetto," and started a family.

And as the months went by, Neil found few reasons to see his parents, or even to call them. Somehow, however, he found a way to let his father know when he bought his first Jaguar, a blue XKE convertible.

Gerry, who was still struggling to keep Columbia Boats afloat and maintain at least the semblance of an affluent public image, was then driving an old, beat-up Thunderbird. When he learned that his oldest son could afford a luxury car so far beyond his father's means, when he thought about how ungrateful his son was, how he had never even offered money when he knew how badly his father needed it, Gerry almost went mad. For weeks he was impossible to live with, and the whole Woodman family paid for Neil's impudence.

When Neil heard that his father had gone bananas over the XKE, he savored his moment of triumph. He would never, ever, be able to forgive Gerry for the year of humiliation, abasement, and penury he'd suffered in Germany, or for the previous years of public mockery and ridicule. He would not, for many, many years, have the courage and self-assurance to confront his father directly. But for a few days, he reveled in the delicious satisfaction of knowing that he had finally found a way to start evening the score.

CHAPTER *Six*

Alibis

SEPTEMBER 26–29, 1985

Holder was surprised to learn, on the way up to Bel Air, that Earvin "Magic" Johnson, basketball superstar and the Lakers' perennial Most Valuable Player, lived on Moraga Lane next door to Muriel and Louis Jackson. So this is how a multimillionaire jock lives, he thought. It must be nice to have enough dough to live up here and watch the sun set over the mountains, and never have to worry about somebody breaking your face on the way to the store for a loaf of bread.

Arriving a few minutes after four, Holder, energy reserves dwindling from lack of sleep, was impressed by the size and appearance of the Jacksons' home. Muriel greeted him warmly, already treating him with the reserved familiarity due some long-lost family retainer.

Even after twenty years on the job, two decades consumed cleaning up after the worst that human beings can do to each other, Holder and Crotsley had not entirely lost their capacity for astonishment. LAPD detectives, who put in a lot of overtime, earn nearly a hundred thousand dollars a year, more than lieutenants with similar seniority. Comfortably middle-class, Holder and Crotsley were bowled over by what greeted them as they followed Muriel Jackson inside her mansion: an interior of exquisite wood paneling. Large, well-lit rooms displaying an assortment of designer furnishings tasteful beyond elegance, and walls hung with all but priceless works of art. Holder himself was a cabinetmaker, good enough to earn a living at it had he chosen to. He knew good work when he saw it, and to his practiced eyes the Jacksons' home was the product of hall-of-fame craftsmen with no budgetary constraints.

Their mouths open in wonder, the detectives declined offers of a drink from a Latino servant at a huge wet bar that would have done credit to any saloon Holder had ever visited, which was, he reflected, more than a few.

Most of Holder's cases have been on the south end of town; unless all the victims were dead, he thought himself lucky if any stuck around long enough to be interviewed. Assembled in Muriel Jackson's living room, however, were most of the surviving adult family members of Jack Covel's clan: Muriel's sisters and almost all their grown children. Holder was amazed; there was nothing in a long and varied career that would have prepared him to expect that all these people would actually be eager to talk to a couple of homicide dicks.

By this time Holder and Crotsley were agreed that, based on what they had heard from Muriel and Lou Jackson and Maxine and Mickey Stern, the top spots on their suspect list were reserved for the brothers Woodman: Neil and Stewart. But the detectives wanted to learn more about the family feud that Muriel had mentioned. And, by training and inclination suspicious sorts, both were eager to see how various other family members behaved. The detectives felt it was not out of the question that one or another of the well-dressed people assembled in Muriel's home might have had some less obvious motive for killing Vera and Gerry, and so would be delighted to let Neil and Stewart take the rap.

But what Holder and Crotsley heard from the assembled family gave them no reason to suspect they weren't hearing the truth—or at least, the family's perception of the truth—about the long, bitter struggle between Gerry and his two older sons. Many of these relatives had given depositions in one or another of the lawsuits brought by the Woodmans.

After listening and making notes on the family's view of events for nearly two hours, Holder began to feel that he was nearly out of gas and would have to find his bed very soon. Rising to his feet, he told Muriel that they had to go. "We've got a lot of investigation to do," he said. "But sometime soon I'd like to have everyone who was at the break-the-fast dinner back here. Is that possible?"

"You tell me the date and the time," said Muriel, "and everyone will be here for as long as you need them."

As Holder and Crotsley headed for the door, Muriel came up to say that Gerry and Vera would be buried on the twenty-ninth of September at one P.M. at Hillside Memorial Park. While Neil and Stewart would not be invited, said Muriel, she thought that they might come nevertheless. So, if Holder and Crotsley wanted to attend the funeral, they would be most welcome.

On their way back to Parker Center, the detectives talked over what they had so far. From the viewpoint of motive, it was looking more and more like Neil and Stewart. But when Holder had asked Sybil Michelson—Stewart's aunt and one of the few people in the family still speaking to him—to describe Stewart, he had been surprised: Stewart, almost six feet tall with brown hair and blue eyes, now weighed something over three hundred pounds.

There was no way, Holder and Crotsley agreed, that any three-hundred-pound, six-foot man would ever vault over the four-foot cinderblock wall between Brentwood Place and the apartment building to the west. So, they concluded, that meant that if Stewart was behind the murders, with or without Neil, he had probably hired someone else to do the killings.

That made the Ninja angle even more intriguing.

Holder got home, too tired to join his wife for supper, and tumbled into bed. A night of uninterrupted sleep left him feeling almost human. He met Crotsley at Parker Center at seven, checked out a car, and drove over to the Medical Examiner's complex on Mission Road. He hung out in the examining room, heavy on stainless steel and tile scuppers for blood and body fluids, while a forensic pathologist performed autopsies on Gerald and Vera Woodman.

The autopsies produced no surprises, confirming that the victims had indeed died from gunshot wounds. Five .38 caliber slugs, soft lead still bearing the distinctive twisting parallel marks left by a short, swift journey down a rifled barrel, and then flattened and distorted by passage through flesh and bone, were removed from the bodies and sent to the crime lab for a thorough examination.

On their way back to the office, Holder and Crotsley stopped at a newsstand to buy a martial-arts magazine featuring a picture of a Ninja warrior in full regalia. This was an evil-looking fellow in vintage Japanese black tights, with a hooded cowl, a mask, and a small armory of knives, swords, circular throwing weapons with razor-sharp points, and ninchucks, an arrangement of chains and wooden handles that can be swung or slung. There was a story with the picture, explaining that Ninjas were a phenomenon of Japan's pre-Commodore Perry days, night-blooming assassins who struck silently and who pledged suicide rather than allow themselves to be taken alive. In the office, Holder photocopied the picture to take back out to Brentwood. He wanted to show it to Roger Backman, the young man who had seen the two gunmen flee Brentwood Place.

The detectives skipped lunch, and spent their afternoon doing paperwork. They left Parker Center before four and headed west on the Santa Monica Freeway, stopping in West Los Angeles for a bite to eat. At five, supported by detectives from West Los Angeles Station and Major Crimes, they began knocking on doors along Gorham Avenue and surrounding streets.

An officer interviewed everyone at each address. Those not home would return to find a business card with a request that they telephone. Those failing to respond were recontacted.

They were fishing. Fishing for someone—anyone—who might have seen the gunmen, seen a car, seen or heard something suspicious. Fishing for clues, leads, something to lead them to the killers, something to tie in a suspect.

Holder and Crotsley reinterviewed Roger Backman, the only witness who had reported seeing black-clad assassins running from the crime scene. He agreed that the gunmen's costumes looked somewhat like the picture of a Ninja warrior that Holder had found in the magazine.

While the daughters of Jack Covel met to share their grief, Neil Woodman had been making and fielding calls from friends and relatives. One, soon after the murders were reported in the media, was from his aunt, Gerry Woodman's sister Betty Mason, who had loaned Gerry seventy thousand dollars. She called from England to ask if it was true that his parents were dead. Neil said he'd find out and call back, then hung up. He didn't call back.

The next day, Nanette Kersh, Betty's daughter, telephoned from San Diego. Neil became argumentative, then abusive. Kersh hung up on him.

Neil called Darrell Vienna, a prominent horse trainer who had worked thoroughbreds owned by Gerry and Manchester. Vienna had seen the newspaper story about the murders—it ran on page one on the second day following the murders—and he asked Neil what he knew about the killings, if what the paper wrote about "black-clad Ninjas" was true.

"These guys will strike again," said Neil. "Like the Night Stalker," he added, referring to a black-clad serial murderer and satanic cultist—ultimately revealed as Texas drifter Richard Ramirez—who for months had invaded California homes, raping and butchering nearly a dozen victims in their own beds. At work, Neil told his employees that he was sure his parents had been killed by a neo-Nazi group simply because they were Jews, and because it was Yom Kippur.

Neil had also been trying to find out where and when his parents would be buried. Where was not hard to figure; there are only a few Jewish cemeteries in the region, and Neil knew that his grandparents were buried in Hillside. Neil's wife, Maxine, called Neil's sisters. They were angrily uncooperative; each accused Neil of being the killer. One finally said that the funeral would be on the 29th of September, the fourth day after the murders and a day later than Jewish law requires—but the Biblical injunction takes no note of the requirements for a coroner's autopsy.

But Maxine still could not find out what time the funeral was scheduled.

Neil telephoned Rabbi Stephen Reuben at Temple Judea, a Reform congregation in nearby Tarzana, and asked for help.

Rabbi Reuben, wiry, nervous, and handsome, a well-dressed man then in his late thirties, had known Neil for several years. The day after the shootings, a congregant had phoned Reuben to say that Neil's parents had been murdered. Reuben had immediately driven to Neil's opulent Encino home.

"Neil's family was totally shook up, distraught, all of them," said Reuben. "Neil was in shock. They acted like any family does when somebody gets murdered. The kids were upset. People were crying. People were coming over. It was a typical crisis: numb, shocked, who, why, what.

"Neil said the things that people say when those kinds of things happen," the rabbi continued. "He said he didn't know what happened, if they were in the wrong place at the wrong time. He said something to the effect of, 'As you know, I wasn't on the best of terms with my parents and we've been having all this fighting, but they were the only parents I had.' It was like he couldn't believe what happened.

"Neil wanted to go to the funeral. His sisters announced that Neil and Stewart had arranged the murders and froze them out, wouldn't tell them when the funeral was. I don't know for a fact that the family arranged this, but when Maxine called to get the time for the funeral, they were given the runaround, and they were told their sisters didn't want them to be there.

"So he asked if I would help. I called over to Hillside to find out when the funeral was, and found out it was one P.M. and told them," added Rabbi Reuben.

"It appeared to be a tremendously painful experience for them—doubly painful because their parents were killed and then, because of all the stuff going on and the anger in the family, they couldn't even mourn, they couldn't participate in their parents' funeral. It's one thing to have lawsuits and business fights with someone in your family. It's another thing when they die. They're still your parents."

Stewart Woodman and his wife, Melody, were also members of Rabbi Reuben's congregation. "I spoke with him, as I would anybody who had a tragedy in their life," recalled Reuben. "And I spoke with Melody. And they all appeared to be in shock and then in double shock because of their frustration with the estrangement of the family.

"Their kids were really upset, because not only were their grandparents murdered, but they'd been cut off from them and never got a chance to redevelop the relationship. They'd been close, years before, and they had very positive memories. They'd been a very tight family," said Reuben.

"Neil told me his father had been his idol, his model, when he was growing up," Reuben continued. "It was painful for him to watch his father deteriorate. His father was this major gambler and owed all this money, and they'd bought him out of the business—according to Neil—because he was ruining it. Gambling all the money away. He was destroying the business, so they forced him out, bought him out one way or another, and he didn't like it. Then he opened up a competing business which didn't succeed, and then he was bitter. He had nothing else going on and his life was about trying to get back at them, I guess."

But Rabbi Reuben never met Gerry Woodman. "I only know what Neil told me," he said, shaking his head at the waves of senseless hatred he felt emanating from the family.

A long evening of canvassing had produced few new clues for Holder and Crotsley. Next morning, they met at Parker Center before driving to the West Los Angeles station to sit down with the other detectives and compare notes. Crime-scene photos were back from the lab, and Holder passed them around.

Just before noon, Holder and Crotsley called their office to check on messages. One was from Rick Wilson, who lived near Parkway Calabasas, in the hills beyond the west end of the San Fernando Valley. Even though it was a long, hot drive in Indian summer heat, the detectives headed for the freeway. Rick Wilson, until the previous July, had been a vice president, the sales manager for Manchester Products, the company now owned by Neil and Stewart Woodman.

Wilson was a ruddy, balding, sandy-haired Canadian in his mid-thirties. He had joined Manchester in 1977 as a sales representative, working his way up to vice president for sales. He told the two detectives that he had heard about the killings from Steve Strawn, Manchester's controller. Strawn had telephoned on the day following the murders.

In his Toronto twang, Wilson explained that for the two years before he left, he was in charge of national sales for the acoustical, electrical, and lighting markets. Since the departure of Gerry Woodman, Stewart had served as Manchester's chief executive officer, while Neil was president. Wilson had met daily with both brothers; they usually went to lunch together, often at Solley's, a deli on Ventura Boulevard in Woodland Hills.

"What can you tell us about the company's financial condition?" asked Crotsley. Wilson gave him a long stare, gathering his thoughts.

"Until two or three years ago, things were going very well," he said. "But in 1983, when the lawsuit with Mr. Woodman—Gerry—was settled, the company had to borrow six hundred eighty-seven thousand dollars to buy back his stock. That was a lot of money.

"Stewart put a lot of pressure on me to increase sales to pay off that debt," said Wilson.

"How did that go?"

"For a while, pretty good. But in early 1985 they bought a new machine, so we could make the latest plastics. 'Polycarbonates' are very-high-impact resins. It's a General Electric product. It's very clear, and very tough. Even a fairly thin sheet will stop a bullet. It's what the industry is switching over to, so it was a good idea for us, too. My salesmen were out selling the new stuff even before the machine was running.

"But they couldn't get the damn thing to work right. I mean, it's still not right. The plastic was too thin, or too thick, or there were scratches in it. We—they—can't—couldn't—ship anything."

Crotsley looked at Holder. They could almost read each other's minds.

"So this poly—this new plastic stuff. Is that the only thing they've got to sell?"

"Uh-uh. They've got machines that make other stuff. But the polycarbonate shipping is all backed up, and they're hurting. They owe a lot of money to Union Bank, that's where they get their financing."

"How bad are they hurting, do you think?" asked Holder.

"Well, when I left, they needed to bring in $40,000 a day—$800,000 a month—in sales to remain afloat."

"And were you doing that?" asked Holder.

"It was harder and harder. Our customers were leaving because so much of what we shipped was poor quality. They'd reject the whole shipment, and we'd have to pay for shipping both ways, and what we got back wasn't worth saving. So, no, as far as I know, they weren't making $40,000 a day. Not since the end of last year," added Wilson.

"Why did you quit?" said Holder.

"Mostly to get away from Manchester. I thought they'll be bankrupt in six months, I'd be out of a job anyway. And, it's crazy . . . working there. And, my girlfriend lives in Arizona, I'm trying to find a way to move there so we can be together."

"Tell us about Neil and Stewart," said Holder. "What are they like?"

"Well, Stewart is a big practical joker. He's always got something going on."

"Like what?"

"Well, once I came back from three weeks' vacation, and I was almost broke. Stewart said he'd put my three paychecks in my office, but when I opened the door there was a huge sheet of plexiglass just inside. And he'd ordered a truckload of plastic foam peanuts and had them pumped in. The room was completely filled—all the way to the ceiling—with these foam pellets. I had to take the plexiglass out and then shovel out the whole room to find my paychecks. He'd crumpled them into little balls and put 'em there with the foam peanuts." Holder and Crotsley exchanged glances. A practical joke on that scale involved careful planning and execution. They were thinking that the man who could put together a prank like that would have no trouble planning a murder.

"Another time," said Wilson, "he hired a stripper, from one of those services . . . you know, like for a party?"

Holder nodded.

"Only, she was dressed like a nun. And Stewart brought her in to the conference room and introduced her as Sister So-and-so, and said she wanted to talk to me about making a donation. Before we went in, he told me he had to leave and I was to just listen and tell her, 'Sorry, we can't help.' But then she said she'd do 'anything' for some plastic, and when I said, 'What does that mean?' she started stripping. Took off all her clothes. She came on to me, and when I responded to her, Stewart and several of the salesmen jumped out of the closet laughing and hooting."

"Okay, he loves a joke. What else?" asked Holder.

"Stewart loves to gamble. Neil, too. In fact, gambling was a way of life at Manchester Products."

Crotsley and Holder exchanged glances again. "Go on," said Holder.

"There's a big-stakes poker game every week in the lunchroom. He's got a satellite dish on the roof to bring in all the games. He subscribes to this service out of Las Vegas—game-day weather, injuries, stuff like that."

"That's it?"

"Oh, no. Bookies—he calls them, they call him. Every day. I'd guess Stewart gambles away maybe fifteen hundred dollars a day."

"Every day?"

"Just about. Well, sometimes he wins. Sometimes he loses even more."

"What does he bet on?"

"Football, basketball, baseball, the fights. Pro games, college games—whatever. Everything. Anything, anyplace he can get action."

"Does he ever go to Las Vegas?" asked Crotsley.

"Yes. All the time. Maybe eight or nine times a year."

"Is there some place he usually stays there?"

"He's got accounts at all the major casinos. We've had sales meetings there, different hotels, and wherever they go, the casinos treat Neil and Stewart like kings. They have a friend, Joey Gambino, who works at one of the casinos. I think he's like a pit boss, or something."

Gambino is an Italian name, not uncommon. It is also the name of one of the five major crime families running rackets in New York City. Anyone working in the Nevada gaming industry is licensed, and so the detectives' first thought was that anyone with a name like Gambino, if they were indeed associated with organized crime, would need a lot of juice to get by the Nevada Gaming Commission, which licenses all casino employees.

But Holder said nothing about this to Wilson, nor did he even look at Crotsley. Crotsley, reading his mind, wrote the name down in his own notebook.

"Tell us, Mr. Wilson, were there any unusual events at Manchester while you were there?" asked Crotsley.

"What do you mean?"

"Anything out of the ordinary. Something you'd remember because it was strange," said Holder.

"Well, every day was strange. The Woodmans had very strange ways. Oh!" inhaled Wilson. "That reminds me. Strange Ways. The racehorse."

"What about him?"

"Her. A filly. She died a few months ago, and the insurance paid off. The money went into the company—two hundred thousand dollars."

"The company owned a racehorse named Strange Ways, and it died?" asked Holder, wanting to get it straight.

"Owned three or four of them. Racehorses. Mr. Woodman, the old man, bought them. Anyway, Strange Ways died, the insurance paid off, the money went into the company's bank account."

"Any other unusual insurance payoffs?" said Crotsley.

"Well, somebody stole Stewart's Rolls-Royce last year. Company car. He bought a Ferrari with the insurance money."

"So, Stewart is a playboy? Fools around with other women?" asked Holder.

Wilson shook his head emphatically. "No. Not him. No other women. Never, not Stewart. He's a big family man."

"What about booze? Drugs?"

"I've never seen him drunk. I'd be shocked if he ever even smoked marijuana. His only drug is food. Stewart loves food. Junk food. Eats a lot."

"Okay," said Holder. "Tell us about Neil."

"Well, I worked mostly with Stewart. Stewart is a tremendous salesman, and that was my area. Neil was in charge of the plant, the manufacturing."

"What kind of a man is he?" persisted Crotsley.

"Neil is very different from Stewart. Very intense. He's got a quick temper. There's no telling what will piss him off. One minute he's calm and friendly, the next he's screaming at you. Sometimes he just acts crazy, like a lunatic or something. A very hard guy to know."

"Were you with the company during the lawsuit?" asked Crotsley. "Against the old man?"

"Oh, sure," said Wilson. "Neil loved every minute of it. He hated his parents, especially his father. Used to say he couldn't wait to see his father dead, that everyone would just be better off if his father was dead."

"He actually said that to you?" asked Holder.

"He said it to everybody. Stewart said it, too, but I think Stewart felt bad about the lawsuit. I think he really cared about his mother. But Neil—Neil just hates everyone in the family. Everyone but Stewart. In some ways, Neil is a lot like his father. Gerry, he was a helluva businessman. A tough cookie, very hard man, but real sharp. When he lost everything, he was so broke he moved in with Wayne, his youngest son. His kids took care of him. I mean, his other kids, not Neil, not Stewart."

"What about Neil and women or drugs?" asked Holder.

"No, not ever. Neil gambles, too. Plays poker, shoots craps, goes to Vegas, bets the games on TV, likes to go to the track. But no drugs, no women, no booze. Never. Not Neil. He's a family man, maybe even a little more than Stewart."

"Mr. Wilson, how bad was Manchester's financial condition when you left?"

Wilson didn't answer immediately. He seemed to be thinking, choosing his words carefully. "I'd say they were in big trouble. They owed Union Bank over a million dollars, and they weren't shipping any polycarbonate, and I could never figure out how they expected to pay off those loans. So I guess I'd say, they were desperate, or pretty close to it."

"Mr. Wilson, aside from what you have just told us, did you at any time ever hear either Neil Woodman or Stewart Woodman say anything that would cause you to believe they may have had anything to do with the murders of their parents?"

"Just that there was an insurance policy on Mrs. Woodman. Everybody in the front office knew about it. And, uh, Steve Strawn, our controller, told me that right after the murders they—Stewart and Neil—seemed very nervous. Everyone knew they hated their father. That's about it," he said, staring at the floor.

"Thank you, Mr. Wilson," said Crotsley. "We appreciate your cooperation. We'll be in touch when we need to ask you anything else. Or if you think of something, anything, that didn't come to

you now, give us a call." He handed Wilson his card, with the telephone number at Parker Center circled. "You can always leave a
message for us at that number."

On their way back to Parker Center, Crotsley and Holder
talked about Wilson. He'd told them some interesting things, but
there was something else, they thought. He was holding back
something, not telling all that he knew.

Neil and Maxine, joined by Stewart and Melody, avoided the
memorial service in the mortuary's family room, where their siblings, aunts, uncles, and cousins prayed, meditated, and consoled
each other. At the graveside service, they stood in the back, behind
the folding chairs where the rest of the grieving family sat.

As Stewart left the area near the grave, a mourner called out,
"Murderer! How dare you come to this gathering!"

Neil went after him, face purple and mottled, fists flying. There
was a scuffle, then Neil, bellowing with rage, allowed his wife to
drag him back to their car.

Stewart, in haste to leave, backed his car into a tree trunk, then
burned rubber as he sped away.

Silently watching this graveside drama from their chairs in the
last row were detectives Crotsley and Holder.

"Think it's about time we go see the brothers?" asked Holder,
and Crotsley nodded, then watched Neil and Maxine leave in their
Porsche.

"First," said Holder, thinking aloud, "let's follow up on the
crime scene, see what else turns up. And let's check out the Ninja
lead over in Hollywood."

"Right, Neil and Stewart can sweat a few days, no problem.
Maybe they'll do something stupid in the meantime."

"Yeah," agreed Holder, rising to show respect as the funeral
director pushed the button that took Gerry Woodman underground.

CHAPTER Seven

Plastics

Gerry Woodman had picked up Columbia Sales from Milton Siegel after Siegel defaulted on payment of the chattel mortgage Gerry held on his vacuum forming machine. Now in possession of a company but without operating capital, Gerry brought in his father-in-law as a partner. When Gerry took over, he changed the company name, first to Columbia Boats. Soon thereafter he had an informative discussion with new partner Jack Covel, and decided to change the name again, to Lancaster Products. After the disastrous episode with fiberglass boats, Gerry, drowning in unsold hulls, began looking for a new product, for some overlooked market niche, for an established product in a business with few competitors.

Success with TV antennas and with sliding doors had made Gerry familiar with fabrication processes and the construction industry. Calculating the manufacturing cost of various items, he decided that there was room in the marketplace for another manufacturer of plastic ceiling panels. By Gerry's estimate, K-Lux and Panelboard, the industry leaders, were selling enormous quantities of product on what he divined were obscenely thick profit margins. Gerry was certain that he could produce and sell panels at a profit for a fraction of what either company charged.

Gerry settled on a single product to launch his new company, something called a prismatic panel. It is used in office buildings, usually beneath ceiling-mounted fluorescent light fixtures. In 1965, prismatic panels were just beginning to see use in residential kitchens and bathrooms. The potential market for this and similar panels, as Gerry correctly guessed, was vast and growing.

For his sixteenth birthday on August 12, 1965, Stewart Woodman got two important presents. One was a brand-new 1966 Mustang, the car of the year, every teenager's wheeled fantasy. The second was a part-time job at his father's company.

"I used to leave [Hamilton High] school at noon, go down to Lancaster and work on the end of the extruding machine until maybe four," recalled Stewart. "In my senior year, when I was seventeen, I went out selling. And by that time, we had a couple of different prismatic patterns.

"We knew by then that we were going to get away from the boats, they were a disaster, and bit by bit we got into flat-sheet plastic. K-Lux and Panelboard were selling at eighty or ninety cents a square foot. We came out at eleven cents a foot. And we thought, at that price, the whole market would be ours," remembers Stewart. "Eventually we did get some of it. But, of course, the competition also cut their prices. We stayed at the low end, let them have the more expensive products."

Jack Covel had become rich long before he decided to become Gerry's partner. He bought in not because he saw the chance for still more money, but because of Vera's repeated urgings. To Vera, her father's presence in the family business would smooth things for Gerry, and that in turn would help make her own life less dramatic. So Covel, always charming, so very good with people, spent part of his week at Lancaster, although he had business interests of his own, including Lancaster Productions and his partnership in Fulltone, a manufacturer of office intercom systems based in Culver City.

"When the stock market opened, Gramps would go into the conference room and watch a television news show that had market ticker tape on it," recalled Stewart. It was all a game to Covel; if the market was down, he cheerfully counted his losses, measuring them in units of Rolls-Royces, then selling for about $18,000 in Southern

California. "Bloody market, I've lost three Rolls-Royces this week," he'd growl, eyes twinkling.

At Lancaster, Covel focused his soothing presence on customers, suppliers, and vendors, making it possible for Gerry to concentrate on manufacturing and distribution. Things ran far smoother when Gerry didn't deal directly with anyone not in his employ.

Nevertheless, Gerry continued to ride roughshod over almost everyone who passed through his orbit, including Covel.

"My father treated Gramps like a piece of shit," said Stewart. Covel, who moved in with the Woodmans after the death of his wife and who had always sought serenity, was greatly perturbed by the constant, bitter domestic warfare rocking Gerry's household. Like many who would come to know Gerry Woodman, Covel had a love/hate relationship with his daughter's husband. When things went his way, Gerry was usually gracious, charming, pleasant to be with, and generous. But if things went badly, when Covel or Vera—or anyone—challenged Gerry on anything, however trivial, he became, almost instantly, a snarling, foulmouthed, red-faced brute.

"I remember Gramps being so mad at my father sometimes, he'd come say, 'I hate him. I hate the man,'" said Stewart. "They fought constantly. Once, Gramps threw something at Dad and it missed but shattered the glass on a huge portrait of my parents and all us children. Down at the office one time my grandfather picked up a chair and threw it at him. Gramps was seventy years old when he did that."

Even the smoothly urbane Covel had a breaking point. After little more than a year under Gerry's roof, he moved two houses down the block to live in greater tranquility with his daughter Muriel and her family.

Neil, by then feuding almost daily with his father, moved down the street into the house Covel had vacated, fully furnished but vacant since his youngest daughter, Gloria, had married and moved to the San Fernando Valley.

All this clan angst notwithstanding, Covel shared with all his sons-in-law an old family business secret, a surefire way to increase the owner's take-home pay by cutting taxes, one of the company's biggest expenses, to almost nothing. Because this technique was frowned upon by certified public accountants, to say nothing of certain state agencies and the IRS, it was most important to Gerry and Jack that it remain a family secret.

For many years, it did.

Unlike his brother Neil, Stewart loved working for his father. "It had been drilled into my head that business was my destiny—I couldn't wait to go out and sell. I went on a work-study program at school; some days I left at 11:00, drove to San Diego, and spent four or five hours there calling on accounts. Or I would go up to Bakersfield. And I loved it. I was opening up a lot of accounts. My own sales were fifty percent of the whole company's sales, and some of those accounts are still with the company," he recalled, still prideful decades later.

Such success did not go unnoticed. Gerry Woodman was very proud of his middle son's achievements. When Stewart landed a new account or brought in a big order, Gerry would boast about his wonderful son. But he could never bring himself to share his paternal feelings with Stewart himself.

"My mother would say that Dad was bragging about me," said Stewart. "He could tell his business cronies, my uncles, customers, even people he barely knew—but he couldn't tell me. He just couldn't."

As far as Gerry was concerned, his older sons didn't need higher education, they needed to learn about the real world: business. So while daughters Maxine and Hilary were allowed to enroll in college—Maxine attended the University of Southern California for one semester before getting married and Hilary spent a year at a community college before her own marriage—Neil had been rushed off to Germany soon after graduating from high school.

So, too, was Stewart dispatched. "In my senior year I drove up to Bakersfield after school one day and opened up nine accounts in one afternoon and my father said, 'That's it, as soon as you're finished with school you can go to Chicago and start there,'" said Stewart.

He graduated from high school in June 1967, on a Thursday. "I was in Chicago on Saturday," recalled Stewart.

Just seventeen but almost six feet tall, Stewart took a room on Michigan Avenue in the Avenue Motel, a small, dingy place that rented for eighteen dollars a week. When Gerry Woodman's boy-hood friend Bernie Lazar came by and saw the place he was appalled. He gave Stewart a bed in his own home that night, and found him a decent motel the next day.

Acting on Gerry's instructions, Stewart rented a warehouse on West State Street. Then he began calling on small home-improve-ment stores and building contractors, selling prismatic panels. A few weeks after arriving, his father called. "Stewart, all the trucks are loaded with plastic. They're on the road to Chicago. Find another warehouse," said Gerry. So Stewart found a second ware-house, and went out to sell the panels on the trucks before the warehouses overflowed.

"My father and I were very close," said Stewart. "Wherever I was, I called the office every day, every night." Stewart also called home to speak to his mother. From the isolated perspective of a young traveling salesman sleeping in lonely hotel rooms, Vera became the lifeline to his comfortable home, his confidant, his best friend. Within a few years, if it hadn't already happened, Stewart became very much the mama's boy, very dependent on Vera for approval and the rewards of filial obedience.

When Stewart set out for Chicago the first time, Lancaster had but two salesmen, Stewart and Dan Cronin, who worked all over the West Coast. After Stewart's success in the Midwest, he and Cronin roamed the country, renting warehouses, opening territo-ries, hiring salespeople to work them, then moving on to the next new territory.

Millions of young men were drafted into the Vietnam War between 1965 and 1973. The brothers Woodman were not among them. Gerry had many business associates, among them some who knew politicians willing to exchange a little influence for a cam-paign contribution, for a favor, for a night on the town—for what-ever pushed their hot button. Each in his turn, Neil and Stewart—the latter a few weeks after drawing number thirty-two in the 1968 draft lottery, which would have ensured an almost immediate draft notice—were accepted by the Army Reserve for six months of active duty for training. Wayne, the youngest Woodman, was never at risk for the draft: he was still too young when the Vietnam War ended.

After Army basic training, Stewart broke a small bone in his back. During his military school days, he had injured the same region in a sledding accident; the new injury compounded the old. Vera, ever anxious about her children and alarmed at the volume of Percodan the Army was pumping into Stewart, prevailed upon her congressman to force a Surgeon General's inquiry. The dosage was reduced.

While Stewart was convalescing in an Army hospital, Vera and Gerry drove three hundred miles to Fort Ord, California, to visit. Vera brought her son his favorite delicacies and a mother's compassion. Gerry brought the strangest of news: Neil had quit his job. Instead of working for brother-in-law Mickey and taking home almost two hundred thousand dollars a year for a leisurely workday, he was again working for his father.

His new salary: three hundred dollars a week.

Vera was proud of herself for engineering this rapprochement. She had convinced her eldest son and her husband to give each other another chance. This was the best news a mother could have brought her ailing son, she believed, and if she noticed that Stewart didn't seem overjoyed, she may have put it down to the constant pain her poor son was suffering.

Before returning to his father's business, Neil had paid cash for a $75,000 house in Encino. That helped as he made do on the comparatively meager salary that Gerry grudgingly offered.

But why had he returned at all? Why had he given up a comfortable life for the constant squabbling and bitter put-downs that marked life and business in Gerry Woodman's thrall?

Until, at his mother's prompting, Neil had begged his father for forgiveness and returned to the family business, Neil had tried to make his wife's family, the Shepards, his own. Maxine seldom missed the opportunity to point out how peaceful *her* family life was, how there was no screaming or shouting or threats. During the first years of his marriage, Neil had spent much of his time enjoying the placid home life of his in-laws. And yet he had missed his own family. He missed the plastics business, the factory noise, the organized confusion, the deals, the drama, the excitement of making a product and selling it.

But that is only part of the answer. The root cause seems to lie in

Gerry's undefinable but undeniably overwhelming familial allure. To his family, Gerry was lord of their manor, king of their clan, the source of all the good things in their lives, a stubborn, difficult, but commanding presence, a black hole of affection that pulled his children closer and closer despite their intellectual judgments. Despite the scorn and abasement he suffered at Gerry's hands and despite the hatred he often felt for his father, despite a facade of rebellious disdain often expressed to friends and siblings, Neil craved his father's love with all the shuddering compulsion of an addict for his needle.

And yet, just like Gerry, Neil could not voice his yearning and feelings in public. Neil's sudden decision to return to his father's business mystified both families.

Neil was not welcomed to Lancaster Products with enthusiasm. Gerry made him serve long months at a desk in an office shared with female clerks and secretaries. He was given no defined duties; mostly he just sat at his desk and did nothing at all. And when Neil asked for something to do, Gerry made it very clear that he didn't think Neil yet capable of handling even sitting at a desk.

Gerry, who took Neil back only to accommodate Vera—and then only because she had made it a prime issue—had decided that the cost to his own male ego for giving in would be balanced by making Neil bear the full burden of his wrath. Gerry seldom missed an opportunity to tell visiting customers, hourly employees—anyone at all—how stupid his oldest son was, how everything Neil did inevitably became a mess, how everything he said or thought was a stupid mistake. And while Gerry wouldn't allow Neil to do anything, he took pleasure in introducing him as "my schmuck son who does nothing all day."

Neil bit his tongue and swallowed whatever Gerry dished out.

"Neil did everything, he bent over every which way he could, to please Dad," recalled Stewart. "I don't know why he did this, but when he blew up with Neil, he'd get real close with me and then when he'd blow up with me, he'd get close with Neil."

Despite the bitterness that marked family relations, Stewart, Neil, Gerry, and the rest of the family did everything possible to maintain a public image of a warm, close family.

"They had family meals together on Sunday, often at Gerry's house," recalled Lynda Beaumont, by then Jack Covel's steady companion. "And I was sometimes invited. Many Sunday afternoons I went there. I thought Neil was a charming, attractive young man. He loved his family. He adored his grandfather. He was a darling to his children. He was extremely attractive, very handsome. They were all wonderful together."

Seeing his grandfather almost daily, Stewart came to idolize Jack Covel. But Stewart had a cruel streak, and a penchant for practical jokes, always at someone else's expense. Not even his beloved Gramps was immune from Stewart's jokes.

"Gramps had a routine," recalled Stewart. "As soon as he came back from lunch he'd go into the office and run right to the bathroom.

"Once, right after lunch but before he could go to the bathroom, he got called in the office. I ran in the bathroom and took out every piece of toilet paper. He goes in, and about five minutes later he screams, 'Stewart, you son of a bitch, where are you?' I never answered him. Ten minutes later he comes out and looks at me and says, 'I knew dollar bills were good for something.'"

In 1968, just after Stewart's release from Army Reserve active duty and his nineteenth birthday, Gerry dispatched his second son to open up European markets. "I spent a month in Germany, a month in France, six months in England, a few days in Belgium, Sweden, Norway," he recalled. The orders began rolling in.

And on every possible occasion, Gerry would pick at Neil's psychic scabs, reminding him that Stewart was the salesman in the family. "[Dad] would always throw it up at Neil," recalled Stewart. "'He can sell the plastic, you can't. You've never done it. Look what you did in Germany. You cost us everything.' This type of stuff, all the time."

In 1968, having outgrown their southern Los Angeles facility, Gerry and Jack moved into a new one in Redondo Beach. They brought in a silent partner, Moe Bauer, who had insider connections with the Santa Fe Railroad. Bauer got the land from the Santa Fe for a song, and put up the money to erect a huge building at 4030 Freedman Boulevard. Bauer would share in Lancaster's profits, but stay out of day-to-day management decisions.

Not long after that, Stewart discovered a family secret. "I was a naive idiot," he said. "Somebody came in with a check, and I told him, just fill in the amount and sign it, but leave the 'Pay to the order of' line blank. Then I went to my dad and said, 'Look, I've got a blank check, make it out to yourself.'"

"He said, 'No, I wouldn't do that.' And instead he puts Lancaster Prod., Inc. on the check. Well, the name of the company was Lancaster Products, so I thought, 'Everything's kosher.' But then one day, right after that, I saw a bank statement on my grandfather's desk. Dad had deposited this check in the account of Lancaster Productions. And suddenly I knew what they were doing."

In California, corporate profits are taxed by the state and by the federal government. Company profits paid as stockholder dividends are also taxed, and all salaries, including those paid to company officers and directors, are subject to income taxes and other payroll deductions.

In other words, every dollar taken out of a company is taxed thrice. Jack Covel had long ago decided that such governmental triple-dipping was unreasonable, and that he wouldn't stand for it. Stewart had stumbled on one of the secret ways his grandfather and father used to siphon tax-free money from the company. The scheme worked because Covel had a bank account in the name of an almost nonexistent company called Lancaster Productions and because Covel and Gerry allowed no one else to open the company mail. Thus, when certain customers paid certain invoices, Covel or Gerry would deposit the check to the bank account of Lancaster Productions, which was a company in name only. Lancaster Productions filed no tax returns and produced no products. It served only to wash cash from one company to another. To keep the balance low, most of the cash was withdrawn almost immediately, then divided between Covel and Gerry.

Against the possibility of an outside audit, for every check they diverted to the "Productions" account, Jack and Gerry voided the original Lancaster Products invoice. Company accountants, who saw nothing sinister about cancelled invoices, a common occurrence, knew nothing of the skim; neither did the California Franchise Tax Board nor the IRS. Nor did partner Moe Bauer ever learn that as much as 20 percent of what passed through Lancaster was skimmed off by his partners.

"My grandfather explained the whole thing to me. He said he

never trusted my father. He said, 'Just know about it, don't use it against him unless you have to, but always know what's going on.'"

Lancaster's customers never caught on to the skimming scheme. When their own auditors went through "accounts paid" invoices, stapled to the back of each they found only a cancelled check bearing the stamp "Lancaster Prods., Inc.," corresponding closely to the invoice addressee, Lancaster Products, Inc.

According to Stewart, however, his aunt and uncle Lou and Muriel Jackson knew all about the skim, the slush fund, and where it came from.

"We all lived in the same block and when he walked the dogs around the block, Dad sometimes stopped at the Jacksons'. Once he walked in and saw a statement from the bank account for Lancaster Productions lying open on the bar in the den. He blew up, he went crazy, because then he knew that the Jacksons knew about it," said Stewart.

That left Gerry feeling vulnerable to the Jacksons. He worried that his in-laws might blackmail him by threatening to tell the IRS. But he worried more that Muriel might tell Vera how much money was flowing through his hands, that she might try to force him to account for what he blew on gambling and women.

But Vera never did. She had accepted Gerry's ways, made her peace with him, and wanted no more quarrels on that subject. If her sister ever shared this kind of information with her, she turned a deaf ear to it.

Jack Covel did not limit his financial support to Gerry. He also helped his other sons-in-law, especially Lou Jackson, who had started Angelette, a company that imported and wholesaled shoes.

"The Jacksons sometimes needed money to keep Angelette going, and Gramps loaned it at times. The Michelsons, too," recalled Stewart.

This did not set well with Gerry. "My father would say, 'You had no right giving him that fucking money. We need it more than they do,'" recalled Stewart. "Maybe, at the time, it was a lot of money to them. But I recall an argument over $50,000 and it was like they were arguing over Fort Knox."

As time went on, Stewart came to notice that there were other ways, including kickbacks on various supplies and services purchased by the company, in which cash was taken out of Lancaster. Once privy to the secret, Stewart became part of the conspiracy, frequently taking checks to a United California Bank branch at Rodeo Drive and La Cienega, many miles from the company, and returning with cash for his father and grandfather.

Despite all the skimming and kickbacks, Gerry and Jack built a booming business. Eventually Neil was allowed out of purgatory and sent to work in the factory. Under his father's skilled if scornful tutelage, he learned about cost estimating, quality control, packaging, managing inventory, and purchasing supplies and raw materials. On the factory floor, working with the men who ran and serviced the enormous extruding machines, he learned to appreciate the subtle mechanical quirks of the plastics business. Meanwhile, Stewart, more than ever the apple of his father's eye, spent most of his time on the road, selling.

Early in 1969, with business booming, Gerry, Moe, and Jack got a very interesting offer from Monogram Industries, a diversified conglomerate whose subsidiaries, including National Screw and Monomatic, a toilet manufacturer, brought in about $250 million a year. Monogram saw Lancaster as a small, thriving company with plenty of physical capacity for expansion. The Redondo Beach factory, with six extruding machines (but only business enough to keep two busy) and over 140,000 square feet of factory space, had the capacity to support production equivalent to sales of thirty million dollars a year.

So Monogram offered to buy Lancaster, keep Gerry on as president and general manager, and retain Jack, Neil, and Stewart in their respective capacities.

Gerry, after consulting with Covel and Moe Bauer, eventually settled on an arrangement that left the partners with five-year contracts and almost three million dollars in Monogram stock, each share then valued at a little over forty-five dollars. The partners could not, however, take possession of the stock—or sell it—until five years had passed.

During the discussion that preceded the agreement, Covel argued that the no-cash buyout was too risky since it would be too long before they could cash in their Monogram stock. Who knew what the stock would be worth in five years? asked Covel.

Gerry shouted down all their objections, and eventually, more to keep peace with Gerry than out of a sense of crafting the best deal, both agreed to accept Monogram's offer.

Despite his bitter experience with holding a single stock—Certainteed—only to see its value suddenly wither, Gerry never worried about the vagaries of Wall Street. He wasn't concerned about what the stock might be worth in five years.

Because just as soon as Monogram owned the company, Gerry set about configuring a system to prevent Monogram's internal auditors from learning the true value of the company's inventory. He had skimmed several hundred thousand tax-free dollars from Lancaster Products every year, and just because the company now belonged to some faceless stockholders, he had no intention of stopping. No intention at all.

Gut Feelings

OCTOBER 1985

The eyeglasses bothered Holder and Crotsley. They'd been found in stall sixty-three of the underground garage, on the floor near the front of the Jaguar, thirty-six feet from Gerry's body. The right lens had somehow popped out and was about two feet away, resting almost upright against the wall. Holder was pretty sure that these glasses had been Gerry's, but pretty sure, in a murder investigation, isn't good enough. And if they did belong to the victim, Holder couldn't imagine how they had gotten so far from his body or how one lens had come loose without shattering. And so he hoped that one of the killers had, for some reason, handled the glasses.

Because then there might be a fingerprint on the spectacles.

The Los Angeles Police Department is a large and, mostly, efficient organization. But its crime lab, among the best in the world, has not for some years been able to keep pace with the hundreds of homicides the LAPD is called upon to solve each year. While any evidence sent in for a workup would eventually get tested, test results often took months to come back.

Given that criminal trials in Los Angeles County are often delayed for several months, or even years, after an individual is arrested, lags in processing clues are merely inconvenient when evidence is needed only to confirm something police already know or when lab reports are used solely as evidence presented to juries during the course of a trial. It does *not* suffice when the clue might help identify a killer still at large.

To the south and east of Los Angeles County is Orange County, a more suburban, less densely populated, and somewhat less crime-ridden area. Holder called a friend in the Orange County Sheriff's Crime Lab and made arrangements for a new laser device to be used to check the spectacles' lenses for fingerprints.

Holder then called Muriel Jackson and asked her to describe the glasses Gerald wore at her home on the night of his death. Jackson could not be precise. Holder put the same question to Wayne Woodman, but the best he could recall was the name of Gerald's optometrist. Holder put the eyeglass issue aside. He'd get back to it.

He sent the clothing worn by the victims on the night of their murder to the LAPD's Special Investigations lab and registered them for a gunshot residue test, a quick, simple procedure. If the test was positive, it would indicate that the killers had fired from close enough to leave traces of gunpowder, a fact—or its absence—useful in reconstructing the crime.

There were two other clues requiring immediate attention. One was a license plate number that one of the Woodmans' neighbors had noted and written down. Holder assigned a couple of detectives in his unit to run the plate through the Department of Motor Vehicles and do follow-up legwork.

The other clue was suspects that Don Riggio, a detective working burglary out of Hollywood, had arrested on March 13, 1984: Daniel Sheppard, nineteen, and Anthony Pierson, eighteen. Dressed in black Ninja gear and carrying a sword, they'd broken into the residence of actress and director Penny Marshall ("Laverne and Shirley," *A League of Their Own*). The sword was a genuine samurai blade, over a hundred years old and razor sharp. Marshall had gone out for the evening, returning home while the burglars were still there. Waving the sword, the intruders took her prisoner. Soon, however, they ran off with their loot, leaving Marshall angry and shaken but unhurt. She telephoned the police.

This being Hollyweird, as many exasperated locals call it, two young men attired in black Ninja getups trotting down the boulevards with swag bags over their shoulders attracted remarkably little attention. But police nevertheless found witnesses who remembered the "Ninjas," and soon tracked down the young men. Apprehended, both pleaded guilty to robbery.

As this was a first offense, their prison sentences were short. Pierson was out of prison and living in a halfway house in Hollywood, pending full release on parole. But on the night of the murders, said Riggio, Pierson had a pass. His parole officer said Pierson had gone to see a movie in Westwood Village.

Westwood Village, thought Holder. That's only about a mile from Brentwood Place, where the murders went down.

Holder drove to the halfway house where Pierson was living to interview him. He asked the young man if he would consent to a polygraph test and, when Pierson agreed, drove him back to Parker Center for the exam.

A polygraph records physiological rhythms during a question-and-answer session. It measures respiration, pulse rate, and blood pressure continuously, and the operator uses the resulting charts to compare responses during "baseline" questions—innocuous queries such as the subject's name and address—with questions about the crime in question. People suffering from certain psychiatric disorders and skilled liars can often beat the polygraph. Other people, innocent of any crime but fearful of the authority represented by police, sometimes experience panic attacks or otherwise lose control of some body functions, thus producing false positives. The test depends on the opinion of examiners, and, considering all the variables, is notoriously unreliable.

Thus, polygraph tests are not admissible as evidence in court. But they are an investigative tool, and many police officers believe in them. For most detectives, a suspect who fails a polygraph exam is thought to show strong indication of guilt. This suspect will be subjected to intense investigation. And, for many detectives, when a suspect refuses to take a polygraph, that decision in itself seems highly suspicious.

"I've had a lot of innocent people say they're not going to take a polygraph," said Holder. "I'm not so sure you could get me in a poly, guilty or not.

"I can show you police detectives who believe that the first thing to do is give polygraphs. I can show you others who never use one. It's a tool and it has to be given that weight. I've seen people that say, 'I didn't do it, no way, give me that poly.' You take them in there, you put them on the poly, the examiner says, 'You flunked,' and they say, 'Yeah, let me tell you about it.' Sometimes it works. But it can't be relied upon," added Holder.

Pierson was a little nervous. His polygraph test was inconclusive.

Every good detective learns to trust intuition, and in his gut Holder did not think Pierson had anything to do with the Woodman murders. Pierson had, reflected Holder, a chance to kill Penny Marshall. Instead, he ran away. Besides, the Marshall case was a burglary, while the Woodman murders plainly were not. Also, the Woodmans were not sliced with an antique sword but shot with a modern gun. Nevertheless, Holder and Crotsley decided that they needed to check out Pierson's alibi for the night of September 25.

It was at this point that Mickey Stern telephoned Holder to say that the victims' family had decided to put up a reward. If men had been hired to kill the Woodmans, then someone else might know something that could help lead them to the killers. Stern agreed to participate in an LAPD press conference, during which he announced a $15,000 reward.

Stern also had a question: Had the detectives interviewed Stewart and Neil yet? "Soon," said Holder. "Very soon."

After Stern hung up, Holder and Crotsley looked at each other across their desks. Crotsley nodded, and Holder dialed Manchester Industries in Chatsworth, a residential and industrial community in the San Fernando Valley's northwest corner. He told the young woman who answered the phone who he was and asked to speak to Stewart Woodman. He was put on hold for several minutes.

"Detective Holder?" said the woman's voice.

"Yes?"

"Mr. Woodman is in a meeting, but he asked me to tell you that he'll be glad to speak with you. Please call his attorney, Mr. Jay Jaffe, to make an appointment." She gave him Jaffe's telephone number.

"Thank you," said Holder. "May I speak with Mr. Neil Woodman?"

"Mr. Neil Woodman is in the same meeting," said the woman. "But he is also represented by Mr. Jaffe."

"So I have to call Jaffe to make an appointment to see Neil Woodman, too?"

"That is what Mr. Neil Woodman asked me to tell you," said the woman, sounding like she was ready to burst into tears.

"Thank you very much," said Holder, hanging up.

Crotsley looked up, anxious to hear the rest of the story.

"Our boys have gone and got themselves a lawyer," said Holder. "Jaffe?"

"Jay Jaffe. If this is the guy I think it is, he was a big jock at USC. Baseball. Had a couple of major league tryouts. Old man was a lawyer, too. Made a bundle back in the fifties and sixties representing bookies. Lots and lots of bookies."

"I'd say that was pretty interesting," said Crotsley. "Them wanting to have their lawyer there when we come over for a little chat."

"Yeah, I'd say so. You ever meet an innocent man who hires a criminal lawyer before he talks to the police?"

"Not yet," said Crotsley. "But there's always a first time."

"I can hardly wait to meet these guys," said Holder, dialing Jay Jaffe's number.

Before meeting the Woodman brothers, Holder and Crotsley had several loose ends to tie up. One was the missing link. Or half link. When the assassins had cut through the bicycle chain securing the side gate, they left half the severed link on the sidewalk. Holder wanted to find the other half, and so he and Crotsley returned to Brentwood Place and pawed through the ivy. After an hour or so, they quit and went to talk to a neighbor couple they'd missed on the first canvas.

After a short, fruitless interview—the norm on canvassing—Holder returned to the planter for one more try. And just as darkness fell, in the dense ivy near the outer gate, he found the larger half of the chain link. Hoping for a fingerprint, he bagged it. Back at Parker Center the next day, Holder matched the half link to its mate, found on the night of the murders. It was a perfect fit.

Holder and Crotsley picked up Anthony Pierson in Hollywood,

then drove him to Westwood to meet with Emma Pierson, his mother. She confirmed that her son had telephoned from the theater about 10:30 on the night of the murders. Mrs. Pierson also consented to a search of the premises. The only thing interesting was some of Anthony's clothing. The detectives asked to borrow it. They planned to subject the clothing to gunshot residue testing to determine if Anthony had recently fired a gun while wearing those clothes.

While still on the west side, Holder, Crotsley, and Pierson went to the movie theater in Westwood Village where Pierson claimed he'd been on the night of the murders. They interviewed ushers and refreshment counter clerks, but none could positively remember that Pierson had been in the theater that night.

The trio then drove east to Hollywood, where the detectives searched the apartment of Matthew Beville, Pierson's friend and part of his alibi for the night of the murders, taking with them all the dark clothing they found there. It, too, would be subjected to tests for gunshot residue.

Then they went to the apartment of another of Pierson's friends, but the young man was not home.

It was nearly midnight before Anthony Pierson was returned to his halfway-house residence on Vine Street in Hollywood. Just as the detectives were leaving, Pierson had a thought. "When I called my mother that night I was almost broke, so I called collect. Wouldn't that call be on her phone bill?"

"Young man," said Holder, "you may have saved us a lot of work."

Pierson's mother produced her telephone bill, proving that Anthony had called from the lobby of the Westwood Theater only two minutes before Gerry and Vera were murdered. There was no way he could have gotten to Gorham Avenue in time to take part in the killings.

Within the LAPD the investigative section that handles illegal gaming is part of the Vice squad, known familiarly as Ad (for administrative) Vice. After talking with Rick Wilson, the former Manchester sales manager, Crotsley had called Ad Vice and asked them to run several names through their computer. If any had been arrested or implicated in illegal gambling, their names would be on file.

Ad Vice came back to Crotsley with the information that neither Stewart nor Neil Woodman had any arrests, but that their names were on record in connection with several known or suspected bookmakers.

Crotsley also sent the Woodmans' names, along with that of Joey Gambino, their pal from Las Vegas, to the LAPD's Organized Crime Intelligence Detail. But O.C.I.D.'s records reflected no information on any of them.

Jay Jaffe returned Holder's call on October 1, leaving word that he and his clients, the brothers Woodman, would be pleased to meet with Detectives Holder and Crotsley in his Century City offices.

Holder, who got the message, showed it to Crotsley.

"Tomorrow at three," he said. "Neil and Stewart and Jay Jaffe."

"Showtime," said Crotsley.

CHAPTER Nine

Manchester

The early seventies were a happy and prosperous time for the Woodman clan. Gerry worked long and hard at Lancaster, and a torrent of money gushed through his hands. Much of it went to make his family secure and prosperous.

Gerry played just as hard, vacationing in Europe each June with Vera, sometimes taking along friends and in-laws, staying in the best hotels, dining hugely at expensive restaurants, and wagering generous sums on the horse races at Ascot, Epsom, Newmarket, Doncaster, Haydock, and Kempton in England, at Longchamp, Vichy, Deauville, and St. Cloud in France, and at Curragh, Tralee, and Ferryhill in Ireland. Back home in California, he went to the track regularly, usually betting hundreds or thousands of dollars each time. There was so much money available to him that he simply didn't care if he won or lost. The bet was the important thing, the feeling of power that rushed through him when he counted out hundreds or thousands of dollars on a single race.

As he aged, Gerry became more civilized in his womanizing, showering Vera with diamonds and furs to make her feel wanted, while conducting a series of affairs—he almost always had a girlfriend or kept a mistress and, often, both—with secrecy and discretion. Unlike the early years, his paramours rarely called Gerry at home, allowing Vera to maintain the pretense that she was unaware of her husband's peccadillos. Nevertheless, she had developed a rule of thumb: the more opulent the surprise gifts she received from Gerry, the more guilt he was feeling. Vera came to regard the diamond bracelets, earrings, and pendants she accepted as campaign medals. Only rarely did she lose control and explode at Gerry.

Little by little, Neil worked his way back into his father's good graces, his acceptance measured in less frequent public humiliation and in gradually increasing responsibilities. Released at last from a desk in the back office, he learned more and more about the subtleties of plastics manufacturing, production scheduling, personnel matters, shipping, and especially about profitably managing a huge and decentralized inventory.

Stewart, too, continued to learn. He still spent most of his time on the road, opening sales offices all over the country and in Europe. Modeling himself after his grandfather, he matured into a consummate salesman, sensitive to his customers' needs, willing to go the extra mile for the good ones. If the customer was an owner or partner and he wanted a vacation, Stewart would see that Lancaster picked up the tab. If he controlled a truly important account, Lancaster might even give him a car—or his wife a mink coat. Even if the customer was only a purchasing agent or midlevel manager, Stewart found ways to keep him happy. A new set of golf clubs, a night on the town with his wife, or even an occasional lunch-hour tryst with a hooker—Stewart discreetly determined what was needed and Lancaster picked up the tab. He did whatever he had to do to keep his buyers happy and giving their plastic panel business to Lancaster. As long as the money flowed, Gerry remained a benevolent dictator, encouraging his sons in crude horseplay, tolerating Stewart's elaborate pranks, and reveling in the role of benefactor. As much as Gerry and his sons argued and fought, they laughed and joked and enjoyed themselves even more. As children, Neil and Stewart, awed as they were by their father's golden touch, had learned the cost of opposing him directly or contradicting him publicly. As adults they came to appreciate that for all his violent fits of foul-mouthed temper, for all his capacity for raging wrongheadedness, their father was a hard-working and astute player, right about business matters far more often than wrong.

And so the brothers, each in his own way, grew into businessmen shaped by their father's peculiar vision. They would look back upon these years with Lancaster, and the four that followed them, as the best and happiest years of their lives.

As Jack Covel's oldest daughter, Vera had seamlessly assumed the role of clan matriarch after the death of her mother in 1962. The daughters of Jack and Lakey, along with their husbands and children, celebrated the major Jewish holidays together, invariably gathering at Vera's home to cook and bake elaborate feasts, to catch up on family news, and to enjoy the pleasure of each other's company.

For the Woodmans, the source of all their wealth was Gerry's business, owned since 1969 by Monogram Industries, but operated by Gerry and his sons almost as though it was still their business.

For the record, Gerry drew a salary of $500 a week, modest compensation, in that era, for a man of his position. But his salary, which he turned over to Vera, was an almost negligible fraction of his income.

Monogram Industries, whose subsidiaries operated with varying degrees of autonomy, had invested healthy sums developing a near-foolproof inventory control system for Lancaster Products. Completed goods were stored on warehouse pallets, easily and rapidly moved around by small, agile forklift machinery. Stapled to each pallet was a punched computer card. Its duplicate was kept in Lancaster's executive offices.

"They used to print inventory cards from one to two thousand," recalled Stewart Woodman. "Monogram sent them over. We'd put one on every pallet in all our warehouses. So we'd put, for example, from one to five hundred in Los Angeles, five hundred and one to a thousand in Chicago, a thousand and one to fifteen hundred in Philadelphia, and the last five hundred in Atlanta. But my father would secretly take a hundred cards out of every stack and send the other four hundred on to the warehouses for inventory. When they took inventory, they'd tear off half the card and put it on the stack, send the other cards back to my father.

"But the auditors didn't realize a hundred cards were missing. So they'd never be able to pull one of those to audit it," Stewart added. "All they could do was go up to a pallet of material and say, 'Pull me the card on this pallet.' And the guy would say, 'There's supposed to be 146 cartons there.' And he'd count them. 'Okay, that's right, let's go to this pallet over here. How many on this one?' And the guy would say, 'The card says 412.' So he counts them and says, 'Okay, you're right.'

"My father and Neil filled out the numbers on the hundred blank cards. They would make up an inventory, maybe two hundred boxes on this pallet, a thousand on this one, seven hundred on that one," explained Stewart.

Thus hundreds of cards filled in by Neil and Gerry accounted for inventory that didn't exist because Gerry had sold it and pocketed the money. "When they counted up *all* the cards, including those my father held back from the warehouses, it all came out even. Neil spent most of his time keeping two inventories. He had one for the company and one for my father and grandfather," said Stewart.

Stewart recalled that his father and grandfather made up a rhyme to keep track of how much they had taken out of Lancaster. "The poem went, 'Roses are red, violets are blue, we're so much short of two million two,' or something like that. They took a fortune out of that company. The last year, just before Gramps died, they took $1,200,000," added Stewart.

In 1971, when Gerry decided that the pleasant confines of Duxbury Circle were no longer suitable to someone of his means, he handed a man named Feintec, an old and valued customer from Fullview, Gerry's patio door company, a brown paper bag containing $39,000 cash, for a lot on Casiano Road in Bel Air, a "view" property behind the new University of Judaism.

"Then he paid two hundred thousand dollars cash, to have a custom house built," recalled Stewart. "A lot of money for a house in those days. Especially for a guy on a salary of five hundred dollars a week."

After hiring a builder, Gerry set a date for when he would move into the new house. "He determined to move in the first week of June and that was it, that was when we moved in," recalled Stewart. "The house wasn't ready to live in. Dad didn't give a shit. We had no windows and it rained the second night—it was insane. We had no power, no water, no carpets. And no electricity. We walked around with candles all night. We had to use a portable outhouse— a block away—for three weeks, until plumbing was in, but my father was determined to move in that weekend, and so we had to move in."

But something magical happened to Stewart that June weekend, something that changed his life. "I was staying in England, opening up accounts there," recalled Stewart. "I returned that weekend to help with the move. And that's the weekend I met Melody."

Melody Placek was two and a half years younger than Stewart, sleek at 115 pounds, with thick, wavy brunette hair, huge brown eyes with dainty, enormous lashes, and but for a slightly Semitic nose, drop-dead gorgeous. Stewart had met her once, while he was still in high school, but she made no impression on him at all. "I was real good friends with a girl named Fran Sandowski," recalled Stewart. "Fran asked me to come with her to take flowers to a friend who was in the hospital with some kind of kidney or bladder problem. And while I hardly remember doing this, the girl in the hospital was Melody. Then for a couple of years after that I used to see her around, driving a pink Mustang. I never knew her name, or that this was the girl from the hospital, but I remembered seeing her because I drove a white Mustang.

"When we first moved into that new house on Casiano, the only thing that worked was the phones. And that was when Melody called," recalled Stewart.

"She said, 'We just moved into a house, my parents and I know you make plastic. We need some ceiling panels.' But then she said, 'That's not really why I'm calling. I'm just calling because I want to meet you.' And so we went out," recalled Stewart.

Melody, like Stewart, had not gone to college. After high school, she found work as a secretary. Stewart felt that they had a lot in common.

"We went out about three or four times, and then there was

the first time she met my family at a Fourth of July party at the Michelsons'. There was a family tradition—all the men played craps at these get-togethers. I will always remember Melody on her knees, rolling the dice, having the time of her life," recalled Stewart.

"I'd warned her about my sister-in-law, Neil's Maxine. I said, 'Don't listen to anything she says.' And it turned out that the first thing Maxine said was that her father wasn't at the party because he was with the Onassises on their yacht. We laughed about that for years afterward," sighed Stewart.

Stewart admits that he was attracted to Melody because he was looking for a wife who would treat him much the way his mother did when he was growing up. Melody offered him that kind of a relationship. "Melody was very easygoing. There were no put-ons between us, and we thoroughly enjoyed each other. We had the same sense of humor," said Stewart.

"We didn't have a lot when we got married. It didn't make any difference—they were the best times of our lives. I can remember Melody going into Sav-On Drugs and switching a shoebrush tag from $5.95 to $.99 because we couldn't afford the $5.95," explained Stewart.

Stewart and Melody became instant best friends. Within weeks of that first call to the house on Casiano Road, the couple announced their engagement. They were married on Columbus Day, October 12, 1971. Stewart, who had been raised to revere and respect his mother but was largely naive about the details of the conjugal bed, had a jolt on his wedding night. Embarrassed or perhaps feeling inadequate, he called Vera from his honeymoon suite and said he wanted to come home.

"You are a married man now, Stewart," said his mother. "This is not your home anymore. You'll just have to learn to be a husband to Melody."

But after that rough start, it was, for the first several years at least, a fairy-tale marriage. "We both believed in the same ways of raising kids. We laughed a lot, and we knew what each other was thinking without saying it," recalled Stewart.

Unlike Neil's wife, Maxine, Melody fit in well with the Woodmans. She got along very well with Gerry, who enjoyed having a glamorous beauty for a daughter-in-law, and with Vera, who treated her as another daughter. In time, however, Melody would grow jealous of Stewart's relationship with his mother. When he traveled, for example, Stewart often called his mother before calling Melody. And he confided to his mother details of his life that he never considered sharing with his wife.

Melody and Stewart had three children: son Ian, born in October 1972, daughter Jaycy, named after Stewart's late grandfather Jack "J.C." Covel, born September 25, 1974, and son Morgan, born in July 1978.

Despite Gerry's elaborate precautions, eventually Monogram Industries management may have begun to suspect that something was going on at Lancaster. But as long as the subsidiary was turning a profit, and as long as Gerry gave them no trouble, Monogram's management said nothing. In 1974, however, Gerry became enraged at a Monogram decision to change the way in which management calculated its bonus stock options. He began to rant and rave at Monogram's top managers.

"Monogram was not making money," recalled Stewart. "Their stock had come way down to under ten dollars a share, and they were not paying my father the salary he thought he deserved. At that time, they had a stock option bonus plan for officers, based on Monogram's annual profit. But when profits went down, management decided to change the basis for their bonus from profits to sales. They began selling stuff below cost just to get the sales up, so they could get their bonuses."

It was all right for Gerry to divert a fifth of his division's sales into a secret bank account, but when his bosses began playing their own sharp angles, he was outraged.

In July 1974, Gerry confronted Monogram's management. "My father said, 'I'm not going to allow you to do it,' " recalled Stewart. "They said, 'Well, who the fuck are you?' He said, 'I'm the one who's going to bring it up at your annual meeting. I'm going to be there and I'm going to tell the stockholders what you're doing,' " explained Stewart.

Monogram's management—Henry Gluck, Martin Stone, and Alan Blau—decided that they no longer needed Gerry Woodman's services. With almost a year to go on his contract, Gluck, Stone, and Blau informed Gerry that Monogram would exercise a buyout clause.

But Gerry had friends in Monogram's higher echelons. When he learned that management intended to fire him and his sons and pay off their contracts, he started making plans.

When the Monogram stock was paid, the shares were down to less than seven dollars a share. Gerry and Jack, instead of raking in nearly a million dollars each for their company, had to settle for just over one hundred thousand.

"My father didn't care," recalled Stewart. "He'd taken more than a million dollars out of that company. Way, way more."

Before the Woodmans departed, however, Monogram asked Stewart, Lancaster's national sales manager, what he thought about various salesmen on his staff, not knowing that Stewart was aware of the company's plans to fire him. Stewart said, "If it was up to me I'd fire every one of your salesmen. As employees, they're a waste of money. The company has to pick up all their fringe benefits, they have to give them vacation and sick leave. I'd get rid of them all and get independent contractors, sales reps, in their place."

What Stewart didn't tell Lancaster's new boss was that Gerry was looking for a vacant factory building. Gerry had decided to start a new company and go into competition with Monogram.

The new company would be called Manchester Products Co., Inc., named for Jack Covel and Gerry Woodman's hometown. Unfortunately, Covel did not get involved. He died on April 16, 1974, after a very brief illness.

"Gramps died bitching at a nurse because he wanted to see the Dodger game on television and they wouldn't bring it into Intensive Care. I went into the next room and brought a TV in and put it on a chair next to his bed, but when I turned it on, he was gone," said Stewart.

After Covel died, something peculiar happened.

"We were always kidding Gramps about dying," said Stewart. "We'd say, 'Make sure the money's going to be where we can find it.' Once I had a miniature coffin brought into his office with his name on it, and on the top I wrote, 'Isn't it about time?' He had a wonderful sense of humor, but we used to drive him absolutely crazy. Little did he know, they stole his money before he was even in his coffin.

"Gramps had at least a million dollars in safe deposit boxes and bank accounts—and we never found it. He kept cash in his room, and jewelry—huge diamonds. When he died it was like a buffet table on Yom Kippur night, the breaking of the fast. They went through it like a cloud of locusts."

Stewart won't say who "they" were. Stewart insists that he doesn't know what happened to Covel's cash, but it wasn't part of his grandfather's estate when it went through probate.

"In his closet, in a shoe, Gramps kept at all times, without any question, between seventy-five and one hundred thousand dollars. No doubt about it. Just a few days before he died, I put more than fifty thousand dollars in that shoe for him. I know he always kept money there, because in 1969, when I went to buy a boat, I asked to borrow some money. He sent me to his shoe closet, I took ten thousand, but there was a lot more there."

Covel also left some stocks and bonds, and some cash in a checking account.

"My Aunt Gloria wrote a check on his account the day he died. He'd left it, signed, with her. I think it was for seventy-one thousand dollars," said Stewart. "She emptied that account out," as Covel had intended.

But where was the rest of Covel's money?

"I know what my father was taking out of Lancaster, and Gramps got half of that. He went everywhere and did everything, but he had no family, no house, and he didn't spend a whole hell of a lot," said Stewart.

Gerry took millions out of Lancaster between 1969 and 1974. Most of it went to bookies, babes, and booze; Gerry was almost broke when his father-in-law died. So the initial capital for the new company came from mortgages on Gerry's and Stewart's houses. Stewart loaned Neil $20,000 and put in another $20,000 for himself. Vera—the house, and almost everything that Gerry owned, was kept in his wife's name to protect against possible lawsuit judgments—put up $40,000.

In July 1975, Gerry rented a vacant factory building on Mason Avenue in the industrial section of Chatsworth, in the northwest corner of the San Fernando Valley. By this time, Lancaster had taken Stewart's parting advice and fired all its salesmen. Gerry hired some of them.

Gerry knew a used-machinery broker named Jerry Winman. After learning that Lancaster had shut down its extruders and laid off all three shifts, he called Winman. "I need a couple of Hobbs machines," said Gerry, talking about a huge assemblage that went for over $100,000 in good used condition. "And I happen to know where you can pick them up, cheap."

Gerry knew because, just before he was fired from Monogram, he told management that they had excess machinery. He said, "We've got to get rid of some of this machinery, we don't use it anymore."

Gerry knew that Monogram was usually eager to dispose of anything that wasn't in use. Monogram's middle management asked Gerry to tell them which machines to sell, and he pointed out two Hobbs extruders. Before the extruders were sold, however, Gerry had pattern rollers put on these machines, the type that turned out the most popular model of plastic sheeting.

A few days after that, the Woodmans were fired.

"So if you know where to buy them, why not buy them yourself?" asked Jerry Winman, the used-machinery broker.

"Because, me they'd charge an arm and a leg. And they don't like me over there anyway," said Gerry Woodman.

"So how much should I pay for these Hobbses?" asked Winman.

"I don't care what you pay," said Gerry Woodman. "But I'll pay you forty-one thousand, and not a cent more."

Winman protested that he worked on commission. "I get fifteen percent over my costs," said Winman.

"I know you guys, how you work. Don't think you can screw me, I'm not like all your stupid customers. I know what's going on. For those two Hobbs extruders I'll pay forty-one thousand dollars, and that's it. Take it or leave it."

"Hold on a minute," said Winman, scribbling on a scratch pad. "I think you'll do better on my price plus fifteen—"

"Forty-one thousand, that's what I'm paying, take it or not."

"Forty-one, then," said Winman.

Winman bought the machines for $28,000. When Stewart tried to tell his father he should renegotiate and pay the usual commission, Gerry exploded and said, "I don't want to know, that's what I'm paying."

Gerry paid Winman $41,000.

"Winman picked up the machines in Redondo Beach, took them to his loading dock in his truck, and we picked them up in bright yellow trucks and had them delivered to our new factory, in the Valley," recalled Stewart. "Later we had to go out and buy another one, an NRM, and it cost one hundred and ten thousand dollars."

Next, Gerry hired production crews, largely the same people laid off by Monogram. Now all the new company needed were customers, and that was Stewart's department.

From his years with Lancaster, Stewart knew Howard Craig, owner of Plastelin, a Glendale company that bought $100,000 a month worth of ceiling panels. Stewart went to see Craig. He asked him to buy some of his panels from Manchester; before Craig would agree, he demanded to see the factory where they would be made.

"Howard came into an empty factory," said Stewart. "There was no machinery in the building, no furniture. He was laughing at us. We promised to have production in the following week. What he didn't realize was that the machines were already coming over from the other plant."

Stewart Woodman is a very convincing salesman. Craig ordered $6,000 worth of panels from the bare-walls company he'd insisted on viewing. In time, he became one of Manchester's best customers.

Once again, Gerry had created a new company virtually overnight, and had done so while risking almost nothing of his own.

And not long after Manchester was formed, Stewart was summoned to his father's office. Gerry told him to go to a branch office of United California Bank and open a new account in the name of Manchester Productions Co. "He had a check sitting on his desk from Channel Companies for about thirty-five thousand dollars," recalled Stewart. "And he didn't want to put it on Manchester Product's books.

"My father said, 'I'll take half and you and Neil can take the other half.' I was making four hundred dollars a week at Lancaster, and now I'm so broke I had to take a mortgage on my house. Eight thousand dollars to me was the world. From there on in, that's how we took money out of the company," said Stewart.

CHAPTER *Ten*

Showtime

OCTOBER 1985

Holder could see the late-afternoon sun reflecting on the showy glass-and-steel highrises of Century City through Jay Jaffe's office windows. A complex of ultramodern office buildings, a shopping mall, and hotels, in the late sixties it had risen from the weedy fields abutting 20th Century-Fox's mammoth film studio north of Pico Boulevard, just west of Beverly Hills. Now, Century City was one of Los Angeles's prestige addresses, boasting the offices of scores of lawyers, several nationally circulated magazines—including the pierced-pubes and nipple-ring variety published by Larry Flynt— and the headquarters of some of Southern Califonia's largest manu- facturing concerns, including Northrop. Century City was a wealthy, busy place, and its streets were full of flashy new cars and fast-walking, well-dressed people.

A pretty good view, thought Holder, looking down at the traffic and pedestrians, then westward through the orange late-afternoon smog toward a slice of blue Pacific, then north toward the green hills above UCLA. He wondered how many killers, rapists, and robbers, how many embezzlers, child molesters, pimps, and book- ies, how much human misery it took every month to pay the freight on this office. Holder knew that the system couldn't work without defense attorneys, but he didn't much care for them.

Crotsley didn't care about the view. He looked around the conference room, stifling his impatience. It was far from the first time he had been kept waiting by what he regarded as scumbags, but it was one of the nicer rooms he'd ever waited in. He found that irritating, as though the opulence of these offices was a calculated insult to the men whose job it was to bust their butts packing the lawyer's clients off to prison.

Holder and Crotsley had driven across town to Jay Jaffe's office to meet and interview his two star clients. Between themselves, the two detectives had already decided that if indeed the brothers Woodman were involved, they hadn't done the dirty work themselves.

"They didn't fit the profile," recalled Holder. "And my clear impression was that they didn't have the *cojones* to stalk down a Brentwood alley in black getups, wait for their parents, then shoot them down like dogs." More to the point, even if his life depended on it, three-hundred-pound Stewart could never get over that four-foot cinderblock wall. As for Neil, "Just my detective's sixth sense," said Holder, "but I couldn't see him hunkering down in a basement garage with a revolver, not when there was grease and oil on the floor and he could stain his trousers."

So what Holder and Crotsley were expecting to hear was that the brothers had airtight alibis for the night of the murders. And what they were expecting to learn this afternoon was what manner of beast they were dealing with, a matter of baiting the brothers to see how they responded.

The door to the conference room opened and Jay Jaffe entered, a tall, boyishly handsome, and graceful man with an impressive head of hair. Jaffe was in his late thirties, well-dressed, immaculate in a dark suit with a power tie. Speaking in a soft, friendly voice, he introduced a second attorney, Steve Revitz.

Revitz was a litigator. He explained that he represented Manchester Products, Inc., in civil matters, including recent lawsuits involving Gerry and Vera Woodman and Gloria Karns, Vera's youngest sister.

Revitz was in his early thirties, a fit, handsome, sandy-haired man, slightly below average height. His suit was expensive and well tailored, but Revitz bristled with so much energy that he seemed ready to burst from his clothes.

Holder thought he looked like a pit bull in a thousand-dollar suit.

After a moment the door opened again and Stewart and Neil Woodman edged into the room, all forced casualness and perfunctory handshakes. Neil was about five feet nine inches tall and on the slender side, owlish behind dark-rimmed glasses. Stewart was nearly six feet, a zeppelin who had once been elegantly handsome but now was morbidly obese. But he, too, was elegantly and expensively dressed.

Holder was well accustomed to interviewing homicide suspects who insisted on having their lawyers present. "That in itself was not unusual," he said. "The thing I've always noticed is that people who do that are all guilty. I've never had an innocent person say to me, 'Yeah, I'll talk to you but I want my lawyer present.' And I never met an innocent person who didn't want to talk to me."

As far as Holder and Crotsley were concerned, the trip to Century City was about what they expected—mostly a waste of time. "They told us a story that we didn't even have to go there to get. We could have sat in our office and made this story up," said Holder, almost amused. "Basically they told us nothing."

Neil and Stewart, occasionally interrupting each other, said that they were home hosting their own break-the-fast dinners when their parents died. And they said that it was true that for several years they hadn't gotten along with their parents. They described the way Gerry had changed after his heart attack, asserting that he had begun to drive the business toward bankruptcy with wild spending and crazy decisions. The brothers admitted that their business had held an insurance policy on Vera's life, but insisted that the reason for keeping up payments on the policy was strictly business. "Mom was over sixty, and even if we had to pay the premium—a few thousand a year—for another ten or twenty years, we'd get half a million dollars when she died," said Neil. "From a business point of view, that was a pretty good investment."

Then Stewart said they didn't really hate their parents, it was just that they didn't get along with them. They were difficult people, explained Stewart, and they had, a few years earlier, brought a lawsuit against their sons, which their parents had lost. And so their parents were bitter, chimed in Neil, and whenever the brothers got together with their parents there was usually an argument. So they had stopped talking to them.

"Did you have your parents murdered?" asked Crotsley, flat out, watching Neil's eyes.

"No, no, of course not," said Neil.

"For God's sake, no!" said Stewart.

"Do you know anything at all about their murders?" asked Crotsley, now looking at Stewart's eyes.

"No," said Neil. "Well. Dad was always a big gambler. He threw away millions of dollars in his lifetime. Las Vegas, the race-tracks, bookies. I think he owed some guy a lot of money. That might have had something to do with it," he continued, "but spe-cific details, who the guy was, who might have done this, no. I have no idea. None at all."

There was one more joker up Holder's sleeve, and now he tossed it on the table, just to see how the brothers would react. "Are you willing to take a polygraph examination—a lie-detector test?" said Holder.

Suddenly the room was very quiet.

"If, as you say, you had nothing to do with all this, and you passed the exam, that could pretty much clear you as suspects," said Crotsley.

Stewart and Neil exchanged glances. The room was silent for another long moment. "I'm not at all sure that a polygraph exam would be appropriate, just now," said Jaffe, in his smooth, low-key way. "But I'll discuss this with my clients, and we'll get back to you on it."

After a few pleasantries, Holder and Crotsley were bowed out of the conference room. Neither spoke on the long elevator ride to the subterranean parking garage, or as Crotsley nosed the bulky police sedan into the traffic on busy Santa Monica Boulevard. Finally, Holder chuckled. "Steak dinner says they won't take the polygraph."

Crotsley snorted. "I'm not giving away my hard-earned money. If you really want to bet, let's bet on how long it takes for Jaffe to call us with the news," he said.

"Two weeks," said Holder.

"Longer," said Crotsley. "A month."

"You're on."

Holder won the bet, but on a technicality: Jaffe called while the detectives were out in the field. Holder returned the call, but Jaffe was out, so he left a message. Jaffe called back a few days later, but Holder and Crotsley were in the field. They played telephone tag with Jay Jaffe for weeks.

In the interim the detectives continued the routine, the minutiae of details. They checked into two other recent murders involving aged Jewish couples, but the *modus operandi* were totally different. They gathered details of Stewart Woodman's many insurance claims. They pressed the crime labs for results. And they waited.

When they came into the office on October 14th, Crotsley had hardly filled his coffee cup when the phone rang. It was Rick Wilson, and he had remembered something that he thought might be important. Crotsley took notes.

As Wilson told the story, there had been some trouble with a customer, Jack Swartz, who owned SoftLight, a company that installed translucent ceiling panels in residential bathrooms and kitchens. SoftLight was in Riverside, about fifty miles east of Los Angeles, and Swartz was a regular customer. In 1982, he ordered some panels after Stewart called him to solicit business. Swartz had a small company with almost no warehouse space, and he was, necessarily, careful with his cash. The deal he made with Stewart on the phone was that Manchester wouldn't ship the panels he ordered for thirty days.

Manchester shipped the panels immediately.

With no place to store them, Swartz left the panels stacked on the floor, where they became a major inconvenience. Angry, he called Stewart and told him to come and pick up the panels, he didn't want them and couldn't pay for them. Stewart had calmed him down, said it was a mistake. After several minutes on the phone, Swartz agreed to send Manchester a postdated check for about $4,000. Manchester would hold it for three months.

Instead, Stewart deposited the check immediately. Swartz didn't have that much in the account, and when the bank called to say that his check had bounced, Swartz called Stewart and told him he had put a stop-payment order on the check.

Manchester sued SoftLight, a legal dispute that lasted three years.

What was most interesting, however, was that Rick Wilson now remembered overhearing Stewart telephoning Swartz and threatening him.

Crotsley called Swartz in Riverside and, with Holder listening on an extension, asked him about Wilson's story.

Swartz said that for three years, Stewart called every few weeks to demand the money. "He said he was going to do me bodily harm. He said he would do something to my family. He even called my home to threaten my crippled daughter in her wheelchair. She called me, crying, wanted to know why this man was bothering her," said Swartz.

On June 5, 1984, his adult daughter, Tracy, who worked for SoftLight, was working in the office. She told her father, "There was a sad-looking character outside." Swartz described him as a man about six feet three inches tall, weighing about 240 pounds, with wild, uncombed black hair and a day or two's growth of beard. He wore ripped blue jeans, a dirty T-shirt, and sneakers with no shoelaces.

Suddenly the man opened the door to SoftLight's office and asked for Jack Swartz. "He isn't here," said Tracy.

"The hell he isn't," said the man, pushing her aside and coming in. The intruder seemed to know all about the legal dispute with Manchester, and mentioned Stewart Woodman's name. He demanded $4,000 he said Swartz owed Manchester.

"He said if I didn't pay, he would 'Break both my legs or snuff out my life, whatever it took,'" said Jack Swartz.

Tracy dialed the police, and the burly intruder fled.

Swartz then telephoned Stewart to tell him what had happened. Stewart denied sending anyone to his business.

The Riverside police came, added Swartz, and while they were in his office the man who had invaded his business cruised by in a beat-up old Buick with Nevada license plates. Not long after this incident, said Swartz, he got a letter from Manchester's attorney,

Steve Revitz, demanding payment. Eventually, Swartz paid Manchester some money and the dispute was settled.

Holder and Crotsley thought this was interesting, that it offered an insight into Stewart's thinking. If what Swartz said was true, here was an example of Stewart sending a thug to muscle a few thousand dollars from what had been a good customer. If Stewart actually had done that, it was much easier to imagine him sending the same guy out to kill someone for half a million dollars.

The detectives made an appointment with Swartz to take his statement.

The next day, Jay Jaffe called and spoke to Holder. His clients were still considering the advisability of taking a polygraph, said Jaffe, but they had not yet reached a decision.

There was something else, said Jaffe. His client Stewart Woodman had reason to suspect that his telephones were being tapped, that he was being followed, and that someone was watching his house.

Holder and Crotsley were amused. Maybe Stewart was just being paranoid, the product of a guilty conscience. But if someone was actually watching him, it wasn't the Los Angeles Police Department.

"It's not us," said Holder to Jaffe. "And, by the way, the Sterns and the Jacksons are holding a press conference this afternoon at two o'clock, to announce an increase in the reward for information leading to arrest and conviction of the Woodmans' murderer. You might like to tell your clients."

Word of the press conference was also put out by the LAPD's press apparatus, which notified the City News Service. Within minutes, teleprinters in newspaper, radio, and television newsrooms were clattering away. When Mike Holtzman, the Jacksons' family attorney, stepped up to microphones in his Century City office that afternoon to announce that the daughters of Jack Covel, along with their husbands and children, were prepared to pay $50,000 to nail the killers of Vera and Gerry Woodman, his conference room was jammed with reporters.

The conference was timed to make the evening television news. It also made the front page of the *Los Angeles Times*. The story was accompanied by a photo of Vera and Gerry, hugging and laughing.

One of the *Times*' million-plus readers was John O'Grady, who had joined the Los Angeles Police Department in 1946 and retired twenty years later. O'Grady looked at the picture of Vera and Gerry Woodman for a long time. He read the article that accompanied it very carefully, and then he found a scissors and carefully clipped it out. There was someone he wanted to show it to, but the guy was taking a vacation in Australia.

Nevertheless, O'Grady called Jean Scherrer's office and left a message on the answering machine. "Call me as soon as you're back," said O'Grady. "I think we've struck it rich."

CHAPTER Eleven

Glory Days

Like her sisters Vera, Muriel, and Sybil, Gloria Covel married young. She was a beauty but just twenty when father Jack gave her in marriage to Hartley Karns in 1956. And as he had for her sisters, Jack Covel started a company, Fulltone Industries, with Gloria's husband as partner. Unlike her older sisters, however, Gloria did not, after marriage, nest along her family's street. She and Hartley, a nice-looking, happy-go-lucky type, moved to the San Fernando Valley. Until the San Diego Freeway linking the Valley to the Los Angeles Basin was completed in the late fifties, the journey from Duxbury Circle to Gloria's home consumed well over an hour, precisely the reason she and Hartley chose to settle there.

Unlike her sisters, however, Gloria did not marry well. She bore two children by Hartley, but the couple squabbled constantly, divorcing when their sons were quite small. Afterward, Jack Covel dissolved Fulltone, which made intercoms, and Hartley returned to live near his parents in Chicago.

Gloria soon married again, but this marriage ended even faster than the first. With only a high school education and few skills suitable for high-paying jobs, Gloria struggled to support herself and her children.

She was aided, over the years, by her father and sisters. She became a travel agent, associated with All About Travel, a neighborhood agency on Pico Boulevard. "She had only two regular accounts," said Stewart Woodman. "Angelette, Muriel Jackson's company, and my father's company. My father made us book our tickets through her. And maybe, whoever she was dating at the time, she got his travel business as well."

Stewart recalls that Gloria rarely went into All About Travel; she just collected commissions for tickets she booked.

When Jack Covel died in 1974, his will provided that most of his estate would go to Gloria, with the rest evenly distributed among children, grandchildren, and great-grandchildren. But little of Jack's supposed millions were found by his executors. To help Gloria, Covel's other heirs signed their inheritances over to her, a total of about $125,000.

This money came with strings, however. Gerald Woodman, who thought nothing of dropping $10,000 or even $20,000 on a weekly visit to the racetrack, expressed concern that Gloria might blow her inheritance on two or three shopping sprees. She might then, worried Gerry, turn up at his doorstep to beg for money to feed her children. Gerry's sisters-in-law shared this concern, and the money turned over to Gloria was conditioned on her investing most of it in some reasonably secure manner.

In July 1975, about the time Covel's estate cleared probate and Gloria got her money, Gerry and his two older sons were putting together Manchester Products. Start-up costs, including overhead for some forty employees, ran well over their anemic cash flow. So Gerry made Gloria an offer: if she would lend Manchester most of her money, about $105,000, he would pay her 12 percent interest on it annually.

Gloria told Gerry that she and her children could not live on $12,600 a year. But Gerry had already begun to count on her money, which was then urgently needed in his business. Gloria, dealing from her position of strength, extracted from Gerry a further concession: "My father said, 'Okay, we'll put you on the payroll and give you medical insurance and two hundred a week in salary,'" recalled Stewart Woodman. In exchange, Gerry insisted that Gloria sign papers saying that Manchester would not have to repay any loan principal for five years, when the entire sum was to be repaid. For the first few years, the interest was paid annually, but Gloria found it difficult to make the money last for an entire year. Gerry agreed to pay her quarterly. Later, she asked for monthly payments, and Gerry, after some grumbling, accommodated her.

Gloria Karns wasn't the only member of the clan to go on Manchester's payroll. Gerry's younger daughter, Hilary, married Mark Sutter. "I still don't know what happened there," said Stewart. "When my sister Maxine got married, it was a big deal—I bet my father spent ten thousand dollars on the wedding. But Hilary— I came home from school one day and my mother and father said they were married."

Like many young couples, Mark and Hilary struggled to make a living while he completed graduate school in architecture. To help out, Gerry often put Mark on Manchester's payroll at a few hundred dollars a week for his occasional services. At times, Mark was given the use of the car and a gasoline credit card. According to Stewart, however, that practice ended after Stewart accused Mark of abusing his father-in-law's generosity.

"We were very, very close, Mark and I," said Stewart. "But I got pissed off when I caught him abusing the privilege. I took it away from him, and all hell broke loose. My father was pissed at Mark, Hilary was pissed at me, and my mother was pissed at all of us."

Stewart thought of himself as very close to his sister Hilary, for most of his life the only sibling he got along with. After each married, they spoke on the phone nearly every day. Often, with their spouses, they visited each other's homes and went out to dinner together. But Stewart, despite his claims of brotherly love, despite sometimes helping his sister financially, could still be mean to his sister and to Mark, whom he cordially despised as a weakling who allowed his wife to dictate how he lived his life.

"We used to go out two or three times a week," recalled Stewart. "And I always paid for them. It was during the time between Lancaster and Manchester, when we had our salaries from Monogram but no company credit cards, no company cars. Once we went to the Spaghetti Castle, in Encino. Hilary told Mark, 'Don't order a Coke now, get it with dinner. You're not going to order two here, we're not paying for this dinner.' If that was *my* wife, I'd have belted her. . . . I used to ask him, 'I wonder why you don't beat the shit out of her,'" recalled Stewart. "He said, 'One day we'll get even.'"

In the mid-seventies, when Stewart and Melody had begun to make regular visits to Las Vegas, they often took Hilary and Mark along. "I walked into the Sahara for the first time, and went to play baccarat," said Stewart. "After about twenty minutes, a casino supervisor asked if I was going to see the floor show, and when I said, 'Yes,' he said, 'You and your wife are comped, whatever you need. If you want to stay here tonight you'll be our guest, and if not, call up next time and we'll have a suite for you.'

"Hilary and Mark heard that. When we went to the show, they ordered champagne and everything else. When the waiter brings the check, he says Melody and I are comped, but he gives Mark and Hilary a bill. Hilary hands it to me. I say, 'What am I going to do with this?'

"She says, 'Well, you always pay for it.'

"I said, 'Not this time.' And that was that. But oh, they were pissed off," chuckled Stewart.

Building a new company from scratch, even with the advantages of cheap machinery and trained personnel that Gerry had maneuvered out of his former employers, was a back-breaking process. Gerry, Neil, and Stewart threw themselves into the company, working long hours and weekends. Under such pressure many people crack, but stress was always Gerry's preferred element. Building a company was what he was born to do.

His sons were still learning. But, just as Gerry had taught himself every detail of his business, so were his sons expected to teach themselves.

"I learned how to sell, a little, from my grandfather," said Stewart. "But some things can't be taught; you have to make your mistakes. You learn by banging your head on the wall, by getting thrown out. I lost a lot of customers by saying, 'My competitor makes garbage,' until I learned to say the competitor makes a great product, almost as good as ours, but our price is a lot lower.' Until I learned not to bad-mouth," said Stewart.

As for Neil, his father rarely sat down and said, "This is how that works." More often Gerry told him, "Get out into the factory, you'll learn what you need out there, not in this office." Often Neil just sat in the factory and watched the machines and the men who ran them.

On the road for three or more weeks a month, Stewart honed his skills as a salesman, selling directly to chain retailers as well as to mom-and-pop hardware stores and generally avoiding jobbers and wholesalers. Sometimes this was a painful experience. "I went to Salt Lake City, one of my first trips. My father had a jobber up there named Owens-Corning, a pretty big company. Dad said, 'Just tell the guy you're going to be selling direct and everything will be fine.' This guy physically threw me out of his office!" recalled Stewart, still not appreciating his father's sense of humor. "After that, I opened up a sales territory in Salt Lake City, and hired a salesman to service it."

In 1975, the income required to pay Manchester's overhead, the "break-even point," was $165,000 a month in sales. "All three of us were working our ass off," said Stewart. "It was hard and stressful, and not everything was fine, and sometimes it seemed like we were never going to get to break-even. We were always scraping to reach our overhead. But finally we did reach break-even.

"About a year after we started we were doing about a quarter of a million dollars a month. Finally cash was coming into the business. And the same way as my father and grandfather did it at Lancaster, we took the cash out, my father, Neil, and me," said Stewart.

But there was one big difference: at Lancaster, Jack Covel had taken enormous risks by putting his name on a bank account to launder untaxed millions that he split with his son-in-law. When Gerry started Manchester, he asked first Neil and then Stewart to open the slush fund account in their own names.

Each refused.

"He got real mad because I didn't want to put my name on the account," said Stewart. I said, 'I don't give a shit anymore. I've got my house. I don't need the money like you do. Your name goes on it or we don't do it.' He screamed and yelled and cried about it."

But neither Neil nor Stewart gave in, and in the end Gerry put his own name on an account opened as Manchester Productions

Co. Had the IRS found this account, Gerry would have faced prison or lifetime exile in England, from where, he firmly believed, he could resist extradition indefinitely. And so the father took from his disobedient sons a measure of revenge in his uniquely calculating way.

"When my father started Manchester, he told us, 'I want us all to be equal partners. When Wayne comes in, he'll be a partner and he'll get twenty-five percent,'" recalled Stewart.

"This was 1975, when Wayne was still in high school. Then he was going on to college. So we agreed. Well, now the cash comes, and Neil and I are expecting to split things three ways. My father says, 'Wait a minute, I've got fifty percent of the company, so I'm getting half the cash.' That was the first time we realized he was fucking his own sons," said Stewart.

And yet this did not, at the time, cause Stewart more than temporary annoyance, because neither he nor Neil knew how much money was flowing through the company, nor how many other ways Gerry had found to divert even more of it to his own pockets. Gerry insisted on opening every piece of mail, and the company's books and payroll remained closed to his sons. The payroll held secrets that Gerry could not allow compromised.

And so, as it had at Lancaster, a torrent of untaxed cash gushed through Manchester. Even a mere quarter of this, Stewart's share, was enough to fulfill some of his childhood dreams. As a little boy accompanying his then-broke father to the beach at Santa Monica, Stewart had admired the yachts sailing in and out from nearby marinas. Gerry would swat little Stewart on the shoulder and say, "Watch, one day we're going to get one."

But it was Stewart who bought a thirty-six-foot Chris-Craft power boat, which he christened *Cutty Sark*, after his grandfather's favorite libation, and kept in a slip on Fiji Way in Marina del Rey. "My father never even came to look at it," sighed Stewart.

Stewart was so anxious to become a real yachtsman that after buying the boat he couldn't wait three weeks for the first opening in a Coast Guard boating safety class. "I figured I'd just go out and come back," he recalled. "But I didn't know it had two engines, so I only put one on." *Cutty Sark* went in circles until a passing sailor set him straight.

Undaunted, Stewart decided to cruise twenty-six miles to the fabled island of Santa Catalina, then return. He couldn't see the low-lying island in the mist, but he knew it was out there, somewhere due west, and it was miles and miles long, so he didn't see how he could miss it.

"I kept going and going and going and missed Catalina by about fifteen miles. After a while I turned around and there was fog at the back of the boat. I knew I was lost, so I made a deal with God, 'You get me out of this and I'm selling this thing.'"

Stewart finally raised the Coast Guard on his ship-to-shore radio. They said, "What are your C.F. numbers?"

"I said, 'I don't know what you're talking about. Just get me out of here.' They towed me back in and I sold the boat. But that wasn't the end of it.

"I only had that boat for four months. About a year after I sold it, my father got a phone call from the FBI. They said, 'Is this Stewart Woodman?' He says, 'No, he's on the road.' And they said, 'Bring him in, we want to talk to him.'

"My father started screaming, 'What have you done?'

"Turns out, I sold the boat to a guy who then used it to smuggle drugs in to Cape Cod from the Bahamas. He'd never changed the registration, so when they caught him, the boat was still in my name," said Stewart.

For over three years, from mid-1975 through late 1978, Stewart roamed the country and the world, selling plastic sheets. As always, he stayed in touch with his father by telephone. Once, while Stewart was in England, Gerry phoned, ordering him to hire his uncle by marriage, Don Hymanson, as a salesman.

But, as Gerry knew, Stewart had hired a salesman only a few days earlier. "Fire him. I want Don," said Gerry.

What made this especially bizarre to Stewart was that he remembered that years earlier, this same man, Don Hymanson, and Gerry's sister, Anna, had lost the half million dollars that Gerry had given them to start a business in California.

But Stewart was used to his father's quirky notions. "At that time, there wasn't a pedestal high enough that I could put my father on," said Stewart. "If he'd told me to jump off a building, I'd have asked what floor. That's just how it was—he was my father. He asked me to stay away from home for weeks and weeks at a time and I did it. I wanted to spend Halloween with my son, just once, but he always made sure that I was out of the country. Once he told me to go to some show that had nothing to do with our industry. For some reason he just didn't want me home then—I don't know why. I was a schmuck, but I did it."

Stewart's obedience—and Neil's—paid enormous dividends. By 1978, Manchester was operating at near capacity and doing over $3 million a year in sales. Gerry Woodman and his older sons were rolling in money. They turned their annual salaries of $100,000 over to their wives, Maxine and Melody—but these paychecks were only a fraction of their take. Beyond their shares of the secret slush fund, Manchester's partners missed few tricks in lining their pockets with untaxed money. The company maintained a petty cash fund, which all three partners dipped into weekly, each taking $1,000, sometimes more. Each of the partners was "reimbursed" for fictitious "business expenses" to the tune of $8,000 or $10,000—every month.

Above that, each partner drew a car allowance: $4,000 a month. But Gerry and his sons drove company-owned and -insured cars, filled their tanks with gasoline bought on Manchester credit cards, and had their cars serviced at dealers that billed Manchester for the work.

Gerry, Neil, and Stewart and their families were covered by medical and dental insurance paid for by the company. Manchester's payroll carried their maids, nannies, housekeepers, cooks, and other servants. If a servant required the use of a car, it was a Manchester car running on Manchester gasoline. When Gerry or his sons took friends to dinner in expensive restaurants or hired caterers for opulent, home-style gatherings, all the bills went to Manchester. If a plumber, painter, or carpenter—even a decorator—was needed at one of their homes, the bill always went to Manchester. Even the several telephones in their homes were charged to the company—and Stewart had a Manchester WATS line installed so that he could call around the country from his home.

It added up to a breathtaking lifestyle. Their wives began to accumulate closets full of exorbitantly priced, one-of-a-kind designer dresses. They each enhanced Mother Nature's feminine bounty with discreet visits to expensive cosmetic surgeons. Neil and Stewart plied their wives with spectacular furs and diamonds, decorated their huge, mortgage-free homes with the finest furniture and accessories, bought their children fabulously expensive toys and games, and indulged their own whims for extravagant cars.

And yet, as much as they spent on luxuries, Melody and Maxine were kept in the dark about their husbands' slush fund, the amount and sources of their secret incomes. "Our wives never knew about the expense checks. They knew about payroll checks and legitimate expenses, some interest checks. We weren't about to let them know what we were really pulling out," said Stewart. "They'd have taken it all, and spent it."

And like their father and grandfathers before them, Neil and Stewart began to indulge their tastes for gambling. They bet on professional sporting events. They went to Las Vegas more frequently. They sat in on weekly crap games and poker sessions in the factory lunchroom.

And yet, as their own affluence swelled, as memories of the lean years of early adulthood faded, as notions of their importance to Manchester grew, the brothers began to resent the sums that their father was losing at racetracks and casinos. While Gerry no longer bet on sporting events, certain bookies still welcomed his action, so long as he had cash up front. Gerry regularly hosted high-stakes poker games, where he might win or lose $4,000 or $5,000 any time he sat down.

As Stewart came to see things, his father's addiction to gambling stemmed from a desire to lose everything. Gerry could only be happy when he was broke, when he was working night and day, scheming to destroy competitors, intriguing to finesse every advantage from a customer, plotting the ruin of someone who had snubbed him. Only at such times, Stewart came to believe, when his father, by the sheer force of an indomitable personality, controlled everyone in his orbit, when his satisfactions came from demonstrating his ability to outthink, outscam, outhustle everyone, when he worked all day, boozed and womanized all night, and pulled off remarkable feats of legerdemain, when he reveled in all his masculine strengths—only then was Gerry Woodman truly happy.

Stewart saw his own gambling quite differently. Admitting that he might drop upward of $10,000 over a weekend, Stewart insists that he never gambled with money that meant anything. He loved to win, said Stewart, and usually made money at the tables or with his bookies. But bookies all but stood in line to get a piece of his action, and over the years Stewart spent virtually all of the millions milked from Manchester, leaving him with few invested assets. Stewart claimed the coveted high-roller's "comp" at half a dozen major Las Vegas casinos—and his brother Neil, whom Stewart recalls as an equally successful bettor, was similarly welcomed by casinos and bookies. None of these facts forced Stewart to confront the logical conclusion that his own compulsive gambling mirrored his father's vice.

Even if his father was determined to lose everything, Stewart, ignoring the contradiction, also came to detest Gerry's single-minded desire to win. "My father was a terrible, terrible sport," he said. "Once, playing poker, he had three jacks on the table. I had a pair of queens showing. From the way Dad had bet, it was obvious he had four jacks. The pot was, maybe, a few thousand dollars. When he won a pot, he always swooped his arm around it and said, 'Next time you should learn how to play poker.' And so I let him get his arm all the way around the chips and pull them toward him—and then I lay down my four queens. Dad went crazy. You'd think I just threw the table over. He stomped upstairs. 'I'm never playing with you again.' Until next week. This went on every single week.

"My father stopped betting on the games because I wouldn't cover his bets anymore," continued Stewart. "He'd say, 'You pay the bookie this week. Take it out of the cash account.' It was six thousand or eight thousand or eleven thousand. I just got sick of doing it. Then, to get money he'd go into my wife's purse, just come over to our house when we were sleeping and empty it out. Or sometimes, right in front of her. What was Melody going to do, was she going to say, 'Don't take any money?' It just got to where it was too much," sighs Stewart.

Manchester's money funded the entire Woodman family. By the time Gerry's youngest son, Wayne, was attending Duke University in North Carolina, his pocket money came from a Manchester pay-roll check. School expenses were also charged to the company, and the youngest Woodman carried company credit cards that he used to pay for weekend trips to New York or Miami, often accompanied by freeloading classmates.

With so many demands on its coffers and the steady siphoning diverted through Gerry's slush-fund account, with Gerry's propensity for dropping huge sums at the track, there were times when Manchester—or one of its owners—needed cash to handle some short-term emergency.

"We never really showed profits in that company," explained Stewart. "It was a private company and the bank understood that. And then a new loan officer comes in from Bank of America and he calls and says, 'Unless you show more profits, you're not going to get the one-hundred-thousand-dollar loan you wanted.' Now, my father could be the sweetest guy in the world and the next minute—well, when he heard that, he went nuts.

"I went into my office and called him and said, 'Don't scream at this guy. I've got the hundred thousand dollars, I'll give it to you, and I'll handle the bank.' He said, 'I won't deal with that bank anymore. You take care of it.' And so I went out and made a deal with Union Bank," recalled Stewart.

If Stewart lived in opulent splendor at home, however, and if his salary was generous and his perquisites breathtaking, he did not always enjoy much comfort on the road, where he spent most of his time.

In Manchester's lean early years, Gerry's notion of corporate travel was the lowest fare, even if it meant catching an all-night flight. His idea of appropriate salesmen's lodgings was the cheapest motel that changed bedsheets between guests. For local transportation, Stewart—like all Manchester salesmen—was expected to rent the least expensive car available. Stewart didn't especially mind this—until he learned that while he was scrimping on the road, Gerry had spent company money on a big shiny Mercedes sedan for his own exclusive use.

Stewart was also getting tired of traveling. For years he was home only two weekends a month. He worried that his three children were growing up without him. One day in 1978, on one of his infrequent visits to Manchester's home offices, Stewart was talking to his father, trying to make him understand. "I don't see my kids growing up," he said, hoping that his father would take the hint, because Gerry was a man who rarely responded to ultimatums except with a tantrum.

"I sat and talked with him and I said, I don't want to travel, I'm not going to travel this month," said Stewart. "We never really got around to discussing it in detail, working out how we would change things, because within about a month of that conversation he had a heart attack."

In October 1978, while Stewart was on a sales trip to Atlanta, he called home to speak to his wife. Melody said, "Your father's in the hospital. You'd better come home."

Gerry, then sixty-one years old, had been at his desk when he was stricken with chest pains. He refused an ambulance and asked Neil to take him to the hospital. But Gerry insisted on driving, evidently bent on proving that he could. The trip was frightening to Neil, with Gerry, who always drove at twice the speed limit, weaving all over the road. Several times Neil thought they would crash, but despite his repeated pleas, Gerry refused to give up the wheel until he lost consciousness in the emergency room driveway.

Stewart rushed home from Georgia to be with his mother while Gerry lay near death in an intensive care unit. Gerry's children—Neil, Stewart, Wayne, Maxine, and Hilary—took turns visiting their father in the hospital. And so did a beautiful young woman named Amy Hearn, who flew in from Denver, even though it had meant borrowing money for airfare.

Amy, trying to be discreet, managed to avoid meeting Gerry's children. But she could not avoid Vera, who for days spent nearly every waking moment at the hospital. One night Vera came by Gerry's room just before midnight. She saw the young woman bent over the hospital bed, and caught a glimpse of the adoring way Amy looked at Gerry. Another of his damn girlfriends, she exploded, this one so stupid and rude she lacked the sense to stay away at such a time.

But Vera was wrong. Amy was not Gerry's doxy. She was his daughter, born out of wedlock in the fifties to one of Gerry's secretaries, with whom he had carried on a long affair. Speaking in whispers in the hospital corridor, Amy identified herself, not concealing her patrimony.

Vera was furious with Gerry. Deeply hurt, she drove home, weeping, then phoned Stewart, begging him to come to her immediately.

"She said, 'The doctor says your father might die tonight,'" recalled Stewart. "'He said he's probably not going to make it. And I hope he dies. I don't want to tell you right now, but he's done something awful, and if he lives, I'm going to divorce him.' I stayed with her until four in the morning, talking." When he got home at dawn, Melody was furious with Stewart for leaving her alone in the middle of the night.

Stewart was concerned about his mother, and about the impact of a divorce on the family. "I knew my sister Maxine wouldn't let Mother live with her. Hilary couldn't afford it. And I didn't want my mother to be on her own. So I talked to her into staying with my father—the biggest mistake of my life," said a rueful Stewart.

It did occur to Stewart that he and his wife, or Neil and his wife, might have found room in their mansions for one tiny old woman. But he could not conceive of continuing to work with his father under those circumstances.

It was two years before Stewart learned what had caused his mother so much anguish. Stewart finally learned about his half-sister in 1981. "I got a phone call one day in my office. A woman says, 'I'm meeting your father for lunch.'

"I said, 'Who is this?'

"She said, 'It doesn't matter. Has your father left the office?'

"I said, 'It's none of your business. Who is this?'

"'I'm your sister. You're going to find out today anyhow.'

"I called my father and said, 'Who the hell is Amy Hearn?'

"He said, 'None of your fucking business. Don't you talk to her.'

"A year or two later, I was cleaning out my father's desk and there's a phone number in Denver. I called, and the number was

Amy's. She had a birth certificate showing my father was her father. He even signed it."

Stewart was delighted to learn that he had a new sister. "She had no money, and so I put her on the payroll, gave her two hundred and fifty or three hundred dollars a week, and I sent her some personal checks," said Stewart. "We talked all the time, and about six months or seven months later she got a job and said, 'Please don't send me any more money,' and that was that.

"I don't blame my father for having an affair," said Stewart. "But I blame him because for years Amy had to live on welfare, while my father had millions of dollars. That pissed me off. Here's a girl that had nothing, and my father was pissing away money left and right."

Weeks before his father's heart attack, Stewart had negotiated the purchase of a cream-colored Rolls-Royce convertible, a $39,000 item. He picked up the car the day his father was due to be released from the hospital.

"I thought I'd surprise him, pick him up at the hospital in the new car," said Stewart. "He comes out in a wheelchair and says, 'Whose car is this?' I said, 'I just bought it.' He refused to get in. Refused to come with me. He came home in a taxi. This was, of course, because *he* didn't drive a Rolls."

To drive home the point that he considered it unseemly for his son to have a better car, for months Gerry refused to let Stewart drive him to the office. "He did, eventually, ride with me," said Stewart. "That was the kind of person he was. He didn't mind what someone else had, as long as he had more."

Stewart traded in his Rolls-Royce about a year later on a new one. "It cost $68,000, and when I took delivery, my father said, 'I'm probably going to die soon. I'd love to have a Clenet, but I don't want to spend the money.' That was his way of saying, 'You go out and buy it for me.' "

To make his father happy, Stewart bought him a new Clenet, a handmade car built to order in Santa Barbara, California. Naturally, Manchester paid the $70,000 price tag.

Not long after Gerry settled into his Clenet, a parking lot vandal broke off the radio antenna. "My father refused to spend the money to get a new one," said Stewart. "He stuck a wire coathanger in there. He's going around in a gorgeous black Clenet with a coat-hanger stuck in it. It was nuts."

Wayne Woodman, the youngest of Gerry's children, graduated from Duke University in June 1978. After a few months on vaca-tion, he joined Manchester. Despite Gerry's 1975 pledge to share the slush-fund cash with all his sons, Wayne drew only a modest weekly salary. Neither his brothers nor his father were willing to let him in on their biggest secret: the source of all their money.

CHAPTER Twelve

The Big O

When Jean Scherrer returned from his vacation trip to Australia, he returned O'Grady's call. O'Grady reminded him of their meeting with Steve Homick and Neil Woodman. "And get this," said O'Grady, "remember the picture he showed us? That was the same picture the *Times* ran. Somebody bumped off the old folks. Ambushed them in their garage, shot 'em down. Didn't take anything, just wasted 'em."

"What do you think?" asked Scherrer.

"I think maybe this guy Homick had something to do with it," said O'Grady. "And I think maybe crazy Neil Woodman hired him, that's what *I* think."

"Why don't I call downtown," said Scherrer. "And then let's you and me go talk to those guys. How much did you say the reward was?"

"Fifty, large," said O'Grady.

"I'll call them right now."

It was with a mixture of pride and amusement that Sergeant John E. O'Grady, "The Big O," pride of the LAPD's Vice Squad, the bane of needle addicts and pot puffers, a man who charmed or frightened hordes of Hollywood hookers into becoming snitches—but was such a tight-assed Catholic prude that he trusted no women but his mother and his wife, and so never, ever sampled hookers' wares—accepted his nickname. The Big O stood six foot three, carrying 190 pounds of bone and whipcorded muscle. His trademark crew cut topped piercing blue eyes set in a handsome, disarmingly guileless face. O'Grady didn't know that suspects had rights, that doors had knobs, or that detectives take a vacation now and then. On his way to becoming the most feared street cop in Los Angeles, he never let lack of a search warrant stand in the way of an arrest.

From 1948 to late 1958, O'Grady was the pride of Chief William Parker's police force. He was brave, but not foolhardy, and utterly devoted to his work. Before his face was splashed across the pages of a dozen newspapers and magazines, O'Grady worked credibly undercover, spouting the lingo of the heroin hipster's demimonde, insinuating himself among the fraternity of the needle until someone offered to sell him drugs.

O'Grady personally arrested over 2,500 narcotics suspects, few of whom avoided jail. It was the Big O who ran jazz legend Charlie "Yardbird" Parker out of town, under threat of arrest on heroin charges. It was he who arrested saxophonists Stan Getz and Jerry Mulligan and trumpet player Chet Baker for possession of heroin. O'Grady feared no one for their wealth or position, and relished high-profile arrests, including Princess Lois Radziwill, who, stark naked, sold O'Grady a gram of heroin. She went down for six years in prison.

But eventually the Big O's approach to narcotics enforcement brought him into contact with people who had more juice than he could bottle. It happened in 1958, when O'Grady busted George A. Hormel, jazz pianist and heir to a $20 million meat-packing empire, for possession of marijuana, and his hundred-pound spitfire girlfriend, actress Rita Moreno, for kicking, biting, and slapping O'Grady and the four officers with him. The arrest made big headlines, but Hormel *père* was not about to let his only son go to prison without a fight.

Hormel hired a phalanx of private investigators to dig into O'Grady's ten years on the vice squad, and legions of hookers, burglars, petty grifters, strong-arm men, street hustlers, and junkies were interviewed. Squads of Hormel's socialite supporters bombarded the police department with calls attesting to young George's character and his many contributions to charity. Hormel had friends in Washington, too: the FBI opened an investigation into O'Grady's record, seeking to determine if he had violated the civil rights of those he had arrested.

No charges were ever brought against the Big O, but to quiet the storm of publicity, Chief Parker transferred him to burglary investigations in a sleepy corner of the San Fernando Valley. There he had so much time on his hands that during the years preceding his retirement, O'Grady completed requirements for a B.A. in public administration, and for certification as a polygraph examiner. When he retired from the LAPD in 1966, with twenty years service, he hung out a shingle as a private investigator.

O'Grady styled himself as "Hollywood's Number-One Private Eye," and indeed he cultivated a celebrity clientele, including Elvis Presley, Flip Wilson, Zsa Zsa Gabor, Jane Russell, the Doors, Peggy Lee, Jim Brown, Andy Williams, Chad Everett, and Sonny Bono.

Despite his high profile, O'Grady never got rich. In his 1974 autobiography, written with screenwriter Nolan Davis, O'Grady said the biggest fee paid for a single case to any private investigator he'd ever known or heard of was $25,000—and that what the man had done, bug the office of an inventor, was illegal.

As he got older and his celebrity clientele faded away, O'Grady continued working as a private eye. By the eighties, the Big O took what he could find. There were times when he worked for people he would have arrested had he still been a cop, and times when he may have nudged or crossed the line between the legal and the illegal.

But there was nothing illegal about the offer he got in the spring of 1984.

O'Grady was acquainted with Lou Cordileone, who had played in the National Football League for several seasons and was peripherally involved as a low-level functionary in a number of Las Vegas–based gambling activities. Cordileone called O'Grady and asked him if he would be available for a one-day security job, and if he could hire one other man, someone with a permit to carry a concealed weapon.

In California, few concealed gun permits are issued to civilians for any reason. The major exceptions to this rule are honorably retired police officers, who by virtue of arrests made during their previous careers have ample reason to expect the occasional armed revenge-seeker. Jean Scherrer had served thirty years on the LAPD, where he had made friends with John O'Grady, and so when O'Grady called to offer him good pay for an easy day's work, Scherrer agreed to meet for a late-afternoon drink at the Brown Derby, not far from O'Grady's office.

Scherrer found his friend O'Grady sitting with Cordileone and a tall, beefy man named Steve Homick. Homick, explained O'Grady, was another former LAPD officer, now acting as a security consultant for a San Fernando Valley manufacturer. One of the owners of that company, said Homick, had asked him to provide security for a family gathering.

Homick promised O'Grady and Scherrer $250 each for the day. The next morning, a Saturday, O'Grady picked Scherrer up and they drove to Page's, a coffee shop on Ventura Boulevard in the Valley community of Reseda. Homick was waiting inside. A few minutes later, an intense, slender, well-dressed man in his early forties arrived. Homick introduced him as their employer, Neil Woodman.

Neil shook hands, then said, "Your principal job is to see to it that my mother and father are not allowed at my son's bar mitzvah, neither at Temple Judea nor at the party at El Caballero Country Club afterward."

Stewart Woodman did not approve of his brother's plan to hire armed guards for his son's bar mitzvah, but Neil would not be dissuaded.

"Neil had this Napoleon complex," said Stewart. "He had power, so he had to use it. This way he could tell people, 'We hired guns to keep them out of there.' But really, he didn't expect our parents would try to crash the temple or the country club. What this was really about, from the beginning, was sending a message to our parents. And that message was, 'You'll never see your grandchildren again, never, never, never. And if you even try, I'll make you wish you hadn't.'"

*   *   *

Temple Judea is a big, busy Reform Judaism congregation with
thousands of members. So until 1984, when Neil's son Paul began
studying for his bar mitzvah, Rabbi Stephen Reuben, one of two
rabbis serving this wealthy congregation, was not well acquainted
with the Woodman brothers.

"I knew them mostly through their kids, some of whom had
been through the bar mitzvah and confirmation experience here,"
said Rabbi Reuben, nervously adjusting modish spectacles.

"I'd describe Neil as a very up, positive, engaging, entertaining,
funny guy. He had a great sense of humor, and appeared to be a
very successful business person. All my experiences with him had to
do with these life-cycle events and my perception was that he was
devoted to his wife and his kids, that his immediate family was very
important to him," said Reuben.

"Neil is not a 'blender-inner' type of person, he is a much more
exuberant human being. I liked him instantly and felt comfortable
around him and his family," added Reuben.

When Neil came to Rabbi Reuben and said he wanted to hire
security guards, Reuben was surprised. "It's very unusual to have
security guards at a bar mitzvah, even in this day and age," the
rabbi said, still perplexed. "It was the only time someone ever came
to me for that, and we had to get special permission from the temple board. I had to talk to the executive director, and to the president.

"Neil explained that he was worried for his son, that his father
was irrational and had a history of acting out, and had a lot of anger
for Neil and Stewart. Because he didn't want Paul's day ruined, he
wanted to quietly make sure that his father wouldn't disrupt things.
He told me that he was afraid his father might try to shoot him.
Neil said, 'I don't know what my father is capable of doing. He
could do anything.'"

But Neil never told his rabbi that the men he hired to come
into Temple Judea would carry loaded guns. "It was my understanding they were *not* armed," recalled Reuben. "Neil assured
the Temple board that there was no danger to anyone. He said
that these were people he knew, professionals. They were ex-

LAPD officers and I didn't have to worry. They'd be very unob-
trusive; under strict orders not to cause any ruckus or hurt anybody. Their only job was to make sure that the father didn't
come into the bar mitzvah. If he showed up, they'd simply stop
him at the entrance to the parking lot and tell him he wasn't
invited."

Neil Woodman sipped coffee in Page's as he described his parents,
Gerald and Vera Woodman. He showed John O'Grady and Jean
Scherrer a photo, an elderly couple laughing and embracing. He
listed the color and make of the cars he thought they might be
driving.

"What happens," asked Scherrer, "if they try to come in? How
are we supposed to treat them?"

"We waste them!" hissed Homick.

Neil Woodman nodded a vigorous assent, his face dark with
anger. "Use your guns, do whatever you have to, just keep them
out," he said.

O'Grady and Scherrer exchanged glances. They thought, Plainly,
this is a loony. They were both armed, but were not about to shoot
anyone if they could possibly avoid it. Neil calmed down and left a
few minutes later. Homick then gave O'Grady an envelope with
$500 in it.

From the coffee shop the men drove to Temple Judea, a
large, low-slung edifice several blocks away in Tarzana. They
found uniformed security guards patrolling the temple parking
lot and main entrance. O'Grady and Scherrer split up, hanging
around the entrances, watching as hundreds of well-dressed
guests drove in and parked. There was no sign of the elder
Woodmans.

Later, at the country club, they stationed themselves discreetly
near the main entrance, occasionally breaking away to roam the
grounds. No one resembling the parents of Neil Woodman ever
showed.

Scherrer and O'Grady leaned back in their booth and looked
around the room. The bar at the Sportsman's Lodge, on Ventura

Boulevard at Coldwater Canyon, was a large, comfortable place, full of stained glass, lots of warm wood paneling, and soft lighting. It was and had been a retired cop hangout for years. At a few minutes after five on the evening of October 23, Holder and Crotsley ambled in. The Big O tuned them in with a glance, and the two bulky men slid into their booth.

"Didn't know you wore glasses, John," said Holder, looking at O'Grady, remembering the Big O in his prime.

"Elvis gave these to me," said O'Grady.

"No shit?" said Crotsley. "*The* Elvis?"

"The one and only."

The two detectives looked expectantly at the older men.

"Got a little story to tell you," said O'Grady, and then he told it, police-officer-on-the-stand style, leaving out very little, and embellishing not at all. Scherrer chimed in, once or twice, with details.

Holder wrote everything down in his notebook.

"This guy Homick, he's retired LAPD?" said Crotsley.

"Not retired. Just on the force for a while, in the sixties," said O'Grady. "Not for long."

"Say where he's living now?" asked Holder.

"Vegas," said Scherrer.

"Mobbed up?" asked Crotsley.

"I'd say connected. Maybe. Just possibly," said O'Grady, not wanting to say why he thought so. A guy has to make a living.

Holder had pulled O'Grady's Administrative Vice file and read it that afternoon. He knew all about O'Grady and his gambler clients, knew everything the Big O had ever been accused of, real or imagined, and he just didn't give a shit.

Holder was a homicide dick, one of the best who ever stood behind a badge. Unless it helped to solve his murder case, he didn't care about arresting gamblers. Holder endured long hours and an almost thankless job for the ineffable pleasure of the "gotcha," an almost religious sensation of accomplishment that he felt every time he sent a killer to prison. A "gotcha" was confirmation that he had made a difference, that he had carried out his oath to protect citizens.

So, on the job, all Holder cared about was nailing killers. With what O'Grady and Scherrer had told him, he was fairly sure he knew who they were.

Now, all he had to do was prove it.

"What are you fellahs drinking?" asked the Big O.

CHAPTER *Thirteen*

Family Drama

Gerry Woodman had always opposed the very notion of life insurance. He thought it was an elaborate con game or a sucker's bet: to win, you had to die. In a similar vein, he thought that drawing up a will, by anticipating his death, was somehow an admission of defeat, an acknowledgment that his life had limitations. But Gerry knew no limits, admitted no weaknesses, and refused to acknowledge his own mistakes. Life was to be lived to the fullest, every minute of every day, and he would go on until he, Gerry, decided it was time to stop.

All this changed after his heart attack. For days, Gerry lay in an intensive-care ward, convinced that his life was over. With nothing else to occupy an always feverishly churning mind, he began to speculate on what would happen to his family after he died.

Vera would be fine, he thought. She was a clever woman and had, he was quite sure, salted money away somewhere without telling anyone. Even if she hadn't, Vera owned a million-dollar house, and her diamonds alone would keep her in comfort for many years. Should Vera ever need help, his sons would care for their mother. Even if they couldn't, her sisters would always be there.

His sons would be all right. He had trained them well, and

though he never told them so—he didn't know how—he was proud of what they had achieved together, building a company like Manchester from nothing to $3 million a year.

But Gerry worried about his daughters.

Neither had spent more than a year in college. Neither had significant job skills. When they were younger, there were many times when he'd had to help them out with cash, buy them a car, loan them money to deal with one of life's little emergencies. They just couldn't take care of themselves, of that Gerry was convinced. Fortunately, they were both married.

But Hilary, the younger one, was constantly squabbling with her husband, Mark—and he had never made much money anyway. As for Maxine and Mickey, they had a long history of marital strife. According to Stewart, they had actually filed for divorce once, but then they couldn't agree on how to divide the property and so stayed together. But Mickey had become wealthy and, as Gerry knew from firsthand experience, moneyed men are most attractive to women. What would happen if Mickey dumped Maxine for a younger woman? What if she wound up with nothing for her years of marriage?

That got Gerry thinking about wills. It had seemed stupid, paying a lawyer good money for something he would never need. And lawyers asked too many questions to suit a man as private as Gerry. But now, lying in a hospital bed with nothing to do but think, he could see the need for a will.

But not *his* will. A will for Vera.

Since Gerry's first business venture, he had insulated himself from lawsuits and judgments by keeping everything of value in Vera's name, including his shares of stock in Manchester Products. When he died, Vera would be left with a fourth of the company. But, worried Gerry, what if, after *her* death, their children fought among themselves for control of the company? How could he protect his children from each other?

Out of danger and on the mend, Gerry left the hospital for what he had supposed would be a few weeks of quiet recuperation at home. The next day, however, a maid serving tea spilled a pot of scalding water on him. Suffering second-degree burns, Gerry was rushed to the burn center at Van Nuys Hospital, where he remained for a week. Vera, still devastated over the discovery of Gerry's out-of-wedlock daughter, Amy, pointedly stayed away.

And even though Stewart had persuaded her not to seek a divorce, Vera, too, thought about life without Gerry, about what he would leave their children, and about all the dark, unmentionable things that run through people's minds when someone close to them has a first brush with death.

When Gerry could finally walk and drive himself, one of the first things he did was make an appointment with his lawyer.

"My parents called and said they wanted me to go to town with my mother to get her will set up," said Stewart. "I went along because many of the attorneys' questions concerned things she didn't know about.

"We met with two attorneys and went over everything, including the business. They asked, 'What are you really taking out of it?' And I couldn't tell them, because my mother was there, and if she'd ever found out, she'd have killed my father. I couldn't ask her to leave the room," added Stewart. "So I just said what I thought the business was worth."

The next day, Gerry, Vera, and Stewart went back to sign the documents that had been prepared according to Gerry's instructions.

"They were trying to protect Hilary more than anything else," said Stewart. "My sister Maxine would cut your throat for ten cents. My mother worried that Maxine would try to get everything, and would never let Hilary have anything.

"Mom and Dad figured that Maxine and Mickey were going to get divorced. Dad wanted to make sure that Mickey and Mark couldn't ever get into Manchester. He never wanted to let an outsider know what was going on—he didn't want to let somebody hold that over our heads.

"And, if my sister Maxine got into the business, she would have brought auditors, and we just didn't want that to happen," said Stewart.

"The [other] concern was over jewelry. There was a tremendous amount of it at that time. There was a twelve-carat diamond ring that she wanted to go to Hilary. There was a bracelet with seventy or eighty diamonds, and Mom wanted it sold with the money going to each of the grandkids."

Stewart was named executor of Vera's will. His younger brother, Wayne, was provided for equally with Neil and Stewart, and though Wayne wasn't yet married, bequests were included for the children Vera and Gerry expected he would eventually father.

Vera's will also provided for the disposal of her house, cars, and furniture, all to be sold and the proceeds divided equally among children and grandchildren. If one of the heirs wanted to buy the house, the property would be independently appraised and they could buy it at market value, with the proceeds shared among the other heirs.

"I was the only one who knew what went on with the will—they didn't want the other kids to know," said Stewart.

As part of the estate plan, an insurance policy was purchased on Vera's life, with Manchester to pay the premiums. After Vera's death, the payout, $500,000 plus dividends, would go to Manchester. The will provided that company management—Neil, Stewart, and Wayne—would decide whether to give the cash to Maxine and Hilary in exchange for Vera's stock, or to keep the cash and allow their sisters to share a 25 percent interest in Manchester.

Stewart had opposed this plan. "We were five children, and I thought that my mother's shares in the company should be divided equally among all of us—we'd each get five percent of the company. But my father—he must always have his way," said Stewart. "He said, 'No, that's not how it's going to be.' And I also didn't think it was fair that the premiums were paid out of the company—but that's how it was."

Vera's inked signatures on the will were barely dry when conflict began between her older sons and Wayne, her youngest.

Wayne had joined Manchester a few weeks after graduating from Duke University in June 1978. Gerry insisted that Wayne draw the same salary as his older sons—but it would be years before he knew about, or shared in, the million dollars a year his father and brothers skimmed from the company.

Gerry suffered his heart attack not long after Wayne came into the business. While he recuperated, Wayne was expected to handle some of the duties performed by Neil and Stewart, so that they in turn could take over some of Gerry's previous responsibilities.

But from his first day in charge of credit and trucking, Neil and

Stewart resented their brother's entry into Manchester as management.

"I started working in that business when I was sixteen. The same thing with Neil. There was no thought of going four years to a university, there was no money to do that, we were expected to go on the road and sell, to start that way in the business, and we did," said Stewart.

"I know an education is wonderful, but you take someone out of business school and put them in the middle of a family-owned business and there's going to be things that they just didn't learn in school. It just doesn't work like that."

Stewart and Neil immediately found fault with Wayne's work habits. "He'd come in at ten o'clock, go have breakfast, come back, then go to lunch with us, and then leave," said Stewart. "So then the arguing started—it was a daily thing, we were all yelling at each other.

"Wayne didn't get along with the workers. Once he was in the factory when the machine caught fire. Everybody was fighting the fire. Afterward, he can barely see through the smoke, but he sees a guy taking a piss against the wall. Wayne fired him. This was the foreman. Well, you don't do that in America. We had to talk to him and bring him back. We told him, 'Wayne, this isn't Duke. This is a factory.' Everything had to be done by the book with him," complained Stewart.

Not that Wayne didn't have fresh ideas or wasn't trying to apply what he had learned at Duke to the family business. But his ideas, from Stewart's perspective, were either grandiose or just silly.

Gerry, however, didn't think they were silly.

Manchester was running at almost full capacity, and Neil had repeatedly recommended that Gerry look for a larger building, buy more machinery, and expand. Stewart agreed. He thought there was plenty of business out there, and Manchester's sales staff, he first among them, would find it.

But Gerry didn't want to invest in new machinery. He didn't want to own a building. He didn't want to increase capacity.

He wanted, instead, to spend his lion's share of the rivers of cash that poured out of Manchester.

But for some reason he embraced Wayne's suggestion that it

was time to improve Manchester's image. "I get a call from my father, at home," recalled Stewart. "He said, 'I want you to do me a favor with Wayne. He got an idea about some advertising agency, and I want you to go ahead and give him a chance.'

"The next morning, Wayne comes in and says, 'I want to hire J. Walter Thompson'—the biggest ad agency in this city—'and I want them to get us into retail stores with a new promotion.' And he wanted them to do the advertising and PR work for our company," said Stewart. Baffled but still backing his father, Stewart went along for the ride. An account executive from Thompson made his presentation at Stewart's home, where he seated himself on a couch among Stewart's fourteen cats. The biggest, Trouble, weighed some forty-five pounds. Trouble crawled into the ad man's lap, and when the executive went to scratch Trouble's stomach, the cat bit his hand, drawing blood.

"This guy thought we were all crazy. He was probably right," recalled Stewart. "But then he says, 'Here's what I'm going to do for you,' and he lays out this elaborate plan. And it was just too high class. We make *dreck*, the lowest-cost stuff you can buy. We're selling to farm stores, mom-and-pop lumberyards. This guy is talking about putting slide projectors in, he had promo purchase sales plans that I didn't understand—and I've got twenty years in the business.

"And my father said, 'Go ahead, we're going to do it.'

"The guy gave us a rough estimate of the costs. I said, 'Before you spend anything, let us know.'

"Next week," continued Stewart, "we got a bill for fifty thousand dollars. And that was just the beginning. I don't know how much we spent, but it was a disaster."

At Gerry's urging, the ad agency brought several people to make an elaborate presentation in Las Vegas at Manchester's sales meeting. For the sales force, these excursions to the desert gambling mecca were simply pep-rally gatherings amid a few days of fun, food, shows, and gambling on Manchester's tab.

Forced to spend hours watching the ad agency's presentation, the salesmen became sullen and angry. This was not why they had come to Las Vegas. They thought the plan was stupid, and said so, privately, to Stewart.

In the end, Manchester gave some $70,000 to J. Walter Thompson. "We came out of it with a new logo, something we put on our stationery, signs, and invoices," sighed Stewart. Stewart later learned that most of the money went for lists—leads for potential accounts. "A guy in Detroit called us later and asked how the lists were working out," said Stewart, disgusted. "You can get these lists for a few hundred dollars and this is what J. Walter Thompson did," he added.

At the time, Neil and Stewart saw the advertising plan as their father's way of humoring Wayne. Later, however, they would come to see Gerry's support for these expenditures in a far different light.

Despite the anxiety his younger brother's presence brought into the workplace, Stewart could still always find time for a gag, especially if the goat was Wayne.

One day Stewart learned from his swimming pool cleaning man, who also serviced Gerry's pool, that Wayne, who still lived with his parents, had gone skinny-dipping with his girlfriend, Susan.

That gave Stewart an idea. "I wrote a note to Wayne," he recalled. "I clipped letters and words out of magazines, like a terrorist. It said, 'Saw you in pool. Will tell parents.'"

Stewart mailed the note to Wayne at the office. "Next day, he gets the letter," chuckles Stewart. "He disappears. Hours later he comes back and says, 'I've got to talk to you. I've just come from the FBI. I'm being blackmailed.'"

Stewart let his brother suffer for two years, a period that included Wayne's marriage to Susan. In 1981, Stewart told Wayne who sent the note. He chose the moment carefully.

"He's helping me move into my new house in Hidden Hills, and at one point he's helping me carry a huge doghouse. I put my end on a brick wall and he's got the other end balanced. So I said, 'You can't move much, can you?'

"He says, 'No.'

"Then I told him the whole story. But he couldn't do anything—if he'd let go of the doghouse it would have killed him."

Wayne, who drew closer to his father during the time after Gerry's heart attack, was well aware of how little his brothers respected him. He began to look for a way out. In the Woodman family, Mickey Stern's bond brokerage had long been the place where relatives could always find a job; Neil had worked there for several years. Even Stewart had quit his father's business a year or so after high school and gone to work for Mickey, though he came back, begging Gerry's forgiveness, in much less than a month.

In 1980, Wayne began to hold secret discussions with his brother-in-law. Mickey told him there would always be a job for him, and so Wayne began to study the materials he would need to master for a bond broker's license. He told no one, not even his father.

The change in Gerry's behavior following his heart attack was far more distressing to Stewart and Neil than Wayne's work habits.

For the first few months of 1979, Gerry came in to the office around six-thirty or seven each morning to open the mail. He left, usually, about ten. Gerry continued to draw his full salary, as well as the cash allowances and half the money skimmed from the business.

"He went to the racetrack almost every day," recalled Stewart. "I don't know if he lost interest in the business, or was just tired. But he acted like he was going to die any day. He was talking like he thought each night would be his last. He drove my mother nuts."

On more than one occasion, Gerry disappeared for several days at a time. Once, when Vera was frantic with worry, Stewart called credit card companies and asked them to check on Gerry's recent charges, eventually tracking him to a Holiday Inn in Mobile, Alabama.

Stewart caught a plane to Mobile.

He found his father in a mental condition that shocked and confused him. Gerry babbled about driving to Israel. In tears, he told Stewart that his day had passed, that it was time for him to turn things over to his sons and retire to enjoy the little time he might still have.

Neil and Stewart had been thinking the same thing for quite some time.

"I was always under extreme pressure with my father in the business," said Stewart, recalling that soon after Manchester first yielded cash he had paid off the mortgage on his home—but a few months later, when Gerry said the business needed more capital to meet unexpected expenses, he'd taken another mortgage on this house for $25,000.

"After I gave him the money, he said, 'If we hit every goal we still can't make it.' But that's what he always did. I'd have ulcers and go to work and then the sales would pick up and we were fine," said Stewart.

Beyond that kind of pressure, Stewart and his brother had a vision about what Manchester *could* become—if only Gerry would allow them to make it so.

"It was a good business," said Stewart. "But my father wouldn't let it grow. Wouldn't put money back in. For example, sometimes we'd get orders for five hundred cartons of an item. The machine produced twenty cartons an hour. So we've got to run all day to fill that. We needed another machine, and he wouldn't spend the money. But if a company stays stagnant, year by year the overhead creeps up. You can't sit where you are. You'll go broke."

Beyond the desire to grow Manchester, and aside from the urge common to most adult children to move out of their father's shadow, Gerry's oldest sons were tormented by curiosity and tempted by greed. In all the years that they were Gerry's business partners, he had never allowed them to open incoming mail or to see the books. Even when Gerry was in the hospital, hovering between life and death, neither son dared to brave his father's wrath by demanding that the bookkeeper show them the records. They did not know how much money was really going through Manchester; for years they suspected that Gerry was taking more out of the business than he told them. They knew he had special arrangements with a few accounts. Obsessed with secrecy, Gerry always sent his sons out of the office when certain customers visited. Stewart and Neil could only speculate about what might be happening: kickbacks, multiple billings, or some other clever trick only Gerry could have devised.

But during the months of Gerry's slow recuperation, Manchester ran very well without Gerry. After years spent learning the business, Neil and Stewart now realized that they no longer needed their father to make money.

Early in 1980, with no prompting from the Woodman family, Harry Fukuwa, a C.P.A. who served as Gerry's personal and business accountant for decades, advised him, "Sell the business. Get rid of it. Sell it to your sons. Otherwise you're going to ruin it." Gerry ignored him.

Not long after that, Stewart, always closest to his mother, spoke to Vera. It was time for his father to retire, said Stewart. Time for Gerry to enjoy the fruits of his years in harness. Time for him to let go, to spend time with his grandchildren.

Vera was all for it.

Gerry exploded with anger and refused to discuss retirement. He couldn't bear to think of loosening his grip on the family or relinquishing control of the business.

"I was getting real restless with the family and he knew it," said Stewart. "When he didn't control me in the business anymore, that was a pivotal moment—because once he saw that the business didn't need him, he wanted to come back into it." In June 1980, Gerry and Vera went to England on their annual pilgrimage to see relatives and go to Ascot and other racetracks. As always, Manchester paid for the trip. But this time, before Gerry left, Stewart took an unprecedented action: he cautioned his father not to spend too much. "I'd just come back from a sales trip, and business was a little down. So I said, 'Look, Dad, before you go, please don't go crazy with money over there. We don't got it.'"

Lips curled with scorn, Gerry replied that there would be plenty of money if only his sons didn't steal so much from *his* company. It was not the first time his father had made such an accusation; as always, Stewart bit his lip and said nothing.

To make the point that Manchester's money was *his* money, Gerry invited his in-laws, the Michelsons, to accompany him to England. He also invited two couples who lived down the block in Bel Air. In all, he would bill Manchester over $45,000 for the two-week vacation.

Gerry was then driving a company-owned Clenet and drawing $3,700 a month for an "automobile allowance," plus several thousand dollars a week in cash "expense money." Beyond his salary, which went to Vera, Gerry took almost $10,000 a week from the slush fund.

Nevertheless, just before going to England, he asked Stewart for a small loan, a little pocket money.

"Stewart, I need to borrow $6,000. I'm going to the races."

"I said, 'I'm not going to give it to you,'" said Stewart. "And the reason was, enough was enough. A few weeks before I was at the Sahara in Vegas, and a pit boss said, 'Your father is down $25,000 and he's signing *your* name to the markers.' The hotel knew me so good, they figured it was fine.

"Well, I *can't* tell a pit boss, 'Fuck you, I'm not responsible.' You *don't* do that. But I told him not to allow it anymore. Dad went crazy when they told him he was cut off."

Stewart told his mother that he wasn't loaning his father any more gambling money. Vera, knowing Gerry would never allow her a moment's rest, decided to keep the peace. She gave Stewart $5,000 to "loan" his father. Stewart gave Gerry the money, never mentioning where it came from.

Returning from England, Gerry strolled into the office and said, "You're lucky. We almost bought a horse. The bidding went to $270,000, but another chap outbid us."

"I said, 'What the fuck are you talking about? You never even told us, and you bid on a horse?'" said Stewart.

A few moments later, Gerry turned to Vera and said, "By the way, I need a couple thousand dollars for the track."

"I thought you took money to England," said Vera.

"I *never* took any money to England," said Gerry, his face all self-righteous innocence. "I didn't gamble there."

"That was the first time I heard my mother swear, ever," recalled Stewart. "She said, 'You're a fucking liar. I gave Stewart the money to give to you, and you blew it all in England, and you're nothing but a liar.'"

Caught in a lie, Gerry threw one of his patented temper tantrums. "He went nuts," said Stewart. "He threw stuff off his desk, he turned over chairs, he broke mirrors and windows. He was cursing me and cursing Neil and cursing our mother. He smashed the doors on the way out. 'I'm through with this fucking place,' he screamed. 'I'm never coming back. It won't run without me.'"

Stewart had been exposed to the fury of many of Gerry's tantrums, but he remembers none to match this one.

Gerry drove north from Los Angeles, and disappeared for more than a week. After that incident, Gerry rarely appeared at Manchester except to pick up money and go through the mail.

And, significantly, it was not long after this tantrum that Wayne was let in on the family secret. Or part of it. "Wayne's name went on the [slush fund] account," Stewart would later tell a federal jury. "He began getting part of my father's share of the cash."

As Stewart and Neil would soon realize, Wayne had become a player in the family drama. In exchange for several thousand dollars a week in cash, he had become their father's eyes and ears at Manchester.

He also became Gerry's best hope for regaining control of the company. Unlike his older brothers, Wayne still worshiped his father and obeyed his orders without question. When he began accepting a share of the money skimmed from Manchester, Wayne became Gerry's tool against Neil and Stewart.

In July 1980, Gerry told his sons that he wanted to start a subsidiary to manufacture ceiling fans. After Gerry saw it through startup, about six months, he would turn it over to Wayne to run. He wanted Manchester to put up half a million dollars to do it.

Even at that price, Neil and Stewart considered the venture feasible. The risk would not be great, because even if the company failed, the inventory could be sold and they would recover most of their investment.

But they balked at Gerry's demand to have Manchester's sales force sell the ceiling fans—and his insistence that he would control the salesmen. "A salesman cannot serve two masters," said Stewart. "Either they would sell plastic, or they would sell ceiling fans; they couldn't sell both."

Next, Gerry tried to hire away Warren Kemp, Manchester's veteran sales director, but Kemp declined. The fan-making subsidiary never happened.

While the ceiling-fan idea was being discussed, Rick Wilson, then one of Stewart's product-line sales managers, telephoned Stewart at home.

"I had lunch with Wayne today," said Wilson, "and he says your father is going to kick you out, put you back on the road, and Wayne is taking over as president."

"Rick, you misunderstood him," said Stewart.

"I understood," said Rick. "Wayne's taking over the business."

"Believe me, Rick, it's not going to happen," said Stewart.

The next morning, Stewart confronted Gerry. "You never told Wayne he was going to be president of the company, did you?"

"What do you think he went to Duke for, to go on the road and sell?" said Gerry, his face flushed, his eyes narrowed.

"After that, the shit hit the fan," said Stewart.

On the evening of July 26, 1980, Vera telephoned Stewart. She said that she was calling a meeting of the board of directors, to be held a few days later. The purpose of the meeting, said Vera, was to go over a list of Gerry's new demands.

These included demotions for Neil and Stewart. "He wanted me to spend virtually all of my time traveling," said Stewart. "I was to travel with every one of our salesmen.

"Neil was to stay in the factory the entire day. He was banned from ever coming into the office.

"My father was to take over all banking activities and purchasing, and would have final approval on all business decisions.

"And Wayne was to take over credit, trucking, and eventually, all my father's authority."

Stewart told his mother that the demands were ludicrous, that Wayne was totally unprepared for major responsibilities, that his father would ruin the company with unrestrained spending. And he told Vera, in detail, all the reasons why Gerry's demands were unfair, and why none would work.

Vera dutifully relayed each comment to Gerry.

Gerry threw another tantrum.

"He was screaming that unless Neil and I did what he said, he'd come down to the plant that night and cripple all the machines," said Stewart.

Stewart told his mother that he was going to call a locksmith and have all the locks changed. "Don't tell Dad," he said, and Vera agreed.

Stewart got on the phone, and within hours all the outside doors and the offices had new locks. Stewart gave a key to both brothers and another to his mother.

Gerry did not attempt to carry out his sabotage threats. He was going through a period of acute mental anguish, ambiguous about his future for the first time in his adult life.

On October 18, 1980, Gerry wrote a letter to Stewart, which came close to an apology for his actions. He told Stewart that he intended to retire and go to live in Israel. "My time has passed, and it was hard for me to swallow," wrote Gerry.

After the letter came, Stewart had a long talk with his mother. Vera agreed that Gerry should retire. She also promised that if he went off the deep end again, if he attempted to take over the company, she would never take his side against her sons. "I would never do that to you," said Vera. "As God is my witness, I will never, ever, sell my shares out from under you—please, do not worry about it."

Stewart was heartened by his mother's assurances. Neil was less optimistic. "Don't bet on it," said Neil. "You know how Mom is. She can't say no to Dad. She always gives in to him."

Gerry did not retire. He did not go to Israel.

Instead, he purchased four racehorses. Manchester paid several hundred thousand dollars for the animals—and Gerry insisted that their ownership be recorded in his name. His older sons were first stunned, then infuriated.

"How can we buy racehorses?" asked Neil. "We can't afford them—and it's asking for trouble with the IRS if we try to justify a racehorse as a company business expense. How do we take depreciation on a racehorse?"

"It's none of your goddamn business what I do with company assets," raged Gerry. "*I* started this company."

The horses cost almost $5,000 a month to maintain at a stable; insurance alone was $15,000 a year. After months of bickering, Gerry finally agreed that if the company paid the upkeep, the horses would be in Manchester's name. His sons felt they had won a moral victory, though the notion of paying equine expenses festered like an open sore, something that irritated them out of all proportion to the money itself.

Through all this Gerry continued to draw his salary and expenses, and he continued to gamble away every dollar he could lay his hands on. He borrowed money from Vera, telling her that her sons had cut off his automobile expense allowance.

None too gently, Stewart explained that his father continued to be paid as before. For the first time, Vera understood that Gerry's gambling was out of control.

When he had recovered from the physical effects of his heart attack, Gerry would no longer admit that he was past his prime. He had spent his entire life building one company after another. The rough and tumble of business was tonic to him, providing proof of his prowess, defining his superiority over all others, fueling his immense ego. Controlling his family through the business helped to hold back the fearsome insecurity that had haunted him since childhood.

Unable to accept that his time was past, Gerry began to look for ways to make certain that everyone realized that Manchester could not survive without him. Plastic extrusion is extremely sensitive to variations in temperature, so much so that factory doors must always be closed when a machine is running. A few degrees deviation soon produces bubbles in the plastic; too many bubbles and the panel is ruined.

One day in early 1981, Neil Woodman, who habitually arrived at the factory around six, came in an hour earlier than usual. The extruding machines had been acting up for several days, spewing tons of worthless panels. They were too thin, or they were too thick, or so fragile they cracked and broke before they could be boxed for shipment. While these panels could be ground up and the plastic recycled, the hundreds of defective products represented a huge waste of energy and costly manpower. Because imperfect panels were made only on the morning shift, Neil wanted to talk to the foreman before work started.

So, instead of going in the front door to his office, Neil parked his car and went in the side door to the factory. Just inside he paused to let his eyes adjust to the gloom. He stood rock still for several seconds.

And saw his father, several feet away, furtively moving from machine to machine. Gerry stopped at each control panel, twisted a few knobs or dials, then moved on to the next.

Neil's jaw dropped open in astonishment. He ducked behind some barrels, waited a few minutes, then left the factory, returning by the front door.

Before nine that morning Gerry was summoned to the factory floor to inspect piles of useless plastic panels. He flew into a towering rage, ripping into the foreman and machine operators.

"Can't you fucking people do anything right!" he raged, throwing a panel down. "Do I have to fucking do every fucking thing in this fucking factory my fucking self?"

Gerry moved to the control panels, looked at the settings, and went into orbit all over again. "Look at these, you stupid assholes! Don't you know how to set up your goddamn machine? What do I pay you for? Are you dumb, or just lazy? Do I have to come in here every day and do your job for you?"

The foreman and operator had no answers. They studied the concrete floor with downcast eyes, cowed by Gerry's ferocity. Finally, out of breath, his face a deep shade of purple, Gerry stopped shouting.

His hands flying over the board, he reset half a dozen controls, then stalked off in a huff. "This place would go to hell in a week if it wasn't for me," he growled over his shoulder.

Neil took in the scene with growing amazement.

The next morning, Stewart responded to Neil's mysterious request to come in at five. Without saying why, Neil asked Stewart to hide with him inside the factory door.

"Don't say anything, just watch," said Neil. Stewart nodded his compliance. A few minutes later, Gerry appeared. Glancing around to make sure no one was in sight, he made the rounds of extruding machines.

And once again, before nine that morning the machines were throwing trash out the business end. Gerry gloried in a repeat performance of sustained outrage. He left the machine operators trembling with fear for their jobs.

After watching this spectacular, Neil and Stewart were convinced that their father had lost his mind.

Stewart called his mother and told her what he had seen.

"But that's crazy," she said. "I don't believe you. You must be mistaken."

"Mama, please believe me. Neil and I have seen this," said Stewart. "Both of us."

"I'll speak to your father," said Vera.

"Go out to dinner, and tell him there," suggested Stewart. "In a restaurant, maybe he'll control himself."

"I wish he would just retire," said Vera. "You boys could run everything."

"You tell him that, Mama. He doesn't listen to us."

Gerry didn't listen to Vera, either.

Gerry stayed away from Manchester for several days after this confrontation. When he returned, his sons did not dare mention his sabotage. Business continued as usual at Manchester, except for one small thing: neither Neil nor Stewart ever trusted Gerry Woodman again.

Manchester's first customer had been Plastalume, a Glendale, California, firm whose owner Stewart had convinced to place a $6,000 order even before the extrusion machinery was delivered in July 1975. By 1981, Plastalume, which installed customized ceiling lighting for residential kitchens, was giving Manchester all of its ceiling panel business, over $200,000 per month.

"This was our biggest account," recalled Stewart. "And I became good friends with the owner, Howard Cray. In September 1981, Cray came to me and said, 'I'm opening a place in Orange County and I'm going to need an extra sixty days on my accounts payable, for about six months, because I need to put the money into the new place.'

"I okayed it. And at that time, I discussed it with Neil, but not with my father, who wasn't coming in very much then. So Cray took his extra sixty days, he made his payments, and everything was fine.

"But Wayne told my father about it. Dad came to the office on a Saturday, with my mother. He called me at home and told me to come down there right away. And he said, 'We're not going to ship any more to Plastalume. We're not going to be his bank, let him borrow from someone else.'"

Stewart was thunderstruck. "But it's our biggest account," he said. "Our oldest customer. He's never been late with a payment. We're *going* to keep shipping to them, if I have to drive the truck myself."

Gerry exploded, cursing Stewart for stupidity.

"Gerald, have you lost your mind?" shrieked Vera. "What on

earth are you thinking? Why don't you let Stewart and Neil run the company?"

His face distorted with hatred, Gerry erupted. "It's none of your goddamned business! This is *my* fucking factory and I'll bloody fucking well do what I fucking well please with it!" Vera moved closer to her husband, concern etched into her face. "But Gerald, what is the *matter*? Why are you *doing* this?" she wailed.

"Goddamn you to hell, it's none of your concern," shouted Gerry, shoving her aside with such force that Vera bounced off a pallet of plastic. Losing her balance, she toppled over, landing, bruised and bleeding, in an awkward heap.

Gerry stalked out of the factory, snarling curses at his sons as they ran to Vera's aid.

Gerry stayed away from the factory for the rest of the week, but before he left he gave instructions to the shipping department: Plastalume was not to be serviced. So Stewart got behind the wheel of a semitrailer and delivered a load to Cray's company.

In October 1981, Gerry told Stewart to have Manchester repay $40,000 of $76,000 owed to Vera. The money would go to pay off the balance on his Clenet.

Stewart demurred, telling his father that since the car loan was held by Union Bank, and it was subordinate to several other loans, the bank would object. He also pointed out that Manchester was paying Vera 20 percent interest on the money she'd loaned the company.

"I don't care how you do it, you have ten days," snarled Gerry.

So Neil and Stewart borrowed $40,000 from Union Bank—at 22 percent interest—and gave the money to Gerry. He paid off the loan on the Clenet.

Relations between Gerry and his older sons, not good since Gerry's heart attack, cooled considerably after the Plastalume incident. When Yom Kippur rolled around in the autumn of 1981, Neil boycotted the traditional break-the-fast dinner at his parents' home.

Stewart, however, felt that the Day of Atonement was a time to put enmity aside. On this day, Jews are commanded to ask forgiveness of all those they have offended in the previous year. For Stewart, Yom Kippur was, perhaps, a time when the family's wounds could begin to heal.

He took Melody and their three children and drove to his father's enormous Bel Air mansion.

He hadn't been there ten minutes when Gerry cornered him.

"You dare to come here?" screamed Gerry. "It's over for you. I'm going to dissolve the company."

Stunned, Stewart asked Gerry what he was talking about.

"You'll find out soon enough. And when we're finished with you, you'll have nothing. Nothing. Your children will sleep in the streets, they'll starve to death, you'll have nothing."

Stewart packed his family in his Rolls-Royce and left without saying good-bye to anyone.

About midnight, Neil telephoned Stewart, waking him.

"I've just been served with papers," said Neil. "Dad wants to break up the company, sell off its assets."

"Like Jack Salzburg did to him at Fullview," said Stewart. "He told Dad, 'We'll both go down together.' Remember?"

"I remember, better than you," said Neil.

"But he can't do anything without Mom's stock, and she said she'd never let him do anything like this."

"I told you, she always gives in to him."

Stewart lived in a million-dollar home in Hidden Hills, a gated security community protected by armed guards. Because he had paid a lot of money for his privacy, he was certain that no process server could find him at home. Safe for the night, Stewart went to bed, exhausted and depressed.

At one in the morning on the night after Yom Kippur 1981, Stewart Woodman's doorbell rang. When he answered, a man in a rumpled suit handed Stewart a subpoena and disappeared into the darkness.

The Homicks

Once Jean Scherrer and John O'Grady came forward with a name—Steve Homick—Holder and Crotsley thought they might be close to cracking what the newspapers and television news took delight in calling the "Ninja Murders" case.

"These guys, Scherrer and O'Grady, said that even if there had been no reward, they would have come forward," said Holder. "I like to think they would have, since they were both retired policemen. So, we call Personnel and they've got no record of a Steven Homick. Now we're thinking, 'What are these guys talking about?' But then we make additional inquiries, we check Police Academy records back to the sixties, and find that Steven Homick *was* LAPD, on patrol out of Wilshire Division. He resigned for 'personal' reasons—the word was he liked to beat up suspects," said Holder.

Scherrer and O'Grady met Holder and Crotsley again for drinks at the Sportsman's Lodge. Another thing he remembered, Scherrer said, was that a few weeks after the bar mitzvah Homick called from out of town and asked to meet him on a Sunday morning in a factory parking lot in Chatsworth. Homick didn't say why they were meeting, so Scherrer assumed it was to talk about another security job.

The factory was Manchester, but instead of another job, Homick had a favor to ask. Homick, who carried keys to Manchester's front door, its various executive offices, and the manufacturing area, took Scherrer to a vacant office and asked him to install a microphone. He wanted it connected to a speaker and amplifier in the office next door, which had Neil Woodman's name on the door. The reason for this hookup, explained Steve, was that management wanted to check on an auditor they thought was cooking the corporate books.

Scherrer went to a Radio Shack store and bought a length of wire, plus components and all the parts necessary to make a sort of public address system. It took only an hour to install a microphone in the unused office. Scherrer hid wires behind a molding and ran them up to the ceiling, through an attic, and down to the amplifier and speaker he'd placed in Neil's office. While Scherrer had accepted reimbursement for his Radio Shack purchases—about $300—he wouldn't accept payment for his time. He figured if he did Homick a favor, he might be hired again for another security job that would pay even better.

In conversation that day, Homick mentioned that he was connected with casinos, and was often in Atlantic City.

To check out the East Coast connection, Jack Holder called the New Jersey Gaming Enforcement Agency in Atlantic City and spoke to a detective. "He said his agency knew Steven Homick; he'd been arrested for possession of stolen property and also on weapons and narcotics charges," said Holder.

"But you guys ought to talk to the FBI," said the Atlantic City cop. "They've got an investigation going against Homick in Las Vegas."

Steve Homick was born in July 1940, in Steubenville, Ohio, the oldest of five children of Steven and Martha. Steubenville, on the west bank of the Ohio River, was established near seams of soft coal in 1797 and grew into a coal-mining and steel-making town. When Steve was a boy, generations of West Virginia miners still came from hundreds of miles away to visit Steubenville's only recession-proof industry, its whorehouses.

Tall and self-assured, Steve "Bucky" Homick decided that there was nothing he wanted in Steubenville. At age thirteen he quit school, lied about his age, and enlisted in the U.S. Air Force. He was only seventeen when he was honorably discharged in 1957.

Steve, who had completed high school through the G.E.D. equivalency program, enrolled at Ohio State in September 1958. But work was hard to find and his G.I. Bill stipend was small. Steve dropped out the following May.

An imposing physical specimen, Steve was a natural athlete, good enough as a semipro outfielder to win a tryout and a 1960 contract with a Philadelphia Phillies farm club. But Steve liked to brawl, and he found curveballs a problem. Philadelphia released him in April 1961, at the start of the season. Homick got one more shot at pro baseball: the Detroit Tigers signed him during the summer of 1961. He played in a dozen minor league games but still couldn't hit what ballplayers call Ol' Mister C. Detroit let him go after 1962 spring training.

Next, Steve trained as a diesel engineer's helper, worked in construction around the Midwest, and eventually went to California, where he passed the tough exam for the Los Angeles Police Academy. Homick was sworn in as an officer in February 1963. After supervisors discovered how much Steve liked beating up suspects, he was encouraged to resign from the LAPD. He did so in April 1964.

Homick returned to construction work, but there never seemed to be enough money. He was arrested on check forgery charges in February 1968, and convicted. As it was a first offense, his sentence was probation. This conviction was set aside on technical grounds in April 1970.

Homick then moved to Las Vegas, where he found occasional work as a carpenter. Preferring management to labor, Steve got a roofing contractor's license.

For many years, however, Homick made a large part of his livelihood by buying knockoffs, cheap fakes of expensive designer jeans, in the Los Angeles garment district and shipping them to Las Vegas via Greyhound for his brother, William, to sell for inflated prices at swap meets.

Steve also dealt blackjack at the MGM Grand Hotel casino, the Riviera, and at El Cortez. But flipping pasteboards at tourists was too passive for Steve Homick. He was more suited to occupations offering an element of physical danger—especially if it meant putting someone else in peril.

Consequently, Steve took a freelance position intimidating deadbeats to collect on markers they had left at the Imperial Palace casino. On behalf of those who profited from a more tranquil labor force, he broke the legs of troublesome union organizers. And he became a security consultant for Tower of Jewels, a chain of Las Vegas jewelry shops.

Steve also dabbled in sideline ventures. He obtained a Federal firearms license and made a deal with a gun shop, Accuracy Gun Distributors, to sell weapons by mail, using Accuracy as his supplier and ordering address.

He also established another direct-marketing business, selling by mail and in saloons and hotels what he told most people were vitamin supplements but which were, in fact, illicit drugs. In his spare time, Steve accepted the sorts of jobs that licensed detective agencies usually refuse: "surveillance" assignments requiring finesse, muscle, and a willingness to ignore criminal statutes. He found clients strictly by word-of-mouth referrals.

Capable of great charm while fostering a reputation for utter ruthlessness, over several years Steve Homick made important criminal contacts, reputedly including mobsters linked to M.C.A. Records. These, in time, led to informal affiliations with peripheral members of New York City's Genovese crime family, one of five Mafia gangs that divide billions of dollars a year from gambling, prostitution, narcotics, several brands of robbery, labor racketeering, and political corruption in the five boroughs. According to news reports, Steve also found time to perform services for Corky Vastola, reputed chief of New Jersey's De Cavalcante crime family. After several years of this, the word got around that Steve Homick was a problem solver.

In June 1982, Steve became vice president of corporate facilities and director of security for American International Airways. A.I.A. operated scheduled and charter flights in the United States, Canada, Mexico, and the Caribbean, and to the Bahamas and Bermuda. A substantial portion of its business was providing air and ground transportation for the hotel casino industry in Atlantic

City, New Jersey. He also dabbled in citizens band radio through a Las Vegas C.B. dealer, Art Taylor.

Steve gave nicknames to almost everyone he knew, and many were favored by several, Steve choosing names to suit the occasion. For example, his brother Robert, ten years younger and a law school graduate, became "Jesse," a reference to the bold bandit Jesse James: Robert eked out his living as a shoplifter. Steve also dubbed him "The Library," a sly, caustic reference to Robert's specialty: stealing law books. At times Robert was the "Fat Man," a nod to his steadily increasing girth.

Steve Homick carried his whole life in a dark briefcase he rarely let out of his sight. In it were diaries and Day Runner organizers going back several years, several personal phone directories, plus a .38 snub-nose revolver and a .45-caliber automatic. Homick jotted down practically everything he did, and almost everything he considered doing. Like the nicknames he hung on people, these notes and reminders were coded to reflect an almost obsessive interest in pop culture. People or places were referenced to movies, songs, television shows, even commercials. Thus a man who habitually carried a comb might become "Kookie," the Edd Byrnes character on the sixties TV caper series "77 Sunset Strip." It was more than a code with many keys; it was the way Steve Homick thought and spoke. Some found it amusing.

For a long time, Art Taylor really liked Steve. After knowing him for several months, Art was pleased to do him a favor when Steve asked him to hold a package for a United Parcel Service pickup. "Steve was a happy sort of fellow," said Taylor. "He seemed very open about the things he did."

After that, Steve asked Art to ship more packages through UPS, sometimes many at a time, and often several days a week. These packages, explained Steve, were vitamin compounds with names like Yellow Jackets and Black Beauties, which he claimed he sold for a company called Romamar. Steve said that because he was on the go so much, doing carpentry work and traveling to New Jersey, he needed a convenient pickup spot. Steve was grateful that Taylor allowed him to use his store to send and accept incoming packages.

As time went on, Steve asked Art for other favors. Steve took out his own Sprint card and asked if he could use Taylor's telephone to make a few long-distance calls. Soon, whenever he was in Las Vegas, Homick used Art's phone several times a day.

"Steve often talked in a code or riddles," said Taylor. "It was, a lot of the time, hard to understand what he was trying to say. And many times when he gave me a message to pass on, I didn't understand what it meant. I would relay the message to somebody, and hope they understood it."

Soon Taylor was passing along coded messages almost every day to people in New Jersey and Los Angeles and most everywhere in between.

One day in early 1984, Steve stopped by the store and asked Art for another kind of favor. "Steve asked me to repair a taillight on his car. When we opened the trunk, he had a large bag of pills which later turned out to be Quaaludes," said Taylor. Quaaludes are a prescription drug, an often abused mood-altering sedative that sells on the black market for several times its licit cost.

"Steve explained that they belonged to another person and he was merely transporting them," added Taylor. The folded plastic bag, about twice as long as the width of a full-sized automobile trunk and nine or ten inches in diameter, was filled with pills.

By this time, Taylor knew that his friend Steve occasionally used cocaine. Soon, however, he began to suspect that he sold it, too. "I'd seen some little plastic bags in Steve's possession. They had a white, powdered substance that Steve later identified as cocaine," said Taylor.

Taylor was alarmed. "I was concerned more for Steve than for anything else," said Taylor. "I went to his wife about it, and to a couple of his other friends, hoping to find some way we could all help him. And they all agreed that Steve might be dabbling in something that he hadn't ought to be, and they tried to talk him out of it."

Homick was coldly furious. He didn't want to be talked out of his cocaine dealership, and he didn't want his friends going around talking about his "problem." It was none of their business, and to make that point, Homick stayed away from Art Taylor for weeks. But Homick needed the convenience and cover of Taylor's store to send and receive his illicit packages. So he went back to see his old friend Art, whom he now liked so much that he hung him with a nickname: "Cowboy."

"Steve kind of said he was going to straighten it out and get away from it, but that didn't happen," said Taylor.

Finally, in July 1984, Taylor began to worry about himself and his three daughters. "I don't like drugs, and I didn't want them to be around me or my children," he said.

Taylor came to the conclusion that if he could not stand idly by and let his friend Steve go down the drain, neither could he any longer risk the chance that Steve's drug dealings might bring him down as well. After all, thought Taylor, he's sending the stuff out of *my* store.

It happened that the day Taylor made up his mind to do something about Homick was July 3rd, 1984. The next day he and his family attended a giant block party. Hundreds of people roamed the usually quiet residential street, eating, drinking, and celebrating Independence Day.

During the festivities, Taylor found a few minutes to chat with a neighbor who worked as a special agent of the FBI.

Soon one of this agent's colleagues, Jack Salisbury, came to see Taylor. Art shared his suspicions about the contents of the packages Homick sent and received. After speaking to his superiors, Salisbury asked Taylor to become an FBI informant. He was to take careful note of everything Steve did, further gain his trust by taking a more active role in Homick's drug business—and report everything he learned to the FBI. In this way, Salisbury explained, the FBI would learn who supplied Homick with drugs. These were the people, said the agent, that the government wanted far more than small fry like his pal Steve.

Taylor agreed. Later on, in consideration of the hundreds of hours that he spent watching and listening to Steve Homick, and of the value of the information he was giving to the FBI, Agent Salisbury put Taylor on the Department of Justice payroll. Over a year of service, he collected about $10,000, all of which went into a vain effort to save his failing C.B. business.

Taylor provided the FBI with photocopies of mailing labels on packages Steve shipped and received. As Art's cooperation became more important to his drug business, Steve began to trust Taylor with holding bags of cocaine to pass on to drop-in customers. He taught Taylor a code to use on the telephone when customers ordered cocaine. "We referenced it as plywood," said Taylor. "An eighth-sheet was one of those small bags we used. A quarter-sheet meant three of them."

Then the middle Homick brother, William—"Moke" to Steve— began dropping off and picking up cocaine at Taylor's shop. "Moke would have the cocaine wrapped inside a newspaper and carry it under his arm," recalled Taylor. On other occasions, Moke, who often called his big brother "Bucky" or "Herman," would use delicate scales to weigh out and bag hundreds of grams of cocaine in small plastic packages.

Among the many casino people Steve Homick cultivated was Joey Gambino, a pit boss at the MGM Grand Hotel & Casino. Joey was aware that Steve often performed small, dirty tasks for "men of respect" who then ran Las Vegas gambling from the shadows and did not wish to dirty their hands.

In 1980, Gambino had tried to pick up Melody in the MGM casino. Instead, she introduced him to Stewart, who in turn introduced Neil.

The Woodman brothers were exactly the sort of customers that casinos love most. They could be counted on to visit the tables once a month or so, always leaving tens of thousands of dollars behind. So it was very much in Joey Gambino's professional interest to cultivate a relationship with them. In time, this may have evolved into genuine friendship. Gambino became a frequent weekend visitor at Stewart's home, and also remained on excellent terms with Neil.

One day, as Joey strolled out of the MGM Grand poker pits with the brothers Woodman, he ran into his other friend, Steve Homick. Joey made introductions, then left.

"We got to talking to Steve," recalled Stewart. "I found out that his brother was interested in the same thing I was: betting on football, baseball, and basketball games. At that time I was betting games on a daily basis. Steve's brother, Robert, only bet college games, while I bet only the pros."

Rich young gamblers, who thought nothing about dropping thousands of dollars, held an obvious attraction to Steve, who had long made his living exploiting human weakness. Steve decided he would like to know the Woodmans better. Maybe they would drop some of that mad money on him.

About a week after this chance meeting, Robert Homick called Stewart. He shared with Stewart some of his insights on betting college games, and made some recommendations. Stewart was intrigued. Collegiate sports were in an entirely new gambling universe, one he quickly embraced.

Soon Robert, who told Stewart and Neil that he preferred to be called Jesse, was betting games through the brothers' bookie, Lenny Bateman. And soon money for bets won and lost went back and forth between Jesse and Stewart, or Neil, and the bookie, Bateman. It was a convenience and a step up for Jesse, who was granted credit only because the Woodman brothers, both important customers, were his sponsors.

Jesse began turning up at Manchester once or twice a week. Eventually he would be there almost daily to use the company's WATS line to make free calls to his family in Ohio.

Neither Stewart nor Neil had any idea who Robert "Jesse" Homick really was. They knew he had gone to college, but they didn't know that he was an attorney. They knew he had worked in a bank, that he had gotten into some trouble and had to leave. But they didn't know that until he latched on to the Woodmans, Jesse made most of his money by stealing law books from UCLA's library and bookstore, and from lifting locker room supplies—towels, handball gear, shoes, etc.—from private athletic clubs. They would have been stunned to know that Jesse rented a single room in a Sawtelle-area apartment, and that most of the floor space in that room was piled almost to the ceiling with newspapers, magazines, books, and junk mail of all descriptions. The Woodman brothers had no idea that Jesse was a man with extraordinary mental abilities and almost no common sense, at times a virtual recluse, who often spent days on end locked in his room, reading, meditating, and doing God knows what.

But because Jesse was such a puppy dog around the Woodmans, hanging around the office, doing little errands and asking nothing but a chance to bet with the big boys, and because with a little menace in his face Jesse was big and disheveled enough to appear genuinely intimidating, Neil and Stewart threw him a few bones.

The Woodmans hired Jesse to collect some of their more intransigent accounts. He got to keep a third of what he obtained. Robert did collect a few, but he was not as effective as two or three other collection agencies with which the brothers maintained relationships.

Nevertheless, Stewart dispatched Robert to Missouri in an effort to end years of harassment by a former Manchester salesman named Gary Henry.

"The guy was just wacky," explained Stewart. "But he could sell, so I hired him. But then he'd go in someplace and start pulling the guy's cash register apart, telling him that he was going to fix it. So after a lot of customer complaints, I fired him and hired a young lady in his place. She was good—and Henry put her through hell. He threatened to rape her, he stuffed her gas tank with mud, and finally she quit.

"Then we started getting calendars. Thousands of calendars that said, 'With love, Gary,' sent to Manchester.

"And then pencils that said, 'Henry does it best.' Ten thousand mechanical pencils. I gave them to the kids at the Round Meadow School," said Stewart.

Unable to find another salesman to cover the territory, Stewart got his star sales supervisor, who worked out of Chicago, to fill in.

"A month later he called and said, 'I'm quitting, I can't take it anymore, my wife got pictures of this nude woman, sent to me, with a note that said, "Thanks for the other night." She's going to leave me. Henry is driving me nuts.'

"This is a guy with nine kids," continued Stewart. "I asked him not to quit, told him I'd send someone down there to straighten Henry out. Robert volunteered."

"Send me," said Robert Homick. "I'll have a conversation with him. He'll never bother you or your people again."

When Robert returned, he told Stewart that Henry had gotten him angry, and he'd thrown a can of oil through his living room door.

But Henry didn't get the message. "It never stopped," said Stewart. "The next year we got calendars and Christmas cards. Thousands of them, through the mail."

Despite his own lack of success, however, Robert "Jesse"

Homick seldom missed a chance to tell Stewart and Neil about his big brother Steve. Steve, said Jesse, was the *real* Jason Bourne, a fearless soldier of fortune whose capers were fictionalized by author Robert Ludlum in several bestselling novels. But Steve's actual exploits, said Jesse, were even more fantastic than anything that had been written. Steve, said his brother, knew exactly who killed John F. Kennedy—and it *wasn't* Lee Harvey Oswald. Steve also knew *why* Kennedy was killed. Steve, said Jesse, was not with the Mafia, though he sometimes dealt with them. Steve's own associates were so tough and ruthless that they made the Mafia look like Boy Scouts by comparison.

Jesse often pointed out news events to suggest that Steve was involved. "I always thought he was joking," said Stewart Woodman. "I mean, everything that ever happened, Steve was responsible for it. If you read something in the newspapers, Jesse would say, 'That was my brother,' or Steve would say, 'That was me.' And it could be anywhere in the world."

Neil and Stewart may have discounted much of what Jesse said, but little by little, as they got to know Steve better and listened to his tales of intrigue and adventure, they came to believe that he was indeed a dangerous man. While they continued to treat Steve as a charming fellow and a good friend, the brothers Woodman, especially Neil, also came to view him as someone they could use, a powerful tool that could give them an unbeatable edge in business.

For his part, Steve cultivated the Woodmans, occasionally carrying out small tasks. Besides bugging an office for them, a job that netted him $600, thanks to the unwitting services of Jean Scherrer, Steve burglarized Neil's home while he and his family were in Las Vegas, taking expensive jewelry so Neil could collect tens of thousands in insurance. To spare Neil's children grief, during the "burglary" Steve chloroformed their dog, leaving him unharmed.

If the big score eluded him, Steve was patient. Sooner or later, the Woodmans would tap him for something major, something to justify all the time he and Jesse were investing in the relationship.

Meanwhile, however, Homick was getting frantic about money. Carpentry no longer interested him, his gun sideline brought in peanuts, and while he bought cocaine wholesale and dealt it retail, his own habit ate up most of his profits. So he was ready for some serious work in March 1985, when his redheaded friend and good coke customer, Ron Bryl, a.k.a. Ronald McDonald, sent him to see Larry Ettinger.

Ettinger owned art galleries in five Hawaiian hotels, including one in the old whaling port of Lahaina, Maui. He also owned a nine-room boardinghouse there, where his gallery employees resided. Ettinger, in the midst of a costly divorce, was desperate for cash. He tried to sell the boardinghouse, but could find no one willing to pay enough to allow him to pay off his mortgage and take a profit.

Instead, according to testimony given before a Federal jury, Ettinger gave Steve Homick $15,000 to torch his house for the insurance.

Homick did not care to risk his own life on arson. He bought a round-trip airline ticket to Honolulu for Michael Dominguez, who traveled under the name "Michael Dome." In the small hours of a sultry Maui morning, Dominguez poured five gallons of gasoline into the building's parlor, then tossed a match and ran. Through a minor miracle, all eleven occupants escaped with their lives. They lost, however, everything else they owned.

Ettinger filed an insurance claim for $219,000, and eventually settled for $155,855.

But someone—a "confidential informant"—had overheard bits of Ettinger's conversations about arson and reported it to the FBI. The informant had the date and target wrong—it was thought to be an art gallery in Florida—but FBI agents went through Ettinger's trash on April 8, 1985.

Among items found in his garbage were memos and phone messages bearing Steve Homick's number.

The fire on Maui occurred five days later, on April 13.

Thanks to Art Taylor, the FBI already knew that Steve Homick was dealing drugs. Special Agent Jim Livingston, who had taken control of Taylor after Jack Salisbury was transferred to another case, got a court order authorizing a "PEN register," a device that monitors a phone line and makes a record of every outgoing call, including the number called and the time and date when it started and ended. It was installed on Steve Homick's line in March 1985.

*   *   *

Following up on the tip from the New Jersey Gaming Enforcement Agency, in November 1985 Holder and Crotsley called Las Vegas FBI agent Jerry Daugherty.

"Jack Holder called, said they were working on a double homicide," recalled Daugherty. "The name Steven Homick had come up. Holder said, 'Tell me if you have anything on him.'

"The guy who worked the case was off that day. I told Holder I didn't know much about it, but I'd look it up and get back to him," said Daugherty.

Ten minutes after their first conversation, Daugherty called Holder back and said, "Sorry it took so long, but it looks like you've got a real good possibility with Homick. We've got a file on him, and we know he flew to Los Angeles the day before the murder, and flew back to Las Vegas the day after it," said Daugherty.

"I've been a cop twenty years, and this is the first time I've ever got a straight answer out of the Federal government," said Holder. "And I didn't have to wait for months. You sure you're really an FBI agent?"

After a good laugh, Daugherty said he thought it would be a good idea if Holder got on a plane and came to Las Vegas. There was a file on Homick, said Daugherty, and in it things that shouldn't be discussed over the telephone.

"I'll get over there," said Holder, "but I've got a few things to clear up first. Can you send me a copy of that file, or even just a summary?"

"Count on it," said Daugherty. "And I guarantee you'll find this guy, Homick, does all kinds of interesting things."

A Fish in the Desert

Jumbled heaps of colossal sandstone boulders, the Santa Susana Mountains shimmer and bounce through the lens of bone-dry air, faded to palest beige by eons of sunshine. Straddling the line between Ventura and Los Angeles Counties, the Santa Susanas made an ideal backdrop for Hollywood horse operas, a purpose they served through sixty years in hundreds of movies starring such screen cowboys as Tom Mix, William S. Hart, Hopalong Cassidy, and Roy Rogers.

Emerging from a tunnel through the Santa Susanas into the northwest corner of the San Fernando Valley are the tracks of the Southern Pacific Railroad. These rails, a spur on the line connecting the cities around San Francisco Bay with those of Southern California, drop down from the mountains, then curve south through Chatsworth, a community in the City of Los Angeles, then southeast to downtown, some forty miles distant.

The low white building used by Manchester Products Co. to extrude plastic panels is on black-topped Mason Street, dead-ended on the north by the railroad. In Manchester's lunchroom, on October 13, 1981, Neil and Stewart Woodman played table-stakes poker with four other men. Tens of thousands of dollars were on the table.

The gamblers were interrupted by the arrival of a stranger. Daniel Raiskin was in his mid-thirties, trim, dapper, of above average height, with a head of thick, prematurely gray hair. An attorney specializing in tax planning and corporate law, Raiskin was a partner in Boren, Elperin, Howard and Sloan. He was there to answer an SOS from Neil and Stewart Woodman.

The game broke up and the brothers took Raiskin, whom they were meeting for the first time, to a conference room. They showed him their subpoenas and expressed annoyance that they had been served on the night after Yom Kippur. They explained that their father wanted to dissolve the company. Gerry had been threatening to do just that for many years, almost every time things got tough. He'd said it so often that his sons had come to believe it was only a bluff. But the papers they handed Raiskin were no bluff.

Raiskin was blunt. "I think your father holds most of the cards," he said. "But that doesn't mean you should just roll over. I'll need to research the law in this area, and if there is anything that suggests a better way out of this, we can go to court, if necessary, to stop your father."

The brothers told Raiskin more about the company, and about their situation. They dared not admit that over a million dollars a year was skimmed from the company. Instead they said that Manchester was selling $3 million worth of plastic a year; if it were to go on the market for the usual high multiple of annual earnings, they would expect bids of no less than $6 million—and perhaps far more.

Dissolving the company, however, meant selling off all its tangible assets and dividing the proceeds among shareholders. That would mean selling idle machinery and used fixtures, not a thriving company, a process that would surely yield far less than $6 million. Neil explained that more than twenty years earlier, his father had been on the other end of an identical situation when his partner, Jack Salzburg, forced the dissolution of Fullview. Raiskin smiled when he heard that name, explaining that one of his law partners was Salzburg's nephew.

Neil and Stewart took this coincidence as a good omen.

The brothers told Raiskin what they supposed was behind their father's action: "Dad can't accept the fact that we no longer need him in the business," said Neil. "He can't accept that we no longer depend on him for everything. So he dissolves the company, takes the little money he gets, and starts something new, with Wayne. He's always known how to start a company, how to make money. He figures that sooner or later we'll come crawling back. He'll let us in, but on his terms—which means everything would be like when we were kids—he runs the show, we can't question his decisions, we don't get a fair share of profits. That's what he really wants."

Raiskin got up from his chair. "I'll take your case on two conditions," he said. "First, you have to know that your father has the upper hand here. And second, this is a family situation, and I don't want to be told, 'Take it easy, don't be so hard on him, don't do this or don't do that.' Because the only way to win this case is to do everything the law allows. I must have a free hand to do whatever is necessary."

The brothers didn't even look at each other. Both nodded yes. "We wouldn't want it any other way," said Neil.

For most of his life, Neil's take on Stewart was the bemused tolerance of an older brother, muffled and warped by their father's constant needling and abuse, and focused in adulthood by Gerry's clearly shown preference for Stewart. Neil felt that his brother did not give him enough respect and that, ignoring the customs of primogeniture, his father had treated him unfairly. He felt that Stewart was good enough at sales, but he was too soft, obeying his heart when he should listen to his head, and lacking the fierce will and drive required to succeed in the business world.

For his part, Stewart had grown up to see himself as smarter, a better son to his parents than his big brother Neil. Stewart felt that he had sacrificed his youth to honor his father's dreams while Neil, however godlike he had seemed during Stewart's childhood, was inclined toward laziness. Stewart resented the occasional weekday afternoons Neil took to play golf. Recalling his own prodigious achievements in business, he measured his brother by them and found him lacking. And yet Neil would always be his big brother, and Stewart would always be just a little intimidated by him.

The lifelong relationship between the two brothers changed when Gerry and Vera filed suit. Suddenly it was them against their family. Knowing they each stood to lose everything, they began to lean on each other, to use each other's strengths and shore up each other's weaknesses. For the first time in their lives, Stewart and Neil began to confide in each other.

Dan Raiskin's first strategy was to try for a negotiated settlement. For days he tried to talk with Gerry. The patriarch refused to take his calls. Nor would he speak to his sons. At Stewart's suggestion, Raiskin contacted Lou Jackson in an attempt to get a dialogue started. But Gerry's blood ran hot. He wanted revenge against his ingrate offspring. Despite Vera's repeated urgings to be reasonable, Gerry told Lou Jackson to mind his own business.

Raiskin's legal research yielded a hopeful item. He telephoned the brothers to say that he had discovered a new law, Rule 2000. In simple terms, Rule 2000 said that if one stockholder or partner in an enterprise files notice to dissolve the company, anyone controlling more than one third of the outstanding stock is entitled to buy out the other partner *at liquidation prices*. In other words, if Gerry persisted with his effort to dissolve Manchester, his sons could force him to sell to *them* at the same price he could expect from his share of Manchester's assets if they were sold at public auction.

Suddenly Neil and Stewart knew that they would win.

Raiskin cautioned them: beating Gerry at his own game would be like trying to land a very big fish on light tackle. Muscle alone would not work; they would need finesse, and some luck, to reel in the slippery leviathan.

The first step: Neil and Stewart called a meeting with Harry Fukuwa, Manchester's accountant; Penny Sneir, a representative of Union Bank; and Raiskin, their attorney.

Sneir was included for two reasons: in 1980, Manchester had established a line of credit with her bank—and now the company owed $1.3 million. Sneir was representing the bank's interest in ultimately recovering its investment.

She was also present, perhaps unwittingly, to participate in a carefully choreographed legal charade which the brothers hoped would result in giving them control of Manchester.

Ostensibly, the purpose of the meeting was to discuss an offer to Vera and Wayne for their stock in Manchester. Neil and Stewart were prepared to offer $300,000 cash and three racehorses owned by Manchester. They would pay their mother and brother a total of $9,429 monthly for forty-two months. Each could keep their company car, Vera's Mercedes and Wayne's Cadillac. The proposed settlement also included agreements that Gerry and Vera would not enter into competition with Manchester, nor say nor write anything to harm the company.

This was a settlement calculated to appear equitable. Certainly it was one which might have served as the basis for a reasonable counteroffer.

But Neil and Stewart knew that their father would never allow Vera and Wayne to settle for so little—or to settle at all. They also knew that their father rarely took advice, that the more his lawyers pressured him to sign the agreement the more he would resist the whole notion of a settlement. If they pressed hard enough, the brothers felt, Gerry would blow them off and do exactly the opposite of what his lawyers advised.

So the real purpose of the "offer" meeting was quite another thing.

Operating on the hypothetical assumption that "Vera and Wayne" would accept the brothers' offer, Sneir was ostensibly present to advise Neil and Stewart where and how to get $300,000 for the buyout.

As she had previously told the brothers privately, Sneir stated for the record that Union Bank was so far out on a limb with Manchester that the bank couldn't authorize an additional $300,000. She added, however, that the bank would be willing to loan the money to Neil and Stewart *personally*.

But, Sneir continued, she would *not* advise the brothers to borrow the money and then simply reloan it to Manchester to proceed with the buyout of Vera and Wayne's stock.

In other words, regardless of who the money was borrowed

from, it was, in Sneir's professional opinion, too much debt for Manchester to carry without acquiring an offsetting asset.

So instead of using the borrowed $300,000 to *retire* stock, Sneir suggested the brothers use it to purchase *additional* stock in Manchester. This prudent step would infuse capital and improve the corporation's important debt-to-assets ratio.

It would also give Neil and Stewart more than 50 percent of Manchester's stock—and control of the company.

The settlement offer was bait.

The charade continued as Raiskin's office drew up settlement papers for Vera's and Wayne's signatures.

As the brothers expected, Gerry wouldn't allow them to sign. Raiskin dickered with Steve Solomon, Gerry's attorney, and set up a meeting with Gerry, Vera, and Wayne in Raiskin's office on October 20. "The purpose of the meeting was to resolve any open issues so that the redemption of shares could be completed," said Raiskin—again, for the record.

After taking a look at the agreement, Gerry erupted, screaming that the offer, which amounted to about $2.2 million, including the four thoroughbreds, was unacceptable. His sons had "intentionally undervalued" the company's inventory, raged Gerry. Manchester was headed for bankruptcy, he roared. Then he stormed out, an awesome, majestic figure, trailed by his dutiful wife and son, unaware that he had just swallowed the hook and was swimming off with it.

Now Raiskin told his clients how to reel their father into the net. In his role as corporate counsel, Raiskin formally advised Neil and Stewart that since they were directors and officers, they "owed a fiduciary duty to the shareholders to protect and preserve the assets of the corporation, and to operate the corporation in the most efficient and profitable manner possible, [and] that immediate steps should be taken to correct any management problems that exist."

Following Raiskin's advice, the brothers called a board of directors meeting for October 22. As required by law, all directors, including Gerry, were delivered formal notice of the gathering twenty-four hours in advance.

On the night of October 21, Ralph Ehrenpreis, then Muriel Jackson's son-in-law and Manchester's former corporate attorney, called Raiskin at his home. He said he was acting, not as an attorney, but as a member of the family. He had spoken to Gerry, Stewart, and Neil, and they had agreed that the offer for Vera and Wayne's stock would be accepted with one modification: payments would be for fifty months, instead of forty-two.

About eleven-thirty the next morning, however, Gerry sent word through his attorney that the directors' meeting was illegal and improper, and he therefore refused to attend.

Half an hour later, the remaining directors—Neil and Stewart—met. Raiskin announced that he had been notified that the offer to purchase the outstanding stock had been accepted by Vera, and recommended that the corporation authorize the issuance of *additional* stock so that Neil and Stewart could invest an additional $300,000 in Manchester.

Neil and Stewart then voted to issue to themselves an additional 1,500 shares of stock at $200 a share.

Their fish was in the net.

While paperwork for a $300,000 personal loan inched through Union Bank's paper mill, sham negotiations with Gerry continued, with an unwitting Lou Jackson acting as the honest broker.

One of the issues raised by the brothers was who would pay a $10,000 stud fee owed for services already provided to Strange Ways, Gerry's prize mare. Gerry refused to pay it. The horse belonged to Manchester when it was put to stud, he said, so the company owed the money.

Gerry's intransigence over the stud fee was expected. After noting that benefits of the stud fee—a foal—would accrue not to Manchester but to the horse's new owners, Vera and Wayne, Neil and Stewart, on Raiskin's advice, agreed to pay the fee from their own pockets. Thus on November 2, each gave Manchester $5,000— money previously skimmed from the till—to pay the stud fee. Each took, in exchange, twenty-five shares of Manchester stock.

The fish was in the boat.

The brothers now owned more than 50 percent of the company's stock. They applied to Union Bank for a letter of credit as guarantee of payment for Vera's stock, a step Gerry had demanded as a guarantee of his sons' good faith. Through Raiskin, they continued a dialogue with Gerry's attorneys.

On November 10, the brothers held another directors meeting, voting to revoke Gerry's previous action dissolving the company.

When Gerry learned that his sons had issued themselves new stock and now controlled the corporation, he realized he'd been tricked. His rage knew no bounds. No longer concerned about money, he now had to prove to his family, and to himself, that he was still a man, still able to control his clan.

Gerry filed a new lawsuit to dissolve Manchester. On November 20, his lawyers called Raiskin and said Gerry would not agree to any deal that left his sons with the company. On the same day, Neil and Stewart held another directors' meeting. The minutes record that the board of directors voted to make Neil president and chief financial officer and Stewart chairman of the board, vice president, and secretary. The minutes also note acceptance of the resignation of Gerald Woodman as president and director, retroactive to October 18, 1981; termination of employment for Wayne Woodman, effective immediately; the removal of Wayne and Gerry as signatories to all corporation bank accounts; the end of salary payments, expense reimbursements, and all other compensation to Wayne and Gerry; and the return to corporate control of Vera's Mercedes 450SL and Wayne's Cadillac El Dorado.

The fish was dead. It just didn't know it.

Gerry hired more lawyers and proceeded to sue his sons, alleging that the procedure by which they had taken control of the company was illegal and restating his desire to dissolve the company.

Until the lawsuit, Neil and Stewart had maintained some contact with the rest of their family. Stewart had occasionally spoken to his mother and aunts, and to his sisters. The suit ended all that. Neil had a high wall built around his house, mostly as a symbol, a message to his parents that they would never see their grandchildren again.

Except for their sister Hilary, Stewart's favorite aunt, Sybil, and a few cousins who remained neutral, all of Jack Covel's clan took sides for Gerry and Vera and against Neil and Stewart. Stewart found this especially painful because he thought of himself as one who had always been exceedingly generous with his sisters, aunts, and cousins.

"What did you expect?" scowled Neil, already reveling in the role of family outlaw.

And then came the depositions.

As in most lawsuits, each side strove to put its own spin on events, to introduce facts most beneficial to its interests, and to discredit the other side. To study the notional worlds created by litigants' assertions is to observe a collision of opposites, of matter and antimatter. The suit between the Woodmans was no exception, and the resulting explosion annihilated the last remnants of goodwill in the Woodman family.

Most of Gerry's "evidence" consisted of allegations, in his and Wayne's depositions, that his older sons were incompetent bunglers who had done nothing to build his company. Neil, according to his father, was always goldbricking in the office instead of in the factory, where his responsibilities were. Stewart, Gerry claimed, was too lazy to make sales trips. The brothers together, asserted Gerry, were driving the business into bankruptcy with their ineptitude, and had intentionally understated the last inventory by $100,000.

Gerry subpoenaed most of the Covel clan to back his allegations that his sons were out of control and had already set Manchester on the road to ruin. To make sure that Gloria Karns didn't testify on behalf of his parents, Neil, through one of his attorneys, conveyed a threat: if Gloria insisted on testifying, Neil would tell Vera about Amy Hearn, Gerry's illegitimate daughter. Gloria, unaware that Vera already knew about Amy, caved in and agreed not to testify.

Outraged that his aunts had sided with Gerry, Neil telephoned Muriel Jackson at her import business, Angelette.

Neil said, "If *we* go down, all Lakey's [his maternal grandmother's nickname] children will go down." It was a veiled reference to the tax-evading, cash-skimming techniques that Neil supposed that his grandfather, Jack Covel, had implanted in each of his daughters' businesses.

Muriel was not cowed.

"Neil, are you threatening me?" asked Muriel. "I don't know what *you* have to worry about, but *I* don't have anything to worry about," she added. Muriel would not forget her nephew's bald attempt at blackmail. Nor would she forget that when her father, Jack, had been seduced by that *shiksa* fortune hunter, Lynda Beaumont, a woman years younger than herself, it was Neil who had introduced them. And when, in the interest of protecting her father, she had forbidden Covel's grandchildren to allow Beaumont in their homes, it had been Neil, most of all, who had defied her. Indeed, Neil had actually encouraged the *shiksa's* relationship with Jack! When the time came, she decided, Neil would be put in his place.

Neil and Stewart's depositions refuted all their father's contentions. Both pointed out that Gerry seemed to delight in kicking Neil out of the factory. He had done this many times, said the brothers, warning Neil not to meddle with the machinery or the work force, cursing him as a "moron" in front of workers, then ordering him to go to and stay in the office. And both brothers pointed out that minutes after each episode, upon finding Neil in the office, Gerry had attacked his son for laziness and ordered him back into the factory.

The sons' depositions also dealt heavily with several of Gerry's costly management mistakes and with his constant gambling.

Stewart quoted Wayne as yelling, in October 1981, "We are going to bankrupt the business and destroy you both!"

Neil and Stewart also brought in outsiders—Manchester employees and suppliers—to give depositions.

Warren Kemp, Manchester's national sales director, testified about Wayne's general ineptitude. "It is my personal opinion," said Kemp, "based on my fifteen years in the business of selling home products, that Wayne Woodman simply was not competent for the job which he undertook."

Later in his deposition, Kemp described Wayne's dealings with Shaw Lumber in St. Paul, Minnesota. "I had sold products to Shaw Lumber for twelve years. . . . Shaw had been a steady account . . . and was considered a good paying customer. I was . . . standing next to Wayne when Wayne was talking to Duane O'berg, purchasing agent for Shaw's entire chain. O'berg told Wayne that he had a problem with concealed damage of merchandise in shipments from Manchester." Wayne told Mr. O'berg that Shaw, contrary to long-standing Manchester policy, should pay one half of the freight costs of reshipping the damaged goods back to Manchester.

O'berg very firmly told Wayne that he had never before had to pay for returning damaged goods, and was not going to pay now. Eventually Wayne conceded the point, then began insisting that O'berg have one of his staff make an exact count of the damaged goods. O'berg said that this was also Manchester's responsibility, a fact that Kemp confirmed.

"Wayne responded with words to the effect, 'If you don't want to do it our way, then you can shove it,'" said Kemp. "From that day, Shaw has never given another order to Manchester."

Rick Wilson, the cheerful Canadian who was then in charge of Manchester's "acoustical applications" line of ceiling panels, said that Wayne "would interfere in aspects of the business over which he had no control and about which he had no expertise. For instance, Wayne would often get into arguments with Stewart or myself concerning pricing policies," said Wilson. "Wayne could not comprehend [no matter how many times it was explained] that on certain key accounts [usually the largest volume accounts] discounts were given for volume purchases. Wayne was of the opinion that even with the largest volume accounts, unit price should be increased, not realizing [no matter how many times the same was explained] that in a business as competitive as plastic extrusion ... large volume accounts were *always* given discounts with the profit being greater to the company because of such volume."

Wilson also observed Wayne's techniques for collecting accounts receivable. "What Wayne did not understand is that there is a close correlation between continued and increasing sales and the methods by which accounts receivable are collected," said Wilson. "Often Wayne's attitude towards collection ... was a more dictatorial approach (e.g., 'Either pay immediately or no more supplies will be shipped.')."

Finally, Wilson described Wayne's habit of picking an argument with one of his brothers, often early in the morning, then storming out of the office and leaving for the day. This "had the effect of creating insecurity among the employees," said Wilson. "Wayne's conduct was so disruptive and demoralizing to the office personnel that Stewart and Neil . . . went to . . . bring him back to the office so as to present a more harmonious front for the benefit of . . . morale."

Shelle Abbott, an office worker, and Steve Strawn, who had been hired to do the collection and shipping work that Wayne was in charge of, also gave depositions about Wayne's general disruptiveness and incompetence.

But the truly damning testimony was reserved for Gerry. Ed Klugman, an able and loyal employee who first worked for Gerry at Lancaster Boat Company in 1964 and had followed him to Lancaster, where he became a foreman, testified that Gerry had always treated him fairly until about 1976, when his "personality and attitude" changed. "Gerald, who had always had a temper, began, when he had a disagreement with an employee, including myself, to use harsh, loud and obscene language," said Klugman. Several longtime employees quit rather than suffer this kind of abuse, said Klugman, naming them.

Klugman added that he once caught Gerry inserting defective plastic sheets in the middle of shipping cartons containing ten or fifteen pieces of perfectly good merchandise. "Don't worry about it," said Gerry. "It's okay if I do it." When Klugman objected, Gerry spouted more obscenities at him.

In July 1980, Klugman, who has a severe heart condition, worked through the night to restart an extrusion machine that had jammed after a power failure left it full of molten plastic. Afterward, feeling that a heart attack was imminent, Klugman tried to leave. Gerry prevented him from leaving, insisting that he continue working. Gerry "gave me a nitroglycerine tablet, told me to take it and I would be 'okay,' " said Klugman. After his shift, Klugman went to see his doctor, who immediately called an ambulance and sent him to a hospital. He spent three days in intensive care and two more in a recovery room. "Gerald came to see me while I was in intensive care," recalled Klugman. "He told me that being in the hospital was a good vacation for me, and that I should be ready to go back to work very soon."

After Klugman was discharged, he went to Manchester to pick up his paycheck. Gerry said that he would not be paid for the days he missed while in the hospital, despite Manchester's long-standing policy on paying such sick leave. Klugman, outraged, appealed to Neil, who eventually arranged for him to be paid.

The stress of dealing with the lawsuit exacted a high price on Stewart's body. Now grossly overweight, his blood pressure soared. He was also plagued with gout and a heart problem that required medication and frequent monitoring.

In January 1982, Stewart suffered a stroke. Unwilling to let Neil alone run the company, Stewart returned to work just four days later, at first spending only half days at Manchester. Within a week he had resumed his previous schedule.

The stroke was a warning to Stewart that he could not indefinitely abuse his body with overeating and lack of exercise. But it was Neil who acted on the message and made efforts to relieve Stewart's stress.

In March 1982, after a preliminary hearing, a Los Angeles County Superior Court judge threw out Gerry's lawsuit against his sons, ruling that the issuance of new stock and election of officers was lawful and that since Gerry was neither a director nor a stockholder, he had no standing to sue.

Neil and Stewart then invoked Rule 2000 against their mother's and brother's interests in Manchester. Independent appraisers were appointed to value Manchester's assets. "My father picked an appraiser, Neil and I picked an appraiser, and the court picked an appraiser," said Stewart.

They came back with a company whose liquidatable assets were valued at $1.375 million. Half of that was the price Neil and Stewart had to pay to be rid of their father's meddling.

Money for this buyout was loaned by Union Bank. They were pleased to structure a repayment plan that equaled the salaries that Gerry and Wayne had been drawing—about $5,000 a week. It seemed that the payback would be less than painless, because the salaries that Gerry and Wayne drew represented only a fraction of the money they actually took out of the company. Neil and Stewart could now split their father's former share of the skim and the inflated "expense reimbursements." They would each have almost twice as much money to spend.

Even better, much of Gerry's settlement went to pay his lawyers.

Vera and Gerry Woodman, 1971: Their marriage was a complex game—and only they knew the rules. (*Courtesy Melody Woodman*)

(*Left to right*) Mark Sutter, Hilary Woodman Sutter, Mickey Stern, Maxine Woodman Stern, Gerry Woodman, Vera Woodman, Melody Placek Woodman, Stewart Woodman, Maxine Shepard Woodman, Neil Woodman, Wayne Woodman, 1971: Stewart and Melody's wedding was a lavish affair. (*Courtesy Melody Woodman*)

Melody and Stewart at their 1971 wedding: She kissed a handsome young prince; thirteen years later he turned into a frog. (*Courtesy Melody Woodman*)

(*Left to right*) Ian, Jaycy, Melody, Morgan, and Stewart in Las Vegas, circa 1979: Melody shopped, Stewart played baccarat, twenty-one, and poker, and the kids fed nickels to slot machines. (*Courtesy Melody Woodman*)

(*Clockwise from lower left*) Gerry, Neil, Wayne, and Stewart Woodman, circa 1978: Before his heart attack, Gerry ruled his roost, playing his sons off against each other. (*Courtesy Melody Woodman*)

Manchester Products: After ousting their father, Neil and Stewart built this new factory building and filled it with expensive new machinery. (*Copyright © 1992, Marvin J. Wolf*)

Side entrance to Brentwood Place: The gunmen cut the chain and slipped inside to wait for their prey. (*Copyright © 1992, Marvin J. Wolf*)

Walkway just west of Brentwood Place: The killers came this way to set up their ambush. (*LAPD*)

Brentwood Place: Last residence of Gerry and Vera Woodman. (*Copyright © 1992, Marvin J. Wolf*)

Subterranean garage at Brentwood Place: The security camera (*top, left*) was a dummy. (*LAPD*)

The death scene: Gerry and Vera were shot as they got out of their car. (*LAPD*)

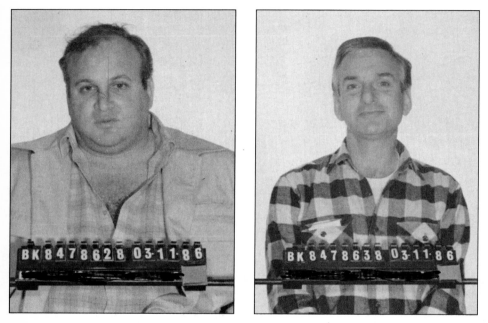

Booking photos, March 11, 1986: Stewart Woodman (*left*) and Neil Woodman. (*LAPD*)

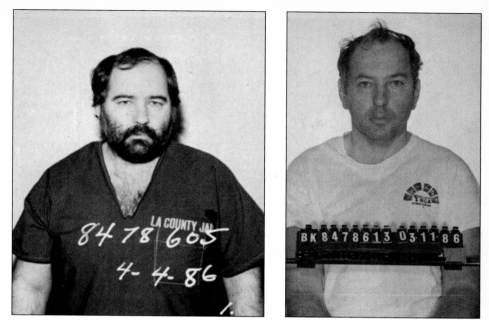

Booking photos, March 11, 1986: Robert "Jesse" Homick (*left*) and Steve Homick. (*LAPD*)

Booking photos, March 11, 1986: Mike "Baby A" Dominguez (*left*) and Anthony Majoy. (*LAPD*)

Bloodhounds: Rich Crotsley (*left*) and Jack Holder. (*Courtesy Jack Holder*)

Attorney Gerald Chaleff: Representing Neil Woodman, he raised an already high profile and sowed enough doubt to hang the jury. (*Courtesy Gerald Chaleff*)

Attorney Jay Jaffe: He was devastated when his client, Stewart Woodman, was convicted of murder. (*Photo: Kim Berly*)

"My father had to pay about four hundred and fifty thousand dollars in legal fees. It cost us only about one hundred and fifty thousand dollars," said Stewart.

The brothers were jubilant. It had been a long, bitter battle, but not only had they caught their fish, they had skinned it and eaten it for dinner.

CHAPTER Sixteen

Leads, Dead Ends, Blind Alleys

OCTOBER 1985

While Jack Holder and Rich Crotsley waited for the FBI file on Steve Homick, they had leads to follow and loose ends to unravel. Solving a murder, proving who did it, also means proving that no one other than the accused is responsible. Sometimes police neglect to do this, and defense attorneys introduce evidence at trial that opens the possibility that someone other than their client might have committed the crime. More than one guilty person has gone free because the jury was persuaded that some other dude might, in fact, have done it.

One loose end was a report from Neil Woodman, sent via his attorney, Jay Jaffe, that a certain Orange County gambling figure had loaned Gerry $4,000 a few weeks prior to the murders. Holder and Crotsley considered that while this might be a genuine lead, it was more likely a red herring—or Neil's rhinoceros-subtle way of trying to build an alibi for a classic defense: "S.O.D.D.I.," Some Other Dude Did It.

Neil had also volunteered, through Jaffe, that Gerry Woodman had fathered an illegitimate daughter, Amy Hearn, who might know about Gerry's gambling, and hence who had reason to kill him. Holder and Crotsley tracked Amy Hearn to San Francisco and scheduled a visit, though they expected to get no more than a good meal on the expense account.

Both Neil and Stewart complained, through Jaffe, that someone was watching their houses from a white minivan that bristled with antennas, and that their phones were tapped. Each hired private investigators, but nothing was found. Crotsley had the telephone company open an underground vault, but they found no evidence of tampering.

Holder and Crotsley concluded that all this was a symptom of guilty paranoia. Neil and Stewart were worried. Their imaginations were playing tricks on them. Or maybe they were studiously trying to build a plausible scenario that could later, if necessary, be used as a defense: that they, too, were targets of whoever had murdered their parents.

Crotsley, seeking to explore every avenue of investigation, asked the LAPD's data department for a printout of recent crimes where entry was made by cutting a lock or chain but could find none suggesting a *modus operandi* like the one used on Gorham Avenue.

Then there were the spectacles that had been found thirty-six feet from Gerry's body, and which, so far, no one in the family had been able to positively identify as belonging to Gerry. Homicide detectives do not like loose ends.

The lenses tested negative for fingerprints but positive for traces of blood matching Gerry Woodman's type. Holder, seeking to confirm that the glasses were Gerry's—and not his killer's—questioned several members of the Woodman and Covel families and checked with two optometrists, several opticians, and every Senator Frames distributor in Southern California. After days of labor, it was a dead end. No one could positively say they were Gerry's glasses.

Holder and Crotsley trekked over to the mid-Wilshire offices of Garry Treadway, who supervised fraud investigation for the California Department of Insurance. Treadway had a file on Vera's life insurance. About two years earlier, she and her sister, Muriel, had written letters and made phone calls to the department and to Presidential Life Insurance, the underwriter, trying to get them to rescind the policy. But the state couldn't force Presidential to cancel unless there was evidence of fraud, and there was none. As long as Manchester paid the hefty premiums, the insurer had no legal justification for cancellation.

Now Vera was dead and her sons' company, the beneficiary, was due for a big payoff. Holder asked Treadway if his department could get Presidential Life to withhold payment until police had enough of a case against the brothers to ask for an indictment from the District Attorney's office.

Treadway said he'd talk to Presidential, but until there was at least an arrest, there was very little the Department of Insurance could do. And, said Treadway, insurance companies that delay payment of death benefits are inviting not only a lawsuit but bad publicity as well.

Another, unwelcome task was to respond to a series of inquiries from the office of Los Angeles City Councilman Hal Bernson. His staffers had called Major Crimes several times, seemingly to wonder why the police were wasting time investigating two upstanding businessmen—and campaign contributors—like Neil and Stewart Woodman. Bernson's staffers were even so bold as to play detective, suggesting to Holder that he check out the *modus operandi* of another recent homicide, the Williams murder. Bernson's chief aide thought that there were obvious parallels between that case and the Woodman murders.

Holder saw no parallels between the cases. The Williams murder was an obscure robbery involving a victim beaten to death, not shot. Holder saw instead the Woodmans' clumsy hands, trying to manipulate politicians into interfering with his investigation. To Holder, this meant that while the brothers had juice enough to make a city councilman stick his neck out, they were also running scared.

Holder liked that. Scared suspects often make mistakes.

Early in December 1985, a confidential file on the FBI's investigation of Steve Homick finally arrived at Major Crimes. It had been forwarded through Las Vegas Metro Police.

To Holder, one of the more interesting items in this file was the revelation that Steve Homick had two brothers, and that one of them lived in an apartment at 1523 Corinth Avenue, in the Sawtelle district, a five-minute drive from the condominium garage where Gerry and Vera Woodman had died.

There was also a description of this brother, Robert, whom the file noted was also known as Jesse. He was thirty-five, tall and heavy, with blue eyes, dark hair, and a full beard. He habitually dressed in tennis shoes, T-shirts, and jeans.

Holder read the description to Crotsley.

"That remind you of anyone?"

"The hood Stewart Woodman sent to muscle Swartz?" said Crotsley. "Guy out in Riverside, with the crippled daughter?"

"Bingo."

Holder called the California Department of Motor Vehicles (DMV) and asked them to run a check on automobiles registered to Robert Homick. There were none. Holder next obtained the utility records for the apartment.

All were in the name of Hassan Abdullah, as was the apartment lease. Apparently Robert "Jesse" Homick had a roommate.

Next, Holder ran Abdullah's and Steve and Robert Homick's names through the LAPD's computer data bases. If either had been arrested or listed as known associates of anyone involved in an LAPD or Sheriff's investigation, if they had been in an automobile accident, or had simply been stopped and interviewed by police for any reason, their names would probably be in the computer.

There was nothing on Hassan Abdullah.

There was nothing on Steve Homick.

Robert's name came up twice.

The first was on June 22, 1985. Robert had been interviewed by an LAPD officer after someone called 911 to complain of a "suspicious" character loitering in front of his apartment at 7:24 P.M. The man who called the police, Eric Grant, lived in an apartment at 11933 Gorham Avenue.

Gerry and Vera Woodman had lived and died at 11939 Gorham—the building next door.

Eric Grant had seen the "suspicious" character because he was moving out of his apartment in the front corner of the building that day. While making numerous trips in and out of the building during the afternoon and early evening, he'd seen a beat-up Buick parked on the street nearby.

The police report from June 22 said that Grant saw Robert Homick parked in a 1960 blue Buick, two-door, with Nevada plates, CSC148. The suspect was "male, white, heavy-set, dark hair, full beard, thirty-five, wearing a black T-shirt."

A patrol unit driven by Officer Jacquelyn Nicholson arrived at 7:40 P.M. She was a well-trained cop, armed with both a baton and a handgun, but she took one look at Robert and fought against a wave of fear.

"What are you doing here?" she asked.

"Reading my newspapers," said Robert, and indeed the car was full of newspapers and empty cardboard boxes. "And I have every right to read them here or anyplace else," said Robert.

Nicholson checked Robert's identification, called his name in to the dispatcher to see if he was wanted for anything, and told him to move on. He drove away.

Holder and Crotsley went out to the West Side and found Grant, a calm, organized, intelligent accounting major who was working his way through UCLA with a thirty-hour-a-week job for the university's parking services department.

The detectives showed Grant an LAPD photo lineup. He picked Robert Homick's picture from several photos he was shown.

Grant said that he had long been interested in cars. As a teenager, he memorized the look of virtually every make and model of American car built since 1925. At about one o'clock, as he walked between his apartment and a storage area, he noticed a twenty-five-year-old Buick or Pontiac with heavily oxidized blue paint. This is an upscale neighborhood, and a car that old and poorly kept was unusual. About two or three hours later, Grant saw that the car had moved. It was now parked across the street, facing the other way. In midafternoon, Grant's neighbor, David Miller, stopped by. He, too, had noticed the car. Miller used a 35mm camera with a telephoto lens to peer at the car's lone occupant, who apparently never left the car all day.

Grant and Miller decided to get the car's license number before calling the police. Grant, pretending to walk his dog, went across the street, then strolled past the car. After strolling down the block to the corner, he turned around and came back, passing the car a second time. Grant memorized the license plate, went back to his apartment, wrote down the number, and called the police.

Holder thought Eric Grant would make an excellent witness.

A few days later, Holder called Muriel Jackson and asked her to assemble everyone who had been at the September 25 break-the-fast dinner so that he, Crotsley, and a team of detectives could interview each of them in detail about the events of September 25.

"Everyone will be here tomorrow for dinner," said Jackson, and Holder marveled again at the cooperation he was getting.

"Before I come over, does the date June 22 mean anything special to you?" asked Holder. "Is that a Jewish holiday of some kind?"

"Not this year," said Jackson, explaining that the Hebrew calendar is lunar-based, with twenty-eight-day months. Every few years an extra month is added, so that a harvest festival, for example, is always celebrated in the autumn.

"Well, does that date mean anything special for your family?" said Holder.

"I shall have to think about that," replied Jackson. "If anything occurs to me, I'll let you know tomorrow."

There was one other report on Robert Homick in the LAPD computer: Jesse himself had reported that he was the victim of a hit-and-run auto accident. A car coming out of an alley had collided with his Buick. According to the accident report, when Robert got out to examine the damage, the other car, driven by young Richard Altman, had sped off.

The accident took place at West End Avenue and the outlet of a blind alley behind Gorham Avenue—less than a hundred yards from Brentwood Place.

The date of the accident was September 25, 1985.

Gotcha! thought Holder, marveling at Robert's stupidity.

"He was seen practically next door to the scene of a double murder only a few hours before the crime—and then he goes out of his way to tell the police about it," said Holder.

Holder and his partner went out to see young Richard Altman, whose car had collided with Robert Homick's Buick.

Altman said he had pulled over after the collision, but took off in fear when he saw Robert—huge, disheveled, and menacing—get out of his car.

Altman said that Robert later telephoned to threaten him, demanding $700 for the little ding in his Buick's door. Under

Holder's questioning, Altman said that there was a passenger in Robert's car, a man with snow-white hair. After the collision, another car stopped, said Altman, and in it was another bulky man, perhaps forty-five or fifty, plus a slender, dark-skinned fellow who seemed barely out of his teens. Robert spoke to the bigger man for a moment. Then the man returned to his car and drove away.

Back at the office, Holder called Jerry Daugherty, the FBI agent in Las Vegas, and described the men Altman saw with Robert Homick. "The little guy sounds like Baby A," said Daugherty. "Real name Michael Dominguez, an associate of Steve Homick. Five arrests—grand larceny, forgery, robbery, like that. He's on parole for possession of stolen property."

"So, a regular sweetheart," said Holder.

"But not very smart," said Daugherty, ringing off.

A few hours later, Daugherty called back. "Got a C.I. [confidential informant] who says Steve Homick likes to fly. I had someone call P.S.A. [Pacific Southwest Airlines] in San Diego and run Homick and Dominguez through their passenger records. And guess what: both of them flew into Los Angeles on September 24, and both of them flew back to Las Vegas on September 26."

"Thanks," said Holder. "I owe you for this."

"Damn right you do," said Daugherty.

When Holder and Crotsley, leading a squad of detectives, arrived at Muriel and Lou Jackson's Bel Air estate, they were firmly told that before any of the two dozen witnesses would be interviewed, everyone would eat.

After the elaborate meal, one of the food-sated detectives interviewed Betty Saul, who with her husband, Marvin, owns Junior's, a delicatessen and the largest independently owned restaurant in Los Angeles. The Sauls had been friends of the Woodmans.

"On the night of the murder, the night of the breaking of the fast, the Sauls were driving to Muriel's when they got into an argument," explained Holder. "They wanted to have a drink. Since it's Yom Kippur, if they go straight to Muriel's they'll have to wait until sundown, an hour, when Muriel can serve. So they stop at A Fine Affair, the restaurant at the corner of Moraga and Sepulveda, to have a drink."

Near the restaurant parking lot, Betty Saul saw a parked car. "It was an old Buick with all kinds of boxes in the back. And, she said, a big, sloppy guy was standing out in front of it," said Holder.

Detective Otis Marlowe, one of the Major Crimes detectives working with Holder and Crotsley, elicited this information from Betty Saul.

She told Marlowe, "I remember that car because it had Nevada license plates. My son goes to the University of Nevada at Las Vegas, and whenever I see Nevada plates, especially in that neighborhood, I look to see if it's a friend of my son's."

Betty Saul also remembered that the car, an old, battered blue Buick, had a decal of a spider on the back window. "The reason I remember all this is that the man and the car just didn't fit the area," said Saul. "He was bearded and scruffy."

Marlowe showed Mrs. Saul a photo lineup.

"Sure enough, she I.D.'d Bobby Homick," said Holder.

A few days later, when Holder put Robert under discreet surveillance, he had photos taken of his Buick. The decal on the rear window turned out to be a California golden bear. But in dim light, from a distance, it did bear a certain resemblance to a spider.

Holder had the streets around Brentwood Place canvassed again, looking for people who might remember seeing an old Buick with Nevada plates. They found a neighbor who remembered seeing such a car parked in front of the victim's house sometime during the previous summer. That neighbor, Dwight Chance, also picked Robert out of a photo lineup.

So two people plus a hit-and-run auto report confirmed that Robert "Jesse" Homick was in the immediate vicinity of the murder scene. Bolstering what the victims' family had said about Neil and Stewart, information from Scherrer and O'Grady linked the Woodmans and the Homicks.

And the FBI put both Steve Homick and Dominguez in Los Angeles on the day of the murders.

It was not yet enough for an arrest, but it was certainly sufficient for a search warrant. Holder and Crotsley had no difficulty convincing Lieutenant Ed Henderson, their boss, to let them proceed to this next step.

"I wanted to see who Robert was talking to, and who the

Woodman brothers were talking to, at home, and at their office," said Holder. "So we wrote out search warrants for their telephone records."

While waiting for the records, Holder and Crotsley made a quick trip to San Francisco to interview Amy Hearn. As expected, she could tell the detectives nothing that would help them find her father's killers. But before Holder and Crotsley left for Nevada and a meeting with Las Vegas Metro Police and the FBI, Maxine Stern telephoned and left a message. Holder called her back.

"You asked my Aunt Muriel about June 22," said Maxine. "That's my mother and father's wedding anniversary. They always went out that night to celebrate."

CHAPTER Seventeen

Clan Clash

Stewart, who had once loved Vera with a fierce, almost unhealthy fervor, was stung by her betrayal. After she supported Gerry's attempt to dissolve Manchester, he saw her as weak and grasping. Rather than defend her sons against their crazy, predatory father, she had played them for fools.

And yet he could not allow himself to believe that his mother did not love him. Not yet.

So, despite Neil's loud objections that any contact with Vera might give Gerry an opening to reimpose himself on his sons, Stewart had tried to maintain a relationship with his mother. Each time he called, however, his father intervened, screaming at Vera, punishing her, belittling and cursing Stewart. It was the last of these failed attempts to make peace with his mother, and his father's furious interference, Stewart believes, that had precipitated his stroke.

Neil was glad when Stewart gave up trying to restore relations with their mother. While physically resembling Vera, Neil from childhood manipulated his mother to gain stature in his *father's* eyes. Rejected, Neil in adulthood adopted many of his father's least pleasant mannerisms. He loved to scream at underlings, to embarrass them, to revel in his own sense of power. Even before Gerry moved to regain control of Manchester, Neil took revenge on his father for a lifetime of public humiliation. He cursed Gerry, wishing him dead not just aloud but in the presence of employees, customers, suppliers, friends, even complete strangers.

Neil now despised his mother no less than his father, often observing that reneging on her promise never to let Gerry control her stock was the cause of the family's bitter schism. Neil's anger toward Vera went far beyond that, of course. Early in his marriage, Vera had severely criticized Neil's wife. Neil passed along her comments, and Maxine recoiled from Vera. For years, the two women had barely been civil to each other. When the lawsuit to dissolve Manchester was filed, Maxine had been quick to point out that such a perverse act could never happen in her own family.

As often as Neil reminded Stewart of Vera's betrayal, however, Stewart could not yet force himself to punish his mother. So, while a court order called for Vera and Wayne to return their company-owned cars to Manchester, Stewart offered to let his mother keep her Mercedes coupe. Gerry, brimming with spite and abashed at losing Manchester, refused to let his wife accept any favors from the *goniff momzers*—thieving bastards—whom he could no longer bear to think of as his own flesh and blood. So Stewart sold Vera the car, purchased for $46,000 only a few months earlier, for $23,000, its depreciated value on Manchester's books.

Both Stewart and Neil, however, took particular delight in snatching back their baby brother's company-owned Cadillac.

It was Hilary, their younger sister, who inadvertently made it possible. After the lawsuit, she alone of the family had maintained a relationship with Stewart and Neil, and especially Stewart. "I spoke to Hilary at least once a day, *every* day," said Stewart. "We talked for hours—it wasn't a call where we just said 'hi' and 'good-bye.' Plus, we were physically with each other at least three times a week. My wife, Melody, and Hilary were the best of friends."

Early one evening in the spring of 1982, Stewart called Hilary. She said, "I can't talk long. We're going out to dinner at The Ginger House," an upscale Studio City eatery on Ventura Boulevard.

"Who are you going with?" asked Stewart.

"Wayne and Susan."

"That's interesting," said Stewart. "I didn't know Susan was a big fan of The Ginger House."

"It's Susan's birthday," said Hilary.

Stewart had never been close to Susan—even before the lawsuit, he had rarely spoken to Wayne's wife. And the reason for that was Susan's strong opposition to gambling. She had, more than once, stopped by the office and caught Wayne playing poker. Each time, Susan became very upset with his brothers.

Hilary knew that there was little love lost between Susan and Stewart; Stewart's sudden interest in her dining preferences rang false.

"Promise me you're not going to do anything," said Hilary to Stewart.

"What are you talking about?"

"Well, I know you're trying to get Wayne's car. So tell me you're not going to do anything."

"Okay. I'm not going to do anything," said Stewart. "I promise."

But after hanging up from his conversation with Hilary, Stewart immediately telephoned Dan Raiskin, his attorney, and told him what he had learned about Wayne's whereabouts that night.

"Can I just go over and take his car?" asked Stewart.

"Take it," said Raiskin. "It's perfectly legal."

Stewart next called Neil, who was dining at one of Stewart's favorite restaurants, The Bistro, and told him what he was up to.

"Go for it," said Neil, warmed by the thought of Wayne's face when his brother discovered that he no longer had a car.

"I drove to the office and got the duplicate keys to Wayne's car," said Stewart. "Melody dropped me off at The Ginger House. I found the Caddy in the parking lot, and I just got in and drove away.

"When I got back to the factory, the security guard recognized the car and thought I was Wayne. He pulled his gun, and I honked the horn and waved until he could see it was me," said Stewart.

Neil and Stewart chuckled over the snatch for days, making jokes about how Wayne had been forced to take a taxi home, about how he'd called the police to report his car stolen, about the way he'd cursed out the parking attendants.

As an unexpected bonus, Stewart claimed, in the glove compartment of Wayne's car were legal documents showing that Gerry had planned the failed *putsch* for more than a year.

"Now we knew why Dad wanted to spend all that money on Wayne's ideas with J. Walter Thompson," said Stewart. "He was planning to sue us and so he tried to drain off the company's cash, to force us to use our own money to fight him."

Gerry was furious when he learned how his older sons had taken Wayne's car. He took well-reasoned revenge a few months later, when Melody's thirtieth birthday was coming up. Guessing correctly that Stewart would celebrate the occasion with a dinner party at his favorite restaurant, The Bistro, Gerry waited until two weeks before the event, then called the manager, identified himself as Stewart, and said Melody was gravely ill. Then he canceled Stewart's party reservation.

When Stewart, Melody, and several friends arrived to find another fête in "their" room, the manager was called in to explain. Stewart understood at once that Gerry was punishing him with the same sort of embarrassment that Wayne had felt upon losing his car.

After Wayne's car was taken, Hilary never again spoke to Neil or Stewart.

The river of untaxed cash that had flowed through Manchester and into Neil's and Stewart's pockets became a Niagara with Gerry's departure. Allowed their first peek at the payroll and the corporate books, the brothers were pleasantly surprised: even more money went through the company than either had supposed.

But hardly had Neil and Stewart taken uncontested control of Manchester when they were confronted with an unpleasant reality: Gerry, whom they assumed was thoroughly beaten at his own game, was far from ready to retire.

By the spring of 1982, Gerry was sixty-five years old. He owned, with Vera, an almost unencumbered Bel Air home that, driven by real estate inflation, was worth over $1 million. And, even after paying his lawyers, he came out of Manchester with over $400,000—more than ten times his original investment.

Many men would have counted their blessings. They would have cashed out their inflated real estate and retired to clip bond coupons and live more modestly but still quite comfortably in England or the south of France or in Palm Springs.

Gerry Woodman was not one of those men. The only thing he loved more than gambling was starting a business, crushing a competitor, demonstrating dominance and manhood to his clan, and especially to its males.

In May 1982, Gerry rented a factory in Glendale, not far from his first business. Then he began recruiting salesmen and plastic extrusion machinery workers. "Salesmen started telling us that Dad had offered them more money to go to work for him," said Stewart. "We lost several. We paid machine operators, then, $400 or $500 a week. He offered them $1,000.

"One day I got a phone call from Miles Thomas, one of our key production people, and he said, 'I just heard from Mario, who says he's walking out, everybody's going with him, and they're taking all the tools—everything. He's going over to Woodman Industries.'

"So now we have a big problem," continued Stewart. "A factory running plastic with no people. We had machines operating; I had to turn them off. We basically lost our whole crew, except for three or four key workers."

But Neil and Stewart were lucky: their three foremen, guessing that the senior Woodman's chances of success were poor, did not run for the money. Instead, they stayed to provide supervision and training to new and relatively unskilled workers. Within a few weeks, the brothers' factory was humming as usual.

Experienced salesmen, however, were more difficult to replace than factory hands. Since ousting his father and becoming chief executive officer, Stewart no longer found time to oversee the minutiae of Manchester's day-to-day marketing effort. That fell to Richard Nuckles, a sales manager, a man nearly sixty years old. But if Nuckles had reason to be wary of Gerry, whom he had served for twenty years, Stewart, with his incessant practical jokes, had also given Nuckles ample cause to jump ship: he had deliberately, and with malice in his heart, embarrassed the older man.

"We had a saleslady, Vicky Wayne, and for years Nuckles tried to get her into bed," said Stewart. "She always turned him down. At a sales meeting at the Sahara in Las Vegas, we had dinner at Trader Vic's, the main restaurant. I told Vicky, 'I want you to tell Richard that this time you want to sleep with him. Get him up in your room. Then leave, and we'll take it from there.'

"During dinner I saw her whispering to Richard. All of a sudden, he smiled. It stayed across his face during the whole dinner. So I dragged dinner out, because I knew he was anxious to get going," explained Stewart.

"Finally, Vicky leaves," he continued. "I'd told her to stall for about ten minutes when they left the restaurant, to give me a chance to get up to her room with Neil, Rick Wilson, and two salesmen. We hid in a closet.

"When Nuckles comes in he tells Vicky, 'I always knew you really wanted me.' Then he starts talking about how he's been screwing me on expenses, how he gets an extra thirty or forty dollars a week without me knowing, about how easy I am to fool. Vicky knew we were there, of course, so to shut him up she said, 'Forget all the talk, let's just hit the sack.'

"She went in the bathroom. He got undressed. I heard his belt buckle hit the floor, and maybe three minutes later he called her, 'Come out, I'm ready for you.' That's when we walked out. He was on the bed, naked.

"We sang, 'When you least expect it, you're elected. You're the star today,' the 'Candid Camera' theme song. He turned white, I thought he was going to have a heart attack! But the best part about the whole thing was, he couldn't tell anybody, because he's married," said Stewart.

It took Nuckles a long time to live down his humiliation. In fact, while he bore his cross with good grace, he never forgave Stewart.

Richard Nuckles left to join Gerry's new company. So did several other Manchester salesmen around the country.

Nuckles's departure alarmed both Stewart and Neil.

"After all, this was my *father*," said Stewart. "And as much as we had a going business and a much bigger one than his, and as much as we had more of a cash cushion, this was the guy who had taught me everything. I had no idea what he was going to do, but I knew what he was, what he was capable of. I was scared; it was the first time in my life that I wasn't working with him, and now he is working *against* us," said Stewart.

Probably no one will ever know just what Gerry's real motives were, whether he thought he could actually build another company—or if he just wanted to destroy his sons.

Either way, he was out to bury Manchester. To get working capital, Gerry took a mortgage on his Bel Air mansion, called in markers from a sister in England, borrowed money from his daughter Maxine—who prudently insisted that he secure it with a second mortgage on his home—accepted cash and important seven-figure loan guarantees from in-laws Lou and Muriel Jackson, forced Vera to sell some of her more ostentatious diamonds, obtained a credit line from Union Bank—and came up with enough capital to rent a factory, buy machinery, and recommence all the business strategies that he had perfected over thirty years.

Gerry's daughters Maxine and Hilary joined the new firm as secretaries, the former to keep an eye on her investment, the latter because even the modest salary was welcome.

As head of Woodman Industries, Inc., Gerry contacted suppliers of raw material, explaining that "Woodman Industries is a new subsidiary of Manchester," that he, Gerry, was running it, and that, with his blessings, his older sons now ran the parent company.

Thus Gerry's suppliers believed that Manchester, Inc., stood behind Woodman Industries, and they shipped raw materials in quantity, at prices and credit terms that few startup enterprises could ever expect to match.

Just as Gerry launched his new venture, Vera suddenly recalled the insurance policy Manchester had taken on her life three years earlier. "The insurance policy really bothers me," she told her sister Muriel.

Unwilling to defy Gerry by calling her sons directly, Vera asked Muriel to talk to them. Muriel telephoned Stewart about the policy three or four times. "The first call I told him that his mother was very perturbed about the policy and would he please cancel it," said Muriel.

"He said he would get back to me after talking to Neil."

Stewart never did.

Muriel made other calls to Stewart to ask if Vera could see her grandchildren, as well as to ask about the life insurance.

"I pleaded with him," said Muriel. "I said, 'Please cancel the policy, your mother is very upset, you'll never be able to live with yourself if you collect money on your mother's life whenever she dies, even in a hundred years.'"

Neil was listening silently on the line. Muriel was unaware of his presence until he said, "Look at the odds," and laughed.

"I just hung up," said Muriel. "I felt sick."

This was last time Muriel spoke to either Neil or Stewart.

Muriel next telephoned Harold Albaum, the insurance agent who handled both Manchester's and Muriel's personal and business insurance. She asked him to cancel the policy.

"I'll take care of it," said Albaum. "No problem."

Later, however, Albaum called back to say that the policy could not be canceled unless Neil and Stewart consented.

Not one to take no for an answer, Muriel called the California Insurance Commission, and later wrote them on Vera's behalf.

But Stewart also wrote to the insurance company, and it became clear to Muriel that nothing could be done. It bothered her "terribly." It bothered Vera even more.

Knowing that their mother and aunt, and possibly their father as well, were exasperated but powerless was tonic to Neil and Stewart. Keeping the policy in effect was, at the time, one of the few things they could do to aggravate their kin. And that, just then, was the biggest reason why they refused to cooperate. And each month that they paid the premiums, they knew, tore the scab from that festering wound all over again.

That made Neil and Stewart feel just a little bit better about themselves.

The money that Gloria Karns had inherited from her father, Jack Covel, and had loaned Manchester in 1975 was in the form of an interest-only five-year note. As Gloria's need for cash increased, Gerry had given her "salary" raises and paid interest monthly, instead of annually or quarterly, as the original agreement called for. In 1980, when Gerry was recuperating from the depression that followed his heart attack, the note came due.

Stewart was planning to buy a lavish new home in Hidden Hills, beyond the San Fernando Valley's western rim. To ensure that there would be money enough to allow him to make the hefty mortgage payments, he had asked his aunt if she would extend the note for another five years.

Gloria said she would roll the note over, but only if Manchester gave her better medical insurance, a raise in her "salary," and a gasoline credit card. Stewart, acting for Gerry and with Neil's approval, agreed and Gloria extended the note through October 1985.

In early 1983, when Gerry had been forced out, but before Woodman Industries was shipping products, Neil asked his aunt to come down and talk about the note. She would later recall that Neil had boasted about stealing Manchester from his father, adding that it had taken him nearly two years to convince Stewart to go along with the plan.

Gloria arrived with a list of demands in exchange for rolling the note over for a second time.

"Gloria said, 'I'm not sure I want to renew, because your father's not here anymore,'" recalled Stewart. "She wanted an immediate increase in salary from four hundred to five hundred a week." Gloria also asked for a company car. "She said, 'If I don't get that, I want a check today, I want to get paid off,'" added Stewart. "I told her to fuck off and get out of the office."

Gloria said, "I see now why your mother changed her will. You're both disinherited. Neither of you will ever see a dime."

It was true. Vera had left everything to her other children.

Upon examining their copy of the original note, Neil and Stewart saw that Gerry had been paying Gloria *monthly* interest payments but that the agreement called for *quarterly* installments. Still reeling from the news of his disinheritance, Stewart called Gloria and said, "From now on, you'll get your interest quarterly. And we'll pay the note off on September 30, 1985."

In a civil suit, Stewart later contended that Gloria then went to Gerry's house and got him to alter the original copy of her note to read "quarterly or monthly," in his handwriting.

"Maybe they didn't realize that we had the original note," said Stewart.

When the first of March 1983 rolled around and no payment check came from Manchester, Gloria filed suit in the Van Nuys branch of Los Angeles County's Small Claims Court. Later she went to the court's West Los Angeles branch and filed another suit for the same sum. The following month, she did it all over again. And the next month, again.

Gloria's choice of Small Claims as a venue was inspired, and perhaps by Gerry. In Small Claims, plaintiffs and defendants must appear personally. For corporations, a company officer must appear.

So every time Gloria filed in Small Claims, either Neil or Stewart had to personally appear. She got no monthly payments, but until May 1985, when Small Claims judges made her take her suits to Municipal Court, Gloria got her pound of flesh twice a month.

Gerry loved it.

Before Gloria's suit went to Municipal Court, however, Neil and Stewart turned the matter over to their lawyers. Dan Raiskin had by then started his own firm, with Steve Revitz as his partner. Revitz drafted a countersuit asserting that $40,000 of the money lent by Gloria was not lent to Manchester, but to Vera personally. It also asserted that until ousting their father in early 1982, Neil and Stewart were unaware of the salary Gloria had received since 1975. The suit claimed that this money, in total about $70,000, was merely camouflaged interest, and so usurious. Since usury was illegal, the suit contended that Gloria was liable for treble damages. Stewart and Neil asked the court to rule that far from owing Gloria even the $60,000 they acknowledged she had lent Manchester, *she* owed *them* about $150,000. In April 1983, when the suit was filed, the brothers ended interest payments to Gloria. They took her off the payroll, terminated her medical insurance, and canceled her company credit card.

It took Gerry months to gear up Woodman Industries for production; not until late in the summer of 1982 was he shipping products for sale. Meanwhile, however, Stewart was desperate to know what his father was up to. He hired his friend Robert Homick to wait near Gerry's home in Bel Air and then tail him to the new factory. After locating the plant on Glenoaks Boulevard, Stewart made frequent visits there to talk to the truck drivers who hauled raw materials in and finished goods out. Stewart knew many of these people, who also serviced his own company; from them he learned what kinds of products Gerry was making, what die patterns he was using in his extruders.

Twenty years earlier Gerry had driven the industry's leaders to the wall by slashing traditional profit margins. Now he started cutting again.

"Dad always told us, 'Don't let a competitor in the door,'" said Stewart. "The only way to keep him out is to make the price such that somebody wouldn't switch for a penny or two, and the competitor couldn't undercut it. Neil and I knew we had to cut the price to where my father couldn't go below it. We came out at $1.59.

"I told Rick, 'If they go below $1.50 they'll be out of business.'" Woodman Industries lowered its price to $1.44.

"When they did that, I knew my father had no interest in staying in business," said Stewart. "His only interest was in ruining both businesses. No way could he come out at $1.44 and make a profit, and he knew it.

"And sure enough, over the next three or four months I heard rumors," continued Stewart. "They weren't shipping because they couldn't make the product, the plastic was no good—too thin. And they were buying re-grind materials, off-grade plastic. Eventually I saw some of it, and it had a greenish tint to all of it. To make the plastic thinner he was pressing it so hard against the rollers that sheets came out with holes in them. You can't sell that."

But almost everything that Woodman Industries did had a negative effect on Manchester, and on Neil and Stewart. Especially Stewart, who reacted to stress with monumental eating binges, consuming junk food the way an alcoholic trapped in a distillery gulps whiskey. Stewart added nearly a hundred pounds in the year after Woodman Industries opened for business. His blood pressure, already high, shot up. His heart labored. Overburdened, his pancreas began to fail.

After Stewart's stroke in January 1982, his medical problems had begun to worry Neil. Since his own background and experience were limited to manufacturing, Neil reckoned that he needed his brother to keep sales humming.

Stewart was in agreement. "At the time of the lawsuit I'd been under my father's reign, so to speak, for so long that I didn't realize that *I* controlled that company," asserted Stewart. "My accounts brought in sixty percent of sales. Many months, even more. I didn't go write up the orders—our salesmen went. But they were *my* accounts. Those buyers would have given their business to me wherever I was."

After the Woodman Industries startup, Neil told Steve Strawn, Rick Wilson, and most of the salesmen not to add to the load Stewart was carrying. According to Wilson, Neil said, "If you bother Stewart at home, I'll kill you."

Later, asking for help in modifying his brother's eating habits, Neil would tell Melody, "If Stewart has a heart attack or dies, I'll make you miserable for the rest of your life."

Gerry not only hired away Manchester's factory force and many of its salesmen. Before leaving, he also copied Manchester's computer records. That gave him access to all his sons' customers and suppliers, and a good sense of the company's financial picture.

Catherine Clemente, hired by Stewart as a receptionist, quickly learned that it was *verboten* even to mention the name of other members of the Woodman clan in front of her bosses. "Neil and I used to talk about thoroughbred horses," said Clemente. "There's a famous horse named Hilary; and I found out by happenstance that Neil's sister had the same name. He got very upset and told me never to mention that name again in the office."

If Gerry had started Woodman Industries with profit in mind, he might have had some chance of success. But if his goal was to knock Manchester out, he was undercapitalized and doomed to fail.

Before that happened, however, he hurt Manchester badly. With computer files on all Manchester customers, Gerry had surrogates call in to his former firm's order desk and pretend to be a customer. "They would place a big order, we would ship it, and the customer would send it back," said Stewart. "I'll bet he did that a hundred times." Not only did Manchester have to pay shipping both ways, but in the process of sorting things out, they lost goodwill with customers. And much of what was ordered was nonstandard sizes, so it couldn't be resold. The best they could do was grind it up for scrap and recycle it.

But Manchester Products had far more cash flow than Woodman Industries. Selling below the cost of manufacture, it was only a matter of time before Gerry folded. On July 1, 1983, Woodman

Industries closed its doors. Union Bank, on the hook for over $2.5 million they had loaned to Gerry, appointed a receiver to dispose of Woodman's assets.

"Union Bank called and said, 'We'd like you to bid on his factory,'" recalled Stewart. "I said, 'I'll go look, but I don't want him to be there.'

"Walking through that factory gave me the most empty feeling I've ever had in my life. I hated him at that point—a guy who robbed me—and here I was going through this factory, bidding ten cents on the dollar for stuff. It was a weird feeling. I didn't buy anything," he added.

Gerry, who had put almost everything he owned into Woodman Industries, was forced to seek the protection of the bankruptcy courts. He lost his house, and with nowhere to go, moved with Vera into the guest room of Wayne's modest Bel Air apartment on Roscomare Road.

When Woodman Industries went under, Neil and Stewart hired back several of their former employees. Richard Nuckles was not among them, but a few salesmen, men who knew their territories intimately and who had been hired by Stewart, were welcomed back into the fold.

The funds required to buy out Gerry had been loaned by Union Bank. Despite the increased amount of cash now available to the brothers, and despite Stewart and Neil's expectation that this money would easily be paid off by converting salaries formerly paid Gerry and Wayne to installments, there never seemed to be as much money around as they could spend. Stewart lavished expensive toys and games on his children, furs and jewelry on his wife.

He had $40,000 worth of video games and old-fashioned pinball machines installed in his Hidden Hills home. The house became the locus of after-school activities for his own children and dozens of neighborhood juveniles.

This was in many ways an idyllic time for Stewart. He was rolling in money and Gerry, it seemed, was at last vanquished. Stewart was free to be lord of his own manor. Life with Melody seemed flawless. "We were the best of friends," he said. "We had a wonderful marriage. And the kind of family I always wanted, the one *I* never had.

"I used to sit *my* kids down and do their homework with them. I never hit them, never spanked them. I never would. I got hit across the face enough by my father," he added.

As yet, while he had created in his home, or at least in his mind, an idealized notion of parenthood, Stewart could never face the realities of his own upbringing. "My complete family was like 'Peyton Place,'" said Stewart. "Neil and I had a very, very good childhood at times. At other times—nobody would believe what went on . . . "

Recalling that he and Neil had been banished to military schools as youngsters, and that their own father was often unavailable, Stewart resolved to do better. "Weekends were always spent with our kids," he said.

Of course, he also visited Las Vegas every few weeks. "Melody usually went shopping. The kids and I went to Circus Circus and played all the games. At the Sahara Hotel, near the casino entrance, are some slot machines. My kids loved playing them. Sometimes I'd give a guy named Billy a couple of hundred dollars when I went in, and he would make sure that no one bothered my kids. He'd give each one a couple of rolls of nickels and they would have a ball for hours." At home, after Ian confessed to losing his allowance playing poker with classmates, Stewart sat him down and explained the fine points of the game. "Not like *my* father," sighed Stewart. "When I played as a kid, he stood behind and screamed at me for throwing away the wrong cards, told me how stupid I was. But with Ian, the neighbors began calling to complain that he had taken all their kids' money," added Stewart, genuinely proud of his son's poker prowess.

Neil, too, was spending money as fast as it came in. "Neil never saved two cents," said Stewart. "One day I went out to buy a car and I guess they ran his TRW credit report by mistake instead of mine. I showed it to him at work the next day and I thought he was going to kill his wife. I think Maxine had spent, that month, something like forty thousand dollars on clothes. For her son's bar mitzvah she spent almost nine thousand dollars on a dress. There was a designer clothing store in Encino where Maxine was such a good customer that, when she was recuperating from a leg operation, they rented a van and clothing racks and took half the store out to her so she could pick out a dress.

"I've never liked the woman," he added. "She's a female version of my father, a very cold, calculating person."

Melody, during this period, sometimes spent as much as $30,000 a month. She didn't spend much on household help—her maid, housekeeper, and gardener were on Manchester's payroll. She didn't spend it on entertainment or dining out—that was all charged to the company. She didn't spend much on car payments or maintenance, because the Rolls, Mercedes, and Bronco were all owned by Manchester, which also picked up the cost of gasoline, oil, tune-ups, and everything else associated with owning a car. Nor did Melody spend any of her monthly $30,000 on insurance, because the company paid the premiums on their life, health, automobile, and homeowner's policies. Even most of the family groceries were charged to the company, as entertainment. Manchester paid their four-figure monthly phone bills as well, and picked up the tab for most of their travel.

Melody spent $10,000 a month on the mortgage payment. The rest went for such household necessities as electricity, gas, water, clothing, furs, and jewelry.

Pressing his sales force, Stewart had increased orders. Output of the factory on Mason climbed to the very limits of multiple-shift capacity. Still, the brothers thought they could do better. But that required more machinery, and more space than the forty-thousand-square-foot building they leased. Gerry had avoided the encumbrance of anything except residential real estate, but Neil and Stewart plunged headlong into it.

Through a friend, they met real estate developer Edward Saunders. Saunders showed them how to get land and a building with no money down: he formed a partnership with his uncle and a cousin. The partnership built a new, sixty-four-thousand-square-foot factory on nearby Prairie Avenue and sold half of the development to Neil and Stewart with no cash up front. Manchester then leased the building for $25,000 a month, which was the same as the mortgage payment. Each year the partnership could take substantial write-offs on depreciation and finance charges, providing the partners with tax savings that exceeded the mortgage charges. Meanwhile, as most California real estate had for decades, the building and land were expected to appreciate. When the building was sold, years in the future, the partners would divide the profits equally.

The size of the building particularly appealed to Neil and Stewart. Not only would they be able to add more machines for their acrylic products, they would have ample room for a new machine that would run the industry's latest material, polycarbonate plastic, a clear, shatterproof, and nearly unbreakable substance that was already much in demand.

The machine they needed for polycarbonates was ordered in the spring of 1983, with delivery timed to coincide with completion of the new building. It cost over $900,000, including installation. Once again Union Bank provided financing.

But just before the Prairie Avenue factory was ready, Gerry deftly poisoned the warm relationships between Manchester and some of its major suppliers of raw materials, dramatically increasing the financial pressure on the company just as his sons were about to embark on the riskiest venture of their business careers.

It made Gerry feel a little better about himself.

CHAPTER Eighteen

Cutthroats, Swindlers, and RICO

DECEMBER 1985

In 1984 and 1985, odd fellows hung around Art's C.B. Shop in Las Vegas. One was Art Taylor himself, a deeply religious and staunchly conservative family man who detested drugs and drug users yet energetically engaged in helping cocaine dealers. Art did a good job, keeping his FBI handlers apprised of everything that went down with the cutthroats and smugglers who had turned his failing business into their headquarters for an expanding list of crimes.

One of Art's frequent visitors was diminutive, baby-faced Mike Dominguez, who worked construction, mostly roofing. Still in his twenties, Dominguez had developed a taste for luxuries far beyond what his irregular paychecks would buy. But Mike didn't mind breaking into houses and stealing valuables to help make ends meet; nor did he flinch from breaking a few legs or even killing someone. If it brought in cash, he didn't mind at all. As his reputation as a burglar and thug-for-hire grew, Dominguez acquired a nickname: he was known on the street and in prison as Baby A.

Dominguez had grown up with Ricky Grey, son of the owner of Accuracy Gun Distributors. Mike often hung around Accuracy, just at the time when Steve Homick was trying to make a go of his mail-order gun business, based at Accuracy. Kindred spirits, Steve and Mike found much to admire in each other.

Taylor met Dominguez in late 1983, when Mike was hired to help tear down and rebuild a nearby restaurant. Homick sent Baby A over to introduce himself—and deliver a message. Now and then, on Steve's say-so, Dominguez borrowed Taylor's pickup truck to make a delivery or run an errand for Steve.

Anthony "Sonny" Majoy was in and out of Art's on trips from Los Angeles, where he sold video products. Sonny had been arrested in various parts of the country for sodomy, contributing to the delinquency of a minor, aggravated assault, robbery, grand theft auto, and unemployment fraud. Now he was trying to get a franchise to distribute blank videotapes from BASF, the German manufacturer. His friend Steve Homick told Sonny that Art Taylor had contacts with BASF and could help set up a deal. Indeed, Taylor knew someone who knew a few people at BASF, but no deal ever came together.

Steve had introduced Sonny to Art in 1984, when he set up a telephone conference call linking Majoy in Los Angeles with Taylor in Las Vegas. Soon Majoy and Steve were passing cryptic messages back and forth, using Taylor as a conduit.

Taylor also got to meet Robert "Jesse" Homick, whose acquaintance he had previously made by telephone because Jesse often called with messages for Steve. Eventually, when Jesse flew in from Los Angeles, he came by the shop.

William "Moke" Homick, four years younger than his brother Steve, was in and out of Art's almost daily, often carrying cocaine or various illicit pills, dropping off packages or picking them up.

From the first months of 1985, Stewart Siegel, sometimes called "Dr. Gold" by Homick but who much preferred to be known as "the Professor," was yet another periodic visitor to Art's, often borrowing Art's phone or his typewriter. He had a big business deal cooking in San Diego County, California, and while it simmered he supported himself by selling forged New Jersey drivers' licenses and Social Security cards. The Professor had excellent contacts in government, official and otherwise, and whenever he used Art's typewriter, he brought along stacks of blank forms, the genuine articles, pilfered from the Social Security Administration and from the New Jersey Motor Vehicle Department.

Siegel would be surprised to learn later that Taylor was an FBI informant. Taylor was *astonished* to learn, at about the same time, that the Professor also regularly sang for the FBI.

Siegel, a balding, bespectacled man of forty-seven with an elfin face, was warm and instantly likeable. In a career spanning almost thirty years, the Professor had become a superbly accomplished con man playing suckers in gambling scams. Had he ever committed his résumé to paper, it would have read like an international Baedeker of casinos, licit and otherwise.

Siegel's relationship with the FBI was a sideline: each time the Professor got nailed, he bargained what he knew about various underworld figures for a lighter sentence. The G-men had come to respect the quality and veracity of Siegel's information. They treasured him as a source, and more than once had allowed him to skate on some slimy scheme simply because they knew that sooner or later, when he ran afoul of local law enforcement, he would be back to barter intelligence they could get from no one else. In addition, many in law enforcement came to genuinely like and admire Siegel, whom they recognized as their professional equal.

Steve Homick brought four Maxxon walkie-talkies into Art's that he'd borrowed from "Professor" Siegel to use in a Los Angeles "surveillance" job, and asked Taylor to check them over.

A few weeks later, on September 24, Steve called Taylor from Los Angeles to ask if he knew where to buy a battery for one of the Professor's walkie-talkies. Taylor put him on hold, consulted a national directory of retailers, then dialed Talley Electronics, a distributor in Santa Fe Springs, California. A woman named Mary at Talley gave Taylor the address for Henry Radio in West Los Angeles, and Taylor relayed this information to Steve.

Steve called Taylor again later that night and said that the radios didn't work well enough to use. When he returned to Las Vegas on September 26, he dropped off the walkie-talkies and a receipt for the battery he'd purchased from Henry Radio. Steve told Art to give the receipt to the Professor, and to collect money to reimburse Steve for the battery.

Siegel, who considered Steve a dangerous fellow to anger, especially about money, decided to pay Homick for the battery. He kept the receipt; it was, he knew, exactly the kind of evidence that law enforcement always appreciates.

In late 1985, San Diego Sheriff's police pounced on the Barona Reservation bingo operation Stewart Siegel was supervising for the Chicago-based Mafia crime family run by Sam Carlisi. Several people were arrested on charges of fraud and grand larceny, Siegel among them.

Always cooperative, Siegel began crooning his usual Mafia tunes. This time, however, he played a few bars of a new song. He told FBI agents that in late September he had loaned walkie-talkies to a Las Vegas thug named Steve Homick, and when he got them back a few days later, Homick had mentioned, in his usual swaggering style, that he had "taken a couple of Jews out for Yom Kippur."

Siegel had seen the newspaper stories. He knew that Vera and Gerald Woodman had been gunned down on the night of the Day of Atonement, and he had filed that away in his prodigious memory.

Later, when he had the opportunity to talk to Las Vegas Metro detectives who were trying to solve a brutal triple murder, Siegel told detectives that Steve Homick had boasted of taking a million in gems from a Paradise Valley residence, where he'd killed three people. Siegel also told the Metro cops that Homick kept a diary, and wrote in it constantly.

Steve Homick had kept Baby A very busy after Dominguez torched Larry Ettinger's Maui boardinghouse. In May, he'd taken Mike along when he paid a house call on a neighbor. Raymond Godfrey was seventy-one and had a heart condition. When Steve knocked on his door, he let him right in, because he knew Steve as his daughter's friend and neighbor.

Steve knew Godfrey as a man who liked to gamble. His daughter had once casually mentioned to one of Steve's other neighbors that her father often kept as much as $50,000 at home, in cash. One neighbor had clucked over this strange habit as he remarked on it to Steve.

Now Steve wanted that money.

"I want to know where the $50,000 is," said Homick.

"I don't have any money," replied Godfrey.

Baby A held Godfrey while Steve hit him. The old man was tough, he didn't scream or yell, and he wouldn't tell the intruders where he kept his money.

Dominguez got some pliers and crushed Godfrey's fingernails.

The old man still refused to talk.

Steve had Dominguez fill the bathtub. Then they forced Godfrey's head under water. The first time they brought him up, Godfrey gasped out a request for his heart medicine.

"Fuck no," said Steve, forcing him back down again. To the end, Godfrey never screamed or yelled. He just looked up at his torturers, his eyes filled with scorn and contempt.

Baby A would remember those eyes looking up at him for a long time.

Godfrey died of a heart attack. When police found his body, his sternum was broken, as were several ribs and his nose and jaw—all, the coroner concluded, from pressure exerted by those holding his head underwater while he struggled.

By the summer of 1985, Larry Ettinger, who would eventually be tried but acquitted of charges that he had hired an arsonist to burn his property, was in the process of divorcing Cheryl McDowell. He owed McDowell $150,000 as part of their property settlement.

After leaving Ettinger, McDowell moved in with boyfriend Craig Maraldo, who owned a house at 3905 Calle Tereon, near Las Vegas. Ettinger and Maraldo had quarreled publicly at the Riviera, where the latter was employed. The confrontation had taken a physical turn, and Maraldo, younger and bigger, had easily knocked Ettinger down.

Ettinger, in a rage, then threatened Maraldo, pointing his forefinger at him, dropping his upraised thumb, miming a handgun. "You're *dead*," said Ettinger.

Ettinger's friend Steve Homick, right there at his side, helped Larry up from the hotel's carpeted floor. Steve gave Maraldo's back a look that might have frozen magma.

About midnight on July 4, 1985, Maraldo returned to his home, accompanied by McDowell. After entering an outer courtyard and locking the gate behind them, they strolled toward the front door.

Mike Dominguez, waiting inside the house, fired through an open window with a silenced .22-caliber handgun. Maraldo was hit in the chest.

Dominguez then turned the gun on McDowell, hitting her left arm. He fired again at Maraldo, and put three more bullets in his chest.

Maraldo ran back through the courtyard to help McDowell escape over a fence. As he went up and over behind her, Dominguez emerged from the house to fire yet again, the bullet penetrating the skull behind Maraldo's right ear.

Maraldo refused to die.

Bleeding from his wounds, he went from house to house, banging on doors until someone let him in and called 911.

Dominguez ran away.

When Maraldo was released from the hospital he was too frightened ever to reenter his house, so he sold it.

Homick was furious with Dominguez. He couldn't understand how he could shoot a man five times and let him live to give police a good description of his assailant.

Even worse, Dominguez's primary mission was to kill Cheryl McDowell, and he had failed at that as well.

Homick decided that the next time he wouldn't trust a .22 to kill. He would use a .38, even though it made more noise. And he wouldn't send a kid like Baby A to do a man's job.

The next time, as it happened, was in an underground parking garage in Brentwood, California, on September 25, 1985. Dominguez was demoted to lookout while Steve and Sonny Majoy did the shooting. Steve enjoyed a big payday, but was obliged to split the take with his brothers and to pay Majoy and Dominguez. There were also expenses; there wasn't much left for Steve from the $50,000-plus he got for murdering Gerry and Vera Woodman.

So Steve Homick went looking for another big score. He was friends with Tim Cadt, owner of Tower of Jewels, a small chain of jewelry stores, and sometimes did security consulting for him. One day, while Steve was hanging around one of the stores shooting the breeze with Cadt, a pretty, middle-aged woman named Barbara Tipton brought in an overnight case full of jewelry for cleaning. Feigning mild interest, Homick asked Cadt what the jewelry might be worth, and was gratified to hear a seven-figure estimate.

Thus Steve discovered Bobbie Jean Tipton, socialite and heir to a Texas oil fortune. Homick duped Cadt into letting him look up the Tiptons' exclusive Paradise Valley address in the store's computer.

A few weeks later, on December 10, 1985, Steve went to Tipton's home on Oquendo. When the maid, Marie Bullock, opened the door, he put a .38-caliber revolver in her face. Homick forced Bullock to take him to Tipton, and Tipton to open a floor safe where her jewelry was kept.

When the safe was open, Homick shot each of the women in the head three times, killing both instantly.

Homick reloaded his pistol, then began removing everything of value from the safe.

The doorbell rang.

A wave of fear jolted Steve Homick. There could be no witnesses. If he *didn't* answer the doorbell, whoever was at the door might take note of his car, parked on the street.

On the stoop was United Parcel Service deliveryman James Myers. Homick opened the door, grabbed Myers by the shirt, and pulled him inside. He herded him back to the bedroom, then shot Myers three times in the head. He took the loot and left.

About six that evening, Homick dialed the Tipton home. Detective Tom Dillard, in charge of the crime scene, answered the call. Homick hung up. Now he knew that the bodies had been discovered. But Homick didn't know that his call was noted by the FBI PEN register monitoring his outgoing calls.

In the sixties Las Vegas began growing like crazy from a sleepy gambling mecca of perhaps twenty-five thousand year-round residents to its present population of nearly a million. Clark County was served by two police agencies, the city police and the county sheriff. In 1973, the two forces merged to become the Las Vegas Metropolitan Police Department, or Metro, as it is popularly called.

Tom Dillard, whose father owned a small business, grew up in Las Vegas. By his early teens he was quite certain that he wanted to be a policeman. And not just an ordinary policeman: a homicide detective. "That's why I never got involved in the promotional process," he said, referring to the odd fact that homicide assignments, in most police departments, are almost exclusively the domain of those who have no ambition to rise through the ranks. These cops prefer, instead, to catch killers. "It took me ten years to get here," said Dillard.

To Dillard the ultimate job was in homicide. "It is difficult to get in," he said. "You have to be lucky or know someone. They try to say that there's a selection process that's fair and equitable, but really, it's whoever they really like the best and happens to be in the right place at the right time."

In 1979, Dillard, a tall, bulky man with blunt features, was in the right place at the right time.

Bob Leonard grew up in Barstow, California, and still speaks with a trace of the Okie twang of rural Californians. He came to Las Vegas in 1967, looking for a job.

"I started working as a busboy and a waiter, and I hated the job so much and I hated the hotels so much I decided I had to do something else," he recalled.

"I applied for both the fire and police departments. The police called first."

Leonard worked patrol until 1974, when he went to the detective bureau. He worked in burglary, then robbery, and finally was assigned to homicide.

"Bob and I got to be partners because the lieutenant we had wanted to get rid of us," said Dillard. "He figured that if he put us together we'd fuck up somewhere and then he could fire both of us at the same time. But we fooled him."

A few days after this unplanned pairing, Leonard and Dillard took the call on the Tipton murders.

Jack Holder and Rich Crotsley flew into Las Vegas on December 13. Waiting at the airport for them were Special Agents Jerry Daugherty and Jim Livingston.

While they waited, Livingston, who had been one of the agents assigned to the Homick brothers narcotics investigation, picked up a copy of the *Sun* and was soon reading the first sketchy details of the Tipton murders. Livingston showed the paper to Daugherty. "This sounds like something that fucking Steve Homick would do," he said. Daugherty nodded his head in agreement.

"As we're pulling into the parking lot with Jerry Daugherty," said Jack Holder, "he's telling us about these murders. Then we come across another agent and he says, 'You know, I checked the PEN register tapes, just on the off chance, and guess what? Steve Homick called the Tiptons' house the day of the murders.'"

It was a fluke, but both police and FBI investigators took it as an omen of good luck.

A careful review of the PEN tapes showed that Steve Homick had also called the Tipton home days earlier, probably to establish when Mrs. Tipton was likely to be home.

The next day, Livingston and Daugherty met with Holder and Crotsley from LAPD and with Tom Dillard of Las Vegas Metro; Dillard's partner, Leonard, was out of town. All three agencies had solid information linking the Homick brothers to a long list of illegal matters; from this initial conference came a recommendation to create an interagency task force. Within a few weeks, supervisors in all three agencies agreed to support the arrangement, with half the funding to come from the FBI.

Murder and robbery are state crimes, but when murder-for-hire is arranged across state lines, it becomes a Federal offense. In addition, the Homicks and their associates had demonstrated a pattern of systematic illegal acts that, under the broad reach of another Federal statute, constituted "racketeering." Under the powers granted by a then somewhat obscure law, the Homicks and all their associates would now be investigated as a Racketeer Influenced Corrupt Organization (RICO).

"RICO gave the Feds jurisdiction," explained Tom Dillard. "Otherwise they couldn't have gotten involved."

With Federal jurisdiction came a commitment of major manpower—dozens of FBI agents and Metro police were assigned to the case. Along with the manpower came access to sophisticated, very expensive wiretapping equipment then unavailable to the cash-strapped Las Vegas Metro Police.

"Jerry Daugherty and Jim Livingston and I compared notes," recalled Dillard. "We discovered we both had an individual close to Homick who was also an FBI source: Stewart Siegel."

After some maneuvering, wiretaps were established on all three phones in Steve Homick's Susan Street home and on the one line in William Homick's Syracuse Drive residence on January 21, 1986. The order was signed by Clark County District Judge Donald Mosely.

Even before the order was signed, the task force geared up for what would become the biggest joint-jurisdiction effort in Nevada history. So many law enforcement officers were involved that no Federal, state, or local office space was large enough to hold it. The FBI rented offices in a downtown Las Vegas high rise, bought desks, chairs, sofas, a refrigerator—everything needed to support an around-the-clock operation.

Unknown to both police and FBI, the building they had rented space in was also home to several "boiler rooms," where banks of high-pressure phone salesmen hawk dubious products or offer fraudulent investment opportunities to the gullible, then move on before authorities can catch up to complaints.

"The first day we went to the building we found a sign in the elevator," recalled Daugherty, who with Livingston, Dillard, and Leonard supervised the wiretap effort. "It was a sheet of cardboard, and somebody had written on it in Crayola, 'FBI surveillance, room such and such.'

"There was a boiler-room operation in there. Maybe they spotted somebody carrying in equipment. They pulled out that day and put a sign up to warn the others. Nobody believed it, evidently, because none of the others left, and later we made some arrests," chuckled Daugherty.

Steve Homick all but lived on the telephone, habitually speaking in coded riddles while cautioning everyone he spoke to that his lines were probably tapped. But judging by what he said, Homick, like the boiler-room gangs, was unwilling to believe that the police were *really* just about to pounce.

CHAPTER *Nineteen*

Pledges

The turning point for the Woodmans came in the autumn of 1983. Gerry, living off the charity of his children, had little to do except annoy and punish his elder sons, taking his pound of flesh in bite-sized morsels.

He relished every scrap.

Before selling his Bel Air mansion to satisfy creditors, Gerry had a plumber fix a stopped-up toilet. Gerry had done business with this particular workman for years, so there was no objection when he told the man to send his bill, something over $300, to Manchester.

Stewart was not amused.

Neil was livid. He sat down to write a sarcastic, spiteful letter to his parents, which detailed many of the brothers' grievances, real and imagined, with their parents. He mailed the letter to them and enclosed the plumber's bill.

"Neil wrote about how our parents could no longer take their whole neighborhood to Europe and have us pay for it. 'Take this letter and flush it down your own toilet'—he said things like that," recalled Stewart.

Their aunt remembers the letter's impact. "I think it was the only time in my life that I saw my sister break down," said Muriel. "She was absolutely demoralized by this letter."

Muriel may be forgiven for perhaps overdramatizing Vera's reaction. And it is remotely possible that her sister never confided her years of shame and angst at Gerry's gambling, his nonstop infidelities, or her reaction to the shattering discovery that her husband had fathered an out-of-wedlock child with another woman. Muriel, of course, sees her late sister through the fond lens of affection, while her nephews are reflected in the dark, pitted mirror of hatred.

Nevertheless, it was a harsh letter, and it inspired Gerry to further acts of harassment. His surrogates continued to call in phony orders, ostensibly from Manchester's better customers. Gerry used an old Texaco credit card to charge a forty-dollar auto repair bill to Manchester. While it would have been cheaper and less trouble to pay, Stewart refused. Texaco canceled the company's charge account and brought suit. Manchester's attorneys had to go to court to defend the company's interests.

Then Gerry rented a car for a few days and had that billed to Manchester. Once again, his sons refused to pay, and the rental agency sued the company. More lawyers, more fees.

Gerry knew he was annoying his sons, but he also knew this was trivial stuff, details to be handled by lawyers.

Poisoning the well of goodwill between Manchester and the giant companies that sold them raw materials was infinitely more satisfying.

Before extending terms to Woodman Industries, Dow Chemical of Midland, Michigan, had asked for personal assurances. Gerry, who made himself Woodman Industries' vice president and owned little of value in his own name, got Wayne, who served as president and treasurer of the company, to make personal guarantees and post a surety bond. When Neil and Stewart learned that their father had gone into business against them, they wrote letters to all their customers and suppliers. The brothers made it clear that Gerry was on his own, no longer connected with Manchester. In the harshest of terms, the letters cast aspersions on their father's character and his motivations in starting the new business. One result of the letters was that some companies put Woodman Industries on their least-risky payment cycle.

When his cash dried up, Gerry was unable to pay Dow. He stalled with a chatty missive while concealing his few remaining assets. He sold his house to satisfy loans from his daughter, Maxine, and sister-in-law, Muriel. The buyer did not pay all cash; Vera also took back a $55,000 note, secured by the property, and collected monthly payments.

So, thanks to Gerry's lifelong habit of insulating himself from lawsuits by putting things in Vera's name, including Woodman Industries, it was *her* property that Dow succeeded in attaching. The chemical giant won a court order to seize her last major asset, the $55,000 note.

That left the elder Woodmans with practically nothing of value except their furniture and a car.

But the attachment did not come close to satisfying the entire debt. Dow, after trying in vain to collect from Manchester, went to court for yet another injunction to keep the senior Woodmans and Wayne from concealing their assets.

Wayne, who lost his house in the Woodman Industries bankruptcy, moved into a small, rented condominium, shared with his parents, and laid low. Dow hired Sentry Investigators to find the Woodmans, but after more than a month, the private eyes came up empty.

Dow turned to Manchester and tried to get Neil and Stewart to pay their father's debt. The brothers refused, citing the fact that Woodman Industries was an entirely separate entity—in fact, a competitor—but Dow's credit and collection *apparatchiks* understandably acted as though the brothers were colluding with their father to defraud them. Dow put Manchester, for many years a valued customer, on cash-only terms while it went after Gerry, Wayne, and Vera.

"My father stuck Dow Corning for six hundred thousand dollars," said Stewart. "He stuck Continental Polymer in Compton for a quarter of a million dollars."

Like Dow Corning, Continental Polymer had taken at face value Gerry's assurances of links with Manchester. When Woodman

Industries went belly-up, Continental management also assumed that Gerry might somehow have colluded with his sons. They let Neil and Stewart know that they were not amused by the Woodmans' shenanigans. Relationships with salesmen and credit managers, solid for years, deteriorated. Then John Altman, who ran Continental, pulled the plug.

This pattern was repeated with other suppliers. "They would call my father," said Stewart. "He'd tell them, 'I used to own Manchester, but I gave it to my sons. So they're responsible because we were just a division of their company.' "

Many suppliers, including trucking companies, cut Manchester off, forcing them to go through third parties or to find other, often more costly, sources. The brothers cursed Gerry at every new turn of the screw.

"We went through a lot of aggravation," said Stewart. "But Neil and I became very, very close."

The brothers blew off steam by gambling, complaining at every opportunity to their friends and employees about the unfairness of it all. "I wish my father would just drop off the face of the earth. Drop dead and leave us alone," said Stewart. Neil was even more explicit in his hatred.

The Homicks, Robert and Steve, were well aware of the Woodmans' problems. "Robert would always say, 'You know, you're crazy to put up with this,' " said Stewart.

And Robert said, "It's driving you nuts. You could just take care of it, so you wouldn't have to worry about it. Let Steve handle it for you."

A few weeks before Manchester moved into the Prairie facility, at a time when suppliers were treating the company like a pariah, Stewart complained to houseguest Joey Gambino about Gerry's latest aggravations.

Gambino offered the same advice that "Jesse" Homick had: "Why don't you let Steve take care of this for you?" he said. "Otherwise, your father's going to drive you into your grave."

Stewart thought about it. He talked to his brother Neil.

They decided that maybe it was time to give Steve Homick a shot. Maybe it was way past time.

"We'll talk to Steve when he comes in," said Neil.

Homick visited Manchester just after the company occupied its Prairie Avenue factory site. "Steve and Neil and I went into the new conference room and Steve brought up the problem that had to do with my father," explained Stewart. "He said, 'I know you got problems with your mother and father. Joey tells me how much it's aggravating you. Let me take care of it. You won't have that problem anymore.'"

To make sure that the brothers knew what was being offered, Steve added, "Stewart, just to make sure he's never in your life again, we'll take care of it for you."

"He didn't have to go any further," said Stewart. "I knew what he was talking about. But Steve always talked about crazy things. I remember him talking about some car that blew up in Las Vegas and the guy lived through it, and Steve said, 'Well, I put those things in perfectly.' You took what he said with a grain of salt."

Explaining that he had a knee problem, Steve said he made frequent visits to his doctor in Hollywood. "Next time I'm in town to see my doctor, I'll come over and we can talk about it some more," said Steve.

When Steve returned, about ten days later, he told the brothers what a hit would cost: about $50,000. To Neil and Stewart it seemed like a fair price. They nodded assent, not quite trusting their voices.

Steve asked Neil and Stewart about their parents' habits, where they lived, what they did, what kind of cars they drove. "My father was living with Wayne on Roscomare Road in Bel Air," said Stewart. "I got the address and gave it to Steve. That was when I realized that Steve was really serious."

Stewart and Neil told Steve about Gerry's idiosyncrasies, how he always drove like a maniac, like it was speed-trial time at the Brickyard and he was trying to qualify, that he sometimes retaliated against motorists who cut him off in traffic by cutting *them* off, even sometimes leaping from his car to break their windshields. At times he had dragged people out of their cars and punched them.

And they told Steve about Gerry's fondness for walking his dog, that one might almost set a watch by their dad's evening strolls.

"He always goes at night, by himself," said Stewart. "Usually he takes a half hour, forty minutes, he makes it that kind of walk even if he's got to walk around the block several times. He's done that since I was a kid."

Stewart paused, remembering a boyhood night when his father had waken him to take Rusty, his cocker spaniel, for a walk.

"Rusty was sleeping with me on August 19, just before my ninth birthday," said Stewart. "My father comes in about eleven-thirty and says, 'I'll take him for a walk.' I said, 'Leave him with me, he's fine.' "

But Gerry always had his way.

"About a half hour later Dad comes upstairs and says Rusty's been run over, he's dead," said Stewart. "I covered him with a sheet and spent the whole night with him until they came and picked him up."

But, added Stewart, Gerry never took Vera with him on his nocturnal prowls. In fact, said Neil, their mother was having vision problems and rarely drove at night. And from all they recalled about her, she rarely went out with Gerry.

"Only on special occasions," said Stewart. "Birthdays, anniversaries, family gatherings."

It would be quite some time before Steve Homick came through on his pledge to rid Neil and Stewart of their parent problem. In the meantime, said Stewart, "I tried to block the end of this out of my mind. But I knew what was going on, what was happening, that he was going to kill both of my parents."

Just after that second conversation with Steve Homick, a new machine was installed at Manchester, an enormous extruder that gave Manchester the capability to make virtually unbreakable panels from a new material. As soon as the machine was installed, however, the brothers found themselves struggling with urgent, overwhelming problems.

So for months Stewart didn't think much about the contract he and Neil had given Steve to murder their parents. He knew what Steve had promised to do, and what he and Neil had pledged in return, but there was an unreal quality about the whole affair, as there was to many of the things Steve said.

But the thought was there, buried in his consciousness, a tiny seedling—hardly more than a sprouted acorn—among a forest of pressing concerns. Now and then Gerry would do something to further annoy Stewart, and it would flash through his mind that soon all that would end. And it was this notion that gave Stewart a sense of freedom and power, a feeling that he and Neil could do anything they pleased.

Anything at all.

CHAPTER Twenty

Conversations

JANUARY 1986

Holder and Crotsley spent a week in Las Vegas, scoping out Steve Homick and his ragtag "gang" of part-time thugs, cokeheads, excitement junkies, and assorted hangers-on. The detectives familiarized themselves with the FBI's file on Homick. It was filled with observations from confidential informants.

By a stroke of luck, Steve was then spending little time in Las Vegas. Instead, he was traveling, mostly on the East Coast, trying to raise money to save his friend Art Toll's bankrupt airline, American International.

So Steve constantly called "Moke," his brother, "Dee," his wife, and his confederates, including Mike "Baby A" Dominguez, Ronald "McDonald" Bryl, and Charles "C.D." Dietz. With taps in place on Steve's and William Homick's home phones, the agents and officers logged hundreds of conversations.

Jack Holder had previously worked in the field with the FBI, and in general, except for agents who tracked down bank robbers, he had a low opinion of Federal law enforcement. It was his experience that the G-men collected information in enormous quantities, much of it quite valuable to crime-solving—and sat on it, sharing it with no one, helping lawmen like Holder not at all.

But this was not like any Federal/local task force Holder had ever experienced. The initial spirit of cautious cooperation quickly evolved to mutual respect, then admiration. Holder and Crotsley became good friends with Dillard and Leonard of Las Vegas Metro and with several FBI agents, especially Jerry Daugherty.

As in most wiretap operations, those listening to the tapes were usually subjected to hours of boredom between calls, and even more boredom from the calls themselves.

But when it came to the Homicks, there were also conversations that left police and FBI agents weak with laughter.

"William—Moke—was always a philosopher," said Daugherty. "He'd call this guy back east and talk in code. He'd say, 'Well, we can talk about cold weather, but I can't stand hot weather. You can't go past naked, but you can bundle up.' I'd bet no one he talked to really knew what he meant—but all of us listening spent a lot of time trying to read meaning into it.

"He'd say things like, 'If you were standing on a ship and you're looking east and a submarine shoots a torpedo at you from the west, that's damage control.' Then he wouldn't say any more.

"Then he'd say, 'What have you got, a potato in your ear?'"

The lawmen just looked at each other and shook their heads.

"We sat and listened," said Daugherty. "He could list fifteen types of doctors. He'd say, 'He's not in pediatrics, he's not in oncology, he's not in podiatry . . .' and he'd go through things like this and the guy on the other end wouldn't know what the hell he was talking about, I'm sure.

"Or he'd call up Domino's, a pizza place, and say, 'How many slices does your large have?' And the guy would say, 'Normally, eight.' Moke would say, 'Thank you,' and hang up.

"He'd sit there and do call after call like that, one pizza parlor after another, and our guys listening would be laughing so hard they had tears running down their faces," said Daugherty, giggling at the memory.

Daugherty could never decide whether Moke had a strange sense of humor or if he knew his phone was tapped and was performing for their benefit, forcing them to tape hours of nonsense, make hundreds of log entries, keeping the wiretappers busy with minutiae that had no value to the case. Or maybe, Daugherty thought, maybe Moke was just a fruitcake.

But the wiretaps also yielded a gold mine of information, much of it incriminating.

One of the most important facts learned this way was that all three Homicks favored pay phones for conversations relating to planning and executing criminal acts. They habitually called each other from one public telephone to another, a practice they referred to as calling "box-to-box." Obviously, this practice was designed to defeat wiretapping—but instead of putting coins in the pay phones, they usually used Steve's telephone credit card, or billed calls to a third-party number, thereby creating a record of the call.

This discovery opened an entirely new dimension to the investigation run by Holder and Crotsley in Los Angeles.

"Like I've always said, I'd rather be lucky than good," said Holder. "And if not for luck, we wouldn't have known about the pay phones and all that."

Eventually the detectives had records of about forty-one thousand telephone calls, including those made from the homes of the Homicks, the Woodmans, and pay phones near these residences, and calls made or charged to Manchester. They now needed to see if they could connect the Homicks with the Woodmans on and before the date of the murders and other times when one of the Homicks was known to be near the scene of the crime. If so, it might be circumstantial evidence of a connection between those who had a strong motive to have Gerry and Vera killed, and those whom other evidence implicated in the actual shootings.

Back in the field, Holder and Crotsley put Robert "Jesse" Homick under twenty-four-hour surveillance. His police watchers carried video and still cameras, and were amazed to catch Jesse working his trade.

Undercover officers photographed Jesse using banks of pay phones along Santa Monica Boulevard near his apartment. These were the same lines whose numbers appeared dozens of times in subpoenaed telephone records.

The FBI had found the names of Steve Homick and Mike Dominguez on P.S.A. passenger manifests between Las Vegas and Los Angeles on the days before and after the Woodman murders. But one may use any name when boarding an airliner; Holder and

Crotsley needed witnesses to identify these two men as actual passengers on the flights where their names had been listed.

"We went to P.S.A. and got a manifest, which showed assigned
seats. Then we ran down the people who sat right near Steve," said
Holder. "We found the stewardess who waited on him. Lo and
behold, some of the passengers remembered Steve and Mike. One
was a girl from Bakersfield, a beautician, who remembered Steve
because of his haircut. Some women who lived in Los Angeles and
were still partying on the return from Vegas remembered Mike
because he was a good-looking kid."

Holder and Crotsley now wanted to make arrests, get the bad
guys off the street before they killed someone else.

"We've got airline tickets and eyewitness I.D.'s. We've got the
traffic accident," recalled Holder. "We've got an I.D. by witnesses
who saw Robert in front of Brentwood Place in June, and another
I.D. on him at that restaurant on Moraga Drive. We've got Art
Taylor, an informant in Vegas, who told the FBI that Steve was
going to Los Angeles to do something for some brothers. We had a
lot of circumstantial evidence, but we didn't have anything really
solid yet. We didn't have a murder weapon, no physical evidence at
all."

Nevertheless, with their boss's blessing, Holder and Crotsley
went to the Los Angeles County District Attorney, seeking arrest
warrants. "We like to say, 'File it on the come, see what happens
afterwards,'" said Holder. "Let's shake some people up, do some
search warrants. But we can't do searches until we serve the arrest
warrants."

The detectives brought their request to a deputy D.A. named
Diane Vizanti. "She said, 'You don't have enough to file yet,'" said
Holder. "So then we went back to Vegas and talked to Stewart
Siegel. He needed help."

At that point, Siegel had been talking to the FBI, trying to get
them to square his beef with the California authorities for the
bingo scam on the Barona Indian Reservation. But the San Diego
County Sheriff was not inclined to let Siegel off the hook to help a
Federal investigation in Nevada. Although Siegel's information
corroborated what Art Taylor had previously given the FBI, that is,
that Homick had borrowed radios from Siegel, it didn't help the

Professor. San Diego authorities had Siegel dead to rights on fraud and gaming violations, and they were ready to nail him.

So when Holder and Crotsley went to see the Professor, Siegel saw another way out: maybe San Diego would give more consideration to its neighbors in Los Angeles.

Suddenly, Siegel's fabled memory improved dramatically.

"The Professor tells us that in 1984 he was trying to put a deal together to buy a casino in Las Vegas. Steve Homick brought Stewart Woodman and another guy to Las Vegas to meet with Siegel; the four of them had a sitdown. Later, the Professor wanted to get poker into the Barona Ranch bingo parlor, and he brought Stewart down as a money man on that. So it gets better and better: the Professor can put Stewart Woodman and Steve Homick together, prove they knew each other," says Holder. "Also, Siegel tells us that in September, just before Gerry and Vera were hit, Homick asked what Jews do on Yom Kippur. Siegel told him about going to temple and fasting all day and then having a big meal afterward.

"So we call Vizanti again and say, 'This is what we've got,'" explained Holder. "We're trying to convince her that she ought to file charges on Stewart and Neil." Under California law, if the D.A. files charges against an individual, one of two kinds of warrants is issued: for arraignment or for arrest. The D.A. has forty-eight hours after an arrest to file charges in Municipal Court so the individual can be arraigned. If a judge then finds sufficient cause exists to justify the arrest, a preliminary hearing is scheduled. If the court finds evidence presented at this hearing sufficiently compelling, a jury trial is scheduled.

"Vizanti was a little bit hesitant because she wanted to have Siegel's information videotaped," said Holder. "At that point he says he won't do that. We contend that a videotape makes no difference because it's not admissible as evidence; if the Professor said, 'I'm not testifying,' we're up shit creek, and we sure can't use his videotape."

Vizanti adamantly refused to file without a videotaped deposition. "So now we go back and forth to San Diego with Siegel to talk to the California Attorney General's Office to try to help him with his bingo-fraud case," sighed Holder.

Finally the Professor made a deal, which included an agreement to plead guilty on fraud charges and to serve hard time in a Federal prison. "Maybe he deserved to be there," said Holder. "But if you ever got to know Stewart Siegel, for a crook he was a nice guy.

"It went right up to the day before we got search warrants," added Holder. "He finally agreed to the videotape the night before the warrants were signed at Parker Center."

While Holder and Crotsley were painstakingly building their case in Southern California, the FBI/Las Vegas Metro investigation was expanding, adding wiretaps to the homes of Homick pals Ronald "McDonald" Bryl and Charlie Dietz. Soon they were playing a bizarre game of cat-and-mouse with Steve Homick and his criminal associates.

Steve Homick continued to roam the country through the early months of 1986, tracked by the FBI through his continuous phone calls to his home and to associates in Las Vegas. He had a lot on his mind, and yet sometimes his family just didn't seem to care about his troubles.

"Homick called in from somewhere and spoke to one of his daughters, then about seventeen," said Daugherty. "And she'd whine, 'I *hate* Mommy, she won't let me get a car, you know how much I want a car, she won't do *anything* for me.'

"Homick said, 'I want you to listen to this. I'm about to be arrested, and it ain't for the Tipton thing, either,' " said Daugherty. "And the kid would say, 'Yeah, but Mommy treats me so bad.' It just went right over her head."

On the phone to family and friends, Steve often said things like, "I know this is wired, I know they're listening to me." A minute later he would make another damning statement.

"Probably the best information we got was from conversations between William, who has a degree in psychology, and Robert in Los Angeles, who graduated from UCLA and has a law degree," said Daugherty. "One would play prosecutor and the other defense attorney, and they'd argue out these cases, the Tiptons, the Woodmans, and we would get it all on the tape."

The circle of the law was closing in on Steve Homick and his employers. By March 1986, Los Angeles County Deputy D.A. Diane

Vizanti had agreed to file murder charges on the Woodman brothers, Sonny Majoy, Mike Dominguez, and the Homick brothers.

The Woodmans, Neil and Stewart, had collected a $500,000 insurance settlement the previous December.

"When they get their money, they think they're home free," said Holder. "They think, 'The cops haven't been around.' They don't know that we are following Steve, Robert, and William, that we've got hundreds of telephone conversations on tape, that the Professor has told us lots about Homick."

A target date was assigned for the arrests, which would require twenty-one separate assault teams to hit as many different locations within moments of each other. In Vegas alone, more than a hundred police, including a dozen LAPD detectives and agents of the FBI, Drug Enforcement Agency (DEA), and the Bureau of Alcohol Tobacco and Firearms (BATF), rehearsed their roles. In Los Angeles, SWAT teams positioned themselves for the arrests, scheduled for seven in the morning.

Mike Dominguez was also scheduled for arrest. But on the ninth of March, Baby A called a friend who kept and sold guns. As detectives listened, Dominguez said, "I need a shotgun, but I can't bring it back. And I've gotta have it today."

"Okay," said the dealer. "I'll leave it outside on the back porch."

It looked like Dominguez was getting ready for another murder. The arrests were put on hold while lawmen struggled with a new dilemma: they needed to get Baby A off the street—but his arrest might cause the others to flee.

"We waited two days," said Daugherty, "and while we were waiting we talked to his parole officer."

With a little shove from the FBI and Las Vegas Metro, officials decided that Dominguez had violated parole by changing his address without notifying proper authorities. He was taken into custody after buying a box of shotgun shells.

Steve Homick considered himself a shrewd judge of character. He had often expressed his confidence that Dominguez would never implicate him.

Mike, allowed phone calls while in custody, called a friend who passed on the word that he was just down for a probation beef, that it was no big deal, nothing to worry about.

The Homick brothers, poised for flight from the moment Baby A went downtown in cuffs, relaxed.

Two days later, the arrests went off without a hitch in Las Vegas and Los Angeles. The Homick brothers, the Woodman brothers, Sonny Majoy, Dietz, Bryl, and Delores "Dee" Homick were taken into custody.

Detectives David Crews and Woodrow Parks, on loan from the LAPD's Foothill Division, were among the six officers, including Holder, Crotsley, and two Bomb Squad explosives specialists, who served a search warrant on Robert "Jesse" Homick's Corinth Avenue apartment. Homick's roommate, Hassan Abdullah, never a suspect, was on hand to show the officers around.

"Homick's room had piles and piles and piles of newspapers, stacked almost to the entire ceiling," said Crews. "In some spots, it was *all* the way to the ceiling. The room was in a state of disarray. There were so many pieces of paper in there. I don't recall seeing a bed." There were also, said Crews, dozens of law books, many still sealed in plastic, heaped everywhere.

On a cluttered desktop, Crews found a pair of fourteen-inch bolt cutters in near-new condition. Visible to the naked eye were slight striations on the sides of the steel blades.

Holder sent this tool to the LAPD crime lab. When the report came back, it said these marks matched perfectly to patterns on both halves of the severed bicycle-chain link that he and Crotsley had found in ivy near the condominium at 11939 Gorham Avenue on September 26, 1985.

CHAPTER Twenty-one

Riding a Tiger

Neil and Stewart felt that their new factory, housing a new H.P.M. extruder that produced polycarbonate panels, would open the way to sales of tens of millions of dollars a year. In a few years, this would propel them far beyond their present affluence and into the realm of the superrich. They would hobnob with the likes of Trump and Iacocca; before long, they, too, would become great industrialists. In the world of movers and shakers, they would be players in the great game.

Demand for polycarbonate products was booming, so their addition to Manchester's catalogue sparked a wave of enthusiasm among the sales force. Many a factory drummer went into the field with a new spring in his step—and visions of fat commission checks danced in his eyes.

But after Manchester's brand-new $900,000 machine was installed in the autumn of 1983, Neil's production team realized that they could not get it to work correctly. While glitches in setting up new machines are to be expected, Neil's crew tinkered for weeks but failed to resolve the problem.

Troubleshooters were summoned from H.P.M.'s Ohio factory. These experts would work at Manchester virtually every day for three months. In the end, almost by accident, the H.P.M. team chief discovered that his company had somehow made the eight-foot screw that pushes molten plastic through the machine about a sixteenth of an inch smaller than its requisite five-inch diameter.

But by the time they made this discovery, Vera's doom was sealed, and Gerry's with her.

For months after the Woodman brothers' conversations with Steve Homick about killing their father, nothing more seemed to happen. Steve, after being introduced by Stewart to Catherine Clemente, Manchester's executive receptionist, as "my man in Las Vegas," was in and out of Manchester frequently. The secretaries were told, "Anytime we need something done, this is our man to do it." They understood this to mean that Homick performed acts of retribution and collected gambling debts.

"If you think the Mafia is tough, Steve's people are tougher," Neil told Clemente.

Homick often telephoned, usually for Stewart. He called himself "Tony Gallante." Recognizing Steve's low, deep voice and slow, deliberate speech, Clemente punched up Stewart's extension. "Steve Homick for you," she always said, and he always took the call immediately.

But when Steve visited the plant, he was most often closeted with Neil. Robert Homick, a more frequent visitor, usually came to see Stewart, who often loaned him money to square his gambling losses, and a few times to pay his rent.

Several times Stewart asked Neil about progress on "the plan." He was told to be patient, to wait, that things were proceeding. Stewart heard that so often that he wondered if Steve Homick was simply hustling him and Neil for a few thousand in expense money. But Stewart never confronted Steve with these thoughts, and he never told Neil, "Let's call it off," or "Get someone else." He still hoped his father would die soon, and he assumed that Steve Homick would be the instrument of that wish.

Even before Gerry left Manchester, Stewart had discovered the joys of receivables financing. Until then, Manchester, and Lancaster before it, had lurched along from feast to famine, responding to the vagaries of its customers' payment habits. If too many accounts were slow in paying, the Woodmans had dug into their own pockets or borrowed from relatives, loaning the company what it needed to meet the payroll and pay suppliers.

Receivables financing, however, allowed them to keep a steady stream of cash flowing into the company. Each time an order came into the factory, an invoice was created. The goods were manufactured, shipped, and billed; a copy of the invoice then went to Union Bank.

Union promptly credited 80 percent of the invoice's face value to Manchester's account. Later, when invoices were paid and checks deposited at Union Bank, the bank immediately deducted 80 percent to repay their loan, plus a small interest charge, and credited the rest to Manchester's checking accounts.

After Manchester moved into the Prairie building in October 1983, Stewart and Neil made a small change in that system. Now, when the sales contract came in to the factory order desk, one copy of the invoice went to the production department for manufacturing while the other went straight to the bank. It might be a few days or even a week before the product was shipped, but Neil and Stewart wanted that money at once.

There was one category of sale that was exempt from receivables financing at Manchester: those invoices that Stewart never put on the company books, the ones he and Neil skimmed into their slush fund account at First Interstate Bank. And as the company's overall sales grew, so did the skim.

Each invoice billed out to a customer carried terms: normally, full payment was required within thirty days, though a few well-established accounts were given sixty, and most of their overseas accounts were allowed ninety-nine days. An invoice that remained unpaid after that period, however, was not considered delinquent until sixty more days had elapsed. The bank would not accept past due invoices as collateral for Manchester's line of credit, so when an invoice went into that category, Union moved it to an "ineligible" list, deducting its value from Manchester's credit line. They collected back their loan by charging the company's checking account.

The process through which an invoice passed from creation until delinquent or paid was called "aging." A computer printout of Manchester's receivables aging went to Union Bank every Friday. In this way, the bank tried to anticipate any problems Manchester might have with its receivables. If the company was in danger of overextending itself, Union wanted to know immediately. The bank considered itself Manchester's partner, and maintained an in-house staff of management experts poised to offer advice and assistance.

If there was one thing that neither Neil nor Stewart wanted, however, it was *any* outsider with access to Manchester's business secrets, especially their cash management system. So while they took Union's money, and gladly, the brothers went to great pains to tell their bankers as little about their company's inner workings as possible.

In October 1983, Manchester's pumped-up sales force wrote dozens of orders for polycarbonate panels. As each order became a production invoice, Union Bank issued cash to Manchester. These products were never shipped, however, because the problem with the machine made their manufacture impossible.

By November, Manchester had taken almost a million dollars from Union Bank on polycarbonate orders they could not ship.

In January, when technicians finally ascertained the problem, they told Neil and Stewart that H.P.M. would have to fabricate a new screw—and that this would take sixty days.

The brothers could have had their salesmen stop taking orders for polycarbonates, told Union Bank of their problem, and worked out a way to repay the millions.

But honesty was not the Woodmans' usual approach to problem-solving.

"I could have gone to the bank," said Stewart. "But I was worried about them saying, 'Well, we're not going to extend you credit anymore.' If they'd said 'stop,' we would have blown everything."

So Stewart told Neil, "We're not going to tell the bank. Let's see if we can get it going by January."

"January comes, we're one and a half million in the hole, and we still can't do it," said Stewart. "But, we're getting real close. We've found out it was a part, and that would be in the machine by March. So I just continued with what we were doing. By then, we were getting close to two and a half million into the hole."

While all this was going on, of course, Manchester was using some of the money Union Bank gave it to pay interest on money it had previously borrowed, a sort of in-house Ponzi scheme designed to buy time. That this might also lead to a debt hole so deep that Manchester could never dig itself out seems not to have occurred to Neil or Stewart.

When the eight-foot screw was finally ready, H.P.M. sent it air freight as far as Chicago's O'Hare International Airport, where a massive ice storm grounded all commercial flights. To save what might have been several days delay, Neil and Stewart spent $10,000 to charter a Learjet at Van Nuys Airport and dispatched it to O'Hare to pick up the part.

Now they were back in the polycarbonate business—but in the five months since their new factory had opened, Neil and Stewart had not only run up some $2.5 million in unsecured debt, they had crossed new criminal frontiers.

Manchester had borrowed the $687,500 it used to purchase Vera's stock, plus over $900,000 for its new extruder. Each month the brothers euchred Union Bank into paying cash against invoices for products it couldn't ship. And each month the company paid $60,000 in interest to service its debt.

The brothers might easily have mitigated Manchester's slide into debt by cutting back on what they skimmed. They might, for example, have foregone their $50,000 annual "car allowances," or taken less than the $100,000 a month that they skimmed from the business, and diverted some of that money to paying down their debt.

They did no such thing.

"If we had suddenly started letting that money go into the company," said Stewart, "the bank would have asked where it came from." If they told the truth, the brothers could expect to say good-bye to the discretionary income to which they had become addicted.

Neil and Stewart were riding a big, hungry tiger, and they dared not dismount.

But oh, what a ride.

Stewart was now dropping about $1,500 a day on sports betting. On his trips to Las Vegas, he was risking as much as $5,000 on a single hand of twenty-one. When Stewart won, he bought Melody a mink or some jewelry. When he lost $30,000 or $40,000, he shrugged it off. Next month there would be more cash. This was money that meant little to him, mad money to piss away on whatever he pleased.

One thing that always made Stewart happy was showering attention on his kids. He loved giving them unique experiences that the children of ordinary people could never hope to match. And, like his father before him, Stewart liked to put on a show of wealth that gave public notice of his status, that let him feel special, gifted, successful—all the things his father never told him he was.

So when Stewart took his children to Las Vegas, he took them not merely to play the slots under the watchful gaze of a casino gofer, or to cavort in artificial snow at Circus Circus, but to see the top shows, to *experience* celebrities. When Bill Cosby played the International Hilton, Stewart waved a thick wad around the Hilton's casino for a few hours, then told a pit boss to get him a front-row table for Cosby's show.

"I go in and give the guy a few bucks and we sit right *on* the stage," said Stewart. "I told him, 'If anybody gets called up, I want it to be my daughter.' Cosby comes out and calls Jaycy, who was seven or eight, on stage. He asks her, 'Is there anything you'd like me to do for you?' Doug Henning was the previous act, he'd sawed a girl in half. Jaycy says, 'Yeah, I'd like you to cut my brother in half.'

"After everything's over with, Cosby says, 'Are there any questions you want to ask me?'

"She looks at him and says, 'How come you have so much hair growing out of your ears?'"

Stewart was in parent heaven. His daughter with a superstar, and *she* was cracking the jokes!

To commemorate this event, Stewart paid a photographer over $1,400 for pictures of Jaycy with Cosby. He bought enough prints to give to almost everyone who knew his daughter—except, of course, her paternal grandparents.

These trips to Las Vegas helped Stewart keep his mind off the excruciating pressures of Manchester's situation. With millions in unshipped orders and debt piling up, however, by mid-1984 Stewart and Neil finally began cutting expenses.

They did this in a manner reminiscent of their father.

Fred Woodard was the plant superintendent. He had first served Gerry Woodman at Fullview Industries, following him from company to company for twenty-three years, including several months at Woodman Industries. For some perverse reason, Neil, over Stewart's token objection, had rehired Woodard when Gerry's company went bankrupt.

Woodard was under no illusions about Gerry's sons. In Stewart's office one day he overheard him say, "The old man is still fucking with us!"

Neil had replied, "We ought to just kill the old bastard and be done with it."

Woodard "didn't feel comfortable" with this sort of talk. He excused himself and went back into the plant.

In 1984, Woodard injured himself on the job and was out ten days. He applied for State Disability Insurance to compensate for the days he couldn't work. Woodard's claim was rejected because his injury was short-term and job-related. The claim was returned with the suggestion that Woodard file for Worker's Compensation Insurance. These claims are paid partly by an insurance company and partly by the employer.

Perhaps fearing an insurance rate increase, Neil chose to meet Woodard's Worker's Compensation claim with outrage.

"I asked Neil how I was going to get paid," said Woodard. "All I wanted was the damn paycheck. He told me, 'If you turn a lawsuit on us, I'll kill you.'"

"You don't have the balls to kill me," said Woodard.

"I've got someone who'll do it for me," growled Neil.

A few days later, Woodard was sitting in his living room when the screen door on his rear entrance opened and Steve Homick walked in, uninvited.

Woodard knew Homick hung around Manchester and played poker with Neil and Stewart. He also knew Steve's reputation as a heavy, someone the brothers sent out to do their dirty work.

Homick's sudden arrival shook him up, but Woodard had fortuitously left a shotgun on the floor next to his chair. He grabbed the scattergun, jacking a cartridge into its chamber with a clicking, metallic sound.

Feigning innocence, Homick pretended to ask directions around the neighborhood.

Woodard said nothing, but kept the muzzle of the gun angled toward Homick's legs.

After a long moment, Homick backed out the door.

Woodard filed a Worker's Compensation suit, and Manchester opposed it with all the resources the brothers could muster. They could have paid Woodard his ten days' salary—less than each of the brothers gave to bookies any day of the week—for far less than the cost of fighting his suit. But Neil and Stewart had gone too far into their power trip for anything as cheap as common sense.

The suit cost Manchester many thousands of dollars to settle.

Another cost-cutting step the brothers Woodman instituted was to delay commission payments to sales staff on invoices that hadn't been collected. Since it was months before the polycarbonate machine was shipping usable products, the impact on individuals was considerable.

One of those affected was Vicky Wayne, a pleasant middle-aged woman who had signed on with Manchester in May 1980. It was Vicky who had played along with Stewart when he had wounded Richard Nuckles's dignity with an elaborate practical joke.

Gerry had tried to hire Wayne away when he started Woodman Industries, but she turned him down. "He offered me an awful good deal," she recalled. "But I really didn't think that Mr. [Gerry] Woodman had a chance. Neil and Stewart were fighting their father and they were bound and determined that he would not succeed, even if they had to give their own product away."

Wayne was one of Manchester's best salespeople. She covered Oklahoma, Arkansas, Kansas, Missouri, Texas, Louisiana, and Mississippi, selling plexiglass, lighting diffusion panels, shower door material, and decorator panels. When polycarbonates came along, Wayne was pleased. Divorced and supporting herself and her children, she could always use extra money from increased sales.

Wayne was paid a "draw" against commissions. In late 1983, however, while her draw and expenses continued as before, commission checks began slowing down. Soon they came only rarely, though Wayne continued to produce sales as usual. Within a year, she was owed $7,500. It was pocket change to either of the Woodman brothers, but money that Wayne desperately needed to pay her living expenses.

Wayne, alarmed at the reduction in her income, began calling Stewart at home to ask about the money owed her. Neil intervened.

"He told me not to call Stewart at home," said Wayne. "Neil didn't want to pay me, he was angry with me."

Wayne would stick it out for almost a year before she resigned. When that happened, Neil told her "that I was not going to get my money and I might as well quit calling," said Wayne. "He said if I were dying of thirst in the desert and he had a swimming pool full of water he wouldn't give me a drop.

"A tornado had just gone through this little town I lived in and killed six or seven of my neighbors, destroyed a third of the town, and tore up my house," explained Wayne. "Neil said he 'didn't care if a fucking tornado blew my house away, along with my whole family.' He told me not to call anymore."

Wayne, too angry for words, put down the phone. Her teenaged son, Stan, seeing she was upset, picked up the instrument and spoke to Neil.

"Stan said something smart to him, and Neil said, 'You know, all I've got to do is make a phone call, asshole.'"

Neil said a few more things. Vicky Wayne understood that her children's lives were being threatened. She hung up.

Neil told Wayne not to call Stewart because he was trying to protect his brother's deteriorating health. By 1984, his weight topped 300 pounds, and he suffered from blackouts and fainting spells. He had diabetes, though it was yet to be diagnosed, and a heart condition.

It wasn't just the business aggravation. Stewart still pined inwardly for his mother, and Gerry still found ways to stir up his sons. And the lawsuit with Gloria Karns was inching through depositions and toward trial. If Karns won, it would put still more strain on Manchester's failing finances.

If Manchester was to survive, Neil needed Stewart to stay healthy. But his brother didn't seem willing to give up junk food binges; his idea of exercise was playing a round of golf from an electric cart. So on a Saturday in the spring of 1984 Neil telephoned his sister-in-law Melody and asked her to come to El Caballero, his Tarzana country club, to discuss Stewart's health.

"Don't tell anyone," said Neil. "And especially don't tell Stewart that you're meeting me."

Melody was alarmed but intrigued. She had never before met privately with Neil.

Stewart was playing golf with his sons, and Melody left their daughter Jaycy at home with a sitter.

Melody arrived at the clubhouse shortly after noon and met Neil. He ordered a drink from the bar and introduced Melody to a few of his friends.

"What is this all about?" asked Melody.

"It's about your husband. You're not being a good Jewish wife," said Neil. "A good Jewish wife would never let her husband eat what Stewart eats. She would help him control his eating habits. She would take care of her husband that way."

"I have always been a good wife to Stewart," replied Melody angrily. "But he's a big boy now. He eats whatever he wants to eat."

"You could help him. Go home, go in your pantry and throw out all the junk food, the frozen pizza and the Ding-Dongs and the Twinkies. He doesn't need that. Feed him vegetables and brown rice. Give him fish, lots of fish."

"I've tried all that. Stewart just goes out and buys whatever he pleases. What am I supposed to do, tell him he has to eat what I tell him? I'm not his mother. Maybe he would listen to *her*—but he doesn't listen to me.

"If you're so damn concerned about Stewart, why don't *you* talk to him? Does he listen to you any better than he listens to me?"

"Stewart is very unhappy," said Neil. "He's trying to commit suicide—digging his grave with his jaws. If you won't help, then at least have the guts to divorce him."

"That's crazy! Stewart doesn't want to commit suicide. He eats when he's stressed, and the reason he's always stressed is because of your damn parents. And because of the damn business. So don't come telling me it's *my* fault, that I'm not a 'good Jewish wife.' Get some of the business off his back. Get your parents off his back."

"Don't worry about that," said Neil. "Everything has been arranged."

"What are you talking about?"

"I don't know where or how, but it's all arranged. Soon our parents won't bother Stewart anymore."

"I don't like this kind of joke, Neil. Say what you mean."

"For a while it will be hard on Stewart, but he'll get over it."

"What are you talking about, for God's sake?"

"I've already said too much. Just be there for Stewart when it happens, and help him get through it."

"I don't want to hear any more," said Melody, rising to go.

"If you don't stand up and do something, Stewart is going to die because of his weight," said Neil. "And if he does, I will personally make the rest of your life miserable."

Melody ran from the club.

Not long after the meeting with Neil, Stewart asked Melody how much she was spending, aside from the mortgage payments. Melody said she usually went through $8,000 to $10,000 a month—and sometimes as much as $30,000.

"Can you cut back a little?" asked Stewart. "Just for a few months, until we get things straightened out at the business. Things are a little tight right now."

Things *were* tight at Manchester. The unsecured debt had risen to over $3 million, and the bank was starting to ask questions that the brothers didn't want to answer.

Diane Eng had been a Union Bank loan officer since 1977. Between June 1982 and March 1984, Eng's duties included monitoring Manchester's financial stability as she provided daily cash advances to the company. She and her supervisors had established that Manchester's line of credit was $1.25 million, a figure never disclosed to Manchester management. But in late 1983 and early 1984, as Manchester's polycarbonate invoices flooded in, the company's balance ballooned. When Eng asked Stewart about this, she was told that business was good and the company was now selling about $1 million a month worth of plastic, triple what it had done in its best month at the old factory.

Nevertheless, Eng asked the brothers if she could do a special audit. They agreed, and after matching the documents Manchester provided to the computer printout, Eng concluded that nothing was amiss.

Based on the audit, Union's management decided to increase Manchester's line of credit, but to monitor the company even more closely than usual. The bankers said nothing of this to Manchester.

In April 1984, Eng left for another job and was replaced by Jonathan Strayer. In June, when the invoices that Manchester had sent the bank the previous October should either have been paid in full or moved to the "ineligible" category, Strayer compared the monthly aging report with previous months and noted a discrepancy.

What troubled Strayer was that Manchester's invoice "aging" was odd. There were very few delinquent accounts, but the sales of certain products, all of them polycarbonate, had doubled and tripled and quadrupled. There seemed to be a lot of products being shipped by the company, but very little cash coming in, except from Union Bank.

The reason for this was that, unknown to Strayer, Manchester was altering its invoices to make them appear current while merchandise had yet to be shipped.

"In other words," Stewart would explain years later, "if an invoice was shipped in January, and it was now June, we were allowed one hundred and eighty days before it became delinquent. So before it hit one hundred and eighty we would go into the computer to find that invoice and put a new shipping date on it. Then it wasn't delinquent, and we could continue to borrow against it."

Strayer didn't know what Stewart was doing, but he set up a meeting with the brothers to tell them that "turnover" (how quickly an invoice was converted to cash) was increasing. Normally, explained Strayer, aging and turnover should move together, and so it had always done at Manchester. Now, however, said the banker, turnover was increasing, while the number of invoices over ninety days remained stable.

Strayer arranged for an audit team to visit Manchester. These accountants sampled fifty invoices and found about $500,000 in merchandise that Manchester claimed to have shipped but had yet to be paid for. Strayer noticed that almost every invoice had been altered to show a later shipping date.

Strayer called a meeting with the Woodman brothers. Knowing all too well what he wanted to talk about, they stalled. Finally, however, on July 18, they sat down with him.

Neil and Stewart told Strayer that to remain competitive, they had extended payment schedules, giving many of their customers as much as 120 days to pay.

Strayer, who knew little about the plastics industry, thought this was odd, but possibly true. Nevertheless, he now added several conditions for extending continued credit to Manchester. The first was that the company would give the bank a daily written summary of all customers who had paid invoices. The second was that hereafter, the bank would take not 80 but 90 percent of all paid invoices, to try to bring down that unsecured balance.

To lessen their exposure, Union Bank demanded second mortgages on Neil and Stewart's homes, to be held as additional collateral against the half million dollars the bankers thought was unsecured. And they asked the brothers to reduce their $200,000 annual salaries.

This was what prompted Stewart to ask Melody to "cut back" a little on household expenses.

The brothers knew that far worse conditions lay ahead of them if their bank were to lose confidence in them. They could be called into receivership. So, as a gesture of "good faith," the brothers gave $85,000 to Manchester, then paid that sum to Union Bank to reduce the unsecured balance.

To get this cash, the Woodman brothers took a leaf from Gerry's book.

"One of the ways that my father had always gotten cash out of the business was with Harold Albaum, our insurance agent," explained Stewart. "We just continued with it. Our actual liability insurance payments to City American were eighteen to nineteen thousand dollars a month. Albaum billed us thirty-five thousand a month, and at the end of the year he kicked back the difference, less his fifteen percent commission.

"So we got one hundred and seventy thousand dollars in little white envelopes, five thousand inside each one," added Stewart.

Three of those envelopes, $15,000, were passed to Robert "Jesse" Homick, whom Stewart met at a Ralph's Market on the corner of Devonshire and Mason, a three-minute drive from Manchester. The money was for additional "expenses" Steve had incurred in setting up the hit on the senior Woodmans.

Half of the $170,000 went through Manchester to Union Bank. Jon Strayer, who had no idea where the money came from, was encouraged by the way Neil and Stewart had responded.

To make sure that everything proceeded correctly, however, Strayer told the brothers that he would be sending an audit team to Manchester more frequently. As in, permanently.

Neil and Stewart were worried about these auditors. They paid Steve Homick to hide a microphone in the ceiling of the office used by the auditors. Homick's fee was disguised as a sales commission to Steve's wife, Delores.

"The auditors didn't know half what was going on; by bugging their office we found out what they knew," said Stewart. "I didn't care if they knew about the invoices. That never bothered me. But they were looking for other things. One of them said, 'We've got to find out where the money is going. We know it's going *somewhere*.' The other said, 'I must find out how Stewart's Ferrari is being paid through the business.'

"But it wasn't," giggled Stewart. "I was paying that myself. They were busy looking for things like that, and they missed everything else. I was only worried that they would go through the invoices, call the customers, and go through the payments, and they would then find the other accounts.

"And that's why the office was bugged, not for the invoices. I mean, they couldn't do anything about that. By then we owed them so much that they needed us to run the business, or they'd never get their money back."

But with a listening device in place, the temptation to handle the bank auditors was irresistible. Each time these accountants went through the printouts, noting specific invoices they wanted to inspect, Neil, Steve Strawn, or Rick Wilson—whoever was listening in Neil's office—noted the numbers they called out. Then Strawn went into Manchester's computer and created a new invoice with dates conforming to those shown on the bank's copy of the printout. Rick Wilson brought the bills of lading to Neil, who changed the dates to make it look as though the products had been shipped. His conscience bothering him, Wilson refused, however, to perform the actual forgery.

These documents were not merely deceptive because of altered dates. They were most often invoices created for goods that were either never manufactured or for defective goods shipped in the knowledge that they would be returned.

For several months Neil's phony invoice team created documents that satisfied the auditors. And the brothers siphoned a little less from the company, using this extra cash to slowly pay down their enormous unsecured balance.

But while funds trickled in to reduce what Union Bank thought was a $500,000 problem, Neil, Stewart, and their confederates went right on falsifying aging summaries and creating phony shipping documents to make the bank's audit team think they knew the extent of the problem.

Disaster of the type Gerry Woodman had often predicted struck in late summer when Manchester shipped more than $600,000 worth of plastic panels for an enormous tunnel system ordered for San Francisco International Airport. The panels came right back: "It was supposed to be a special light gray," said Stewart. "It turned out almost purplish black. It happens, it's a new product, new machinery," explained Stewart. "Continental Polymers shipped us the wrong stuff and we didn't realize it."

Many months later, after a lawsuit, Continental eventually replaced the plastic, but Manchester had to eat the energy and manpower expense of running and shipping it.

Not long after that setback, a bookkeeper named Mary Snyder mistakenly sent the wrong set of aging printouts—one that showed the actual status—to Union Bank. Suddenly the bank understood the true nature of the Woodman brothers' deception.

"The shit hit the fan," in Stewart Woodman's description of Union Bank's reaction to this information.

This time auditors asked for every piece of paper in the business. They found $1.7 million in ineligible receivables.

"Of the unsecured $1.7 million, $550,000 was prebilling, merchandise not yet shipped," said Strayer. "The remaining was credit memos, issued primarily for defective merchandise. I find it hard to believe that management of any company wouldn't be aware that they were shipping [that much] defective merchandise."

The game was up.

But Stewart was right: Union Bank did not want to risk closing Manchester down, because the only way they might still get their money back was to keep them in business. So the brothers finally came clean with their bankers.

Well, sort of clean.

"We showed the bank exactly how much it was that we'd re-aged," said Stewart. "We showed them how we reaged the invoices. And we made an agreement that we would catch up, it would take us about two and a half or three years. And they said, 'If we find how you're taking cash out of the company, we'll stop this.' But they never came close, nobody ever did, to finding out how we did it.

"If the bank didn't think we were catching up, they would never have loaned us more money," added Stewart. "Actually, I think they knew all along, but never said a word, because any banker could see that the aging was current all the time. We had five million dollars' worth of current invoices and we're only doing one million dollars a month—and that's impossible.

"They knew we were taking cash out, but they had no idea how. They said, 'Will you at least slow that down?' "

Money was tight around Manchester. Most of the cash coming in, except for the skim, which never stopped, was going to pay Union Bank, and the company was involved in several lawsuits.

In early 1985, Manchester suffered yet another blow when Gloria Karns won her suit against the company. The judge said that Neil and Stewart's assertions that they hadn't known their aunt was on the payroll were ludicrous.

Manchester was ordered to pay Karns $95,000, plus back interest, before September 30, 1985. Further, the company was ordered to make interim interest payments to Karns *monthly*. Manchester was also assessed court costs.

A few days later, Gloria dropped the other shoe, filing a lawsuit asserting that Manchester's previous suit against her was "frivolous" and charging malicious prosecution. Manchester, the brothers personally, and one of their attorneys were named as defendants. Gloria gleefully announced that her chief witnesses would be Gerry and Vera Woodman.

Neil, sledgehammer subtle as always, clipped an article from *Los Angeles Magazine* and sent it to Gloria. It was an in-depth report on the growing phenomenon of Southern Californians using hired killers to settle business and personal disputes.

Neil and Stewart asked their insurance company, Commercial Union Assurance, to defend Karns's new suit, but the underwriters declined, citing the limits of their coverage. So the brothers filed yet another suit, this time against Commercial Union, asserting that this failure to defend them made the brothers "ill, nervous and upset," and that this was "intentional infliction of emotional distress."

Besieged by costly, time-consuming legal conflicts on all sides, their every business move second-guessed by bean-counting bankers, forced to endure the humiliation of telling their wives to economize, Neil and Stewart could almost hear their father laughing at the mess they had created.

To any detached observer, it looked like Gerry was right all along: his sons *were* incapable of running the company.

The brothers could not bear even to imagine their father's exultation if Manchester went into receivership.

CHAPTER Twenty-two

Endgames

By 1985, Rick Wilson had had it up to *here* with the Woodman brothers and Manchester Products. It wasn't just Stewart's incessant practical jokes, although those were bad enough. Wilson would never forgive Stewart for tricking him into downing a dozen glasses of sherry, the last several laced with soy sauce, which had caused him to vomit all over the front seat of his new Mercedes and into his briefcase.

Or the time Wilson's hemorrhoids were acting up, and Stewart, feigning sympathy, said he had just the thing to help and sent someone out for an economy-size tube of Preparation H. But Stewart secretly made up a fake instruction sheet, and Wilson, following it, had used the whole tube, most of which had leaked out to stain his underwear and trousers.

And it wasn't just Neil's normal nastiness and his hair-trigger temper. If Wilson would never understand why Neil had responded to one of his lighthearted remarks by throwing a tantrum and urinating all over Wilson's new car, shaming Wilson in front of Neil's wife, he did understand that Neil was the boss. Even the constant screaming and the four-letter words that daily flew from the Woodmans' mouths didn't bother him that much, and he could live with the perpetual gambling, the poker and crap games, and the parade of bookies that were a part of workaday life at Manchester Products.

What scared Wilson was the daily deceit, the wholesale fraud unfolding before his eyes. Moreover, it looked like the company might go belly-up any time, what with hundreds of orders being returned because the goods were substandard.

Wilson reported to Stewart and supervised the sales force; Stewart had made it plain that their company needed to take in $40,000 *a day* just to break even and stay in business. But as 1985 went along, more and more defective panels were coming back. Soon many established customers started looking elsewhere. It got harder and harder to make sales.

So, in Wilson's version of events, he did the manly thing: He went to Stewart and said that he would be leaving in about six months.

This scared the hell out of Stewart. Men like Wilson, who put up with petty indignities and blatant lawlessness for fifty thousand a year and a company-owned Mercedes turbo-diesel, do not scuttle down the hawsers until they know the holes in the hull are too big to patch.

Stewart, angry, said that he hoped Wilson wasn't going to work for a competitor.

Rick assured Stewart that what he had in mind was moving to Arizona or Denver, where he could be with his girlfriend. Stewart replied that Wilson could move to Arizona and still work for Manchester—but Rick didn't want to work for the Woodmans anymore, even if it was in Timbuktu.

An intense rivalry between Strawn and Wilson had developed after Gerry was forced out of the company, and Stewart did nothing to discourage it. As a result, the two men each found opportunities to tell Stewart not to trust the other. Now, when Strawn insisted that Wilson was planning to leave for a similar job with a competitor, Stewart became even more suspicious of Wilson. He had the receptionist listen in on certain calls of his. Then he thought better of that, and instead had the phone bugged so that he and Neil could listen themselves.

In July 1985, Wilson learned about the telephone tap. He left soon afterward, vowing never to speak to a Woodman again.

Stewart insists to this day that he had evidence that Rick betrayed him by accepting a job with a rival plastics company. Whatever the reason, Wilson's departure put further strain on the company, and much of that settled on Stewart.

Even before Wilson abandoned ship, Stewart was feeling the load. If only his father were dead, he thought, then life might be bearable. Stewart again asked Neil about the hit on Gerry, and was told, as before, to be patient.

To help Steve Homick track his quarry, the brothers had pumped horse trainer Darrell Vienna, who innocently told them when their father was likely to be at Vienna's ranch to watch the workouts. And they had given Steve the dates when their parents were likely to go out: Vera's birthday—never Gerry's, he hated birthdays—their wedding anniversary, and those Jewish holidays when the whole clan gathered.

Initially, Stewart had objected to Robert "Jesse" Homick's involvement. "He was well known around the office, and he was just a klutz," said Stewart. And Steve had agreed to keep Robert out of the actual murders.

But that had changed by Passover 1984. "Robert came into the office and told Neil and me that they had missed him," said Stewart. "He said that my father was driving like a maniac, they couldn't catch up with him, so they called it off."

On that occasion, Gerry was alone in his car.

Stewart, growing antsy, discussed the attempt to kill their parents with Neil. "Neil told me, 'You're going to have to stay strong through this, because obviously, you know, they're going to have to kill them both,'" said Stewart.

"Neil said, 'They can't just do Dad, because it will come directly back to us. But you're very close with Mom, so no one will ever believe that you had anything to do with this.'"

After the unsuccessful Passover attempt, Robert asked the Woodmans for $6,000 in expense money. "Neil and I always kept a lot of cash on us," explained Stewart. "We drew this money out of expenses for ourselves and gave it to Robert."

But 1984 ended and Gerry and Vera remained very much alive. When they testified on behalf of Gloria Karns to help her win her suit against Manchester, the brothers were furious. Stewart's blood pressure soared.

"What the hell is going on with Steve?" he asked Neil.

"Just be patient, it's going to happen," said Neil.

Gerry and Vera's forty-fifth wedding anniversary was on June 22, 1985, a day Jesse spent parked in front of their Brentwood condominium. Less than an hour after he was rousted by police responding to a neighbor's call about "a suspicious man," Gerry and Vera were slated to join Wayne, Maxine, Hilary, and their spouses at an anniversary dinner at Guido's Restaurant in Santa Monica. But Vera wasn't feeling well, and the dinner was postponed.

As their company's problems grew, Neil went to greater lengths to shield his brother from stress. When Union Bank discovered the aging scam, Jon Strayer had been brutally direct with Stewart.

"One day Neil called," said Strayer. "In the past I'd always dealt with Stewart. . . . Neil told me to leave his brother alone because of his health—or something might happen to me."

Neil had second thoughts, however, and called Strayer back to apologize.

Neil, of course, was subjected to the same stresses that had bloated Stewart to well over three hundred pounds and inflated his blood pressure. But Neil's reactions to this stress, if different from Stewart's, were oddly in consonance with his hated father's ways. Beset from all sides, Neil took solace from the notion that he could cause physical harm to enemies real and imagined. Steve Homick became a blunderbuss for Neil to wave at anyone who defied him. Intoxicated with the idea that such a gifted thug was his to command, Neil found occasion to offer Steve's services to friends and business contacts.

"I don't know if Neil really believed it, or if he was just acting like a big shot. Neil wanted people to look at him like he was ten feet tall," added Stewart.

By September 1985, Manchester was again skirting disaster. Union Bank was taking most of the incoming cash, customers were increasingly wary of product quality, sales representatives were owed back commissions, legal expenses for the assorted lawsuits were rising—and while Neil and Stewart had negotiated extended terms from some suppliers, others were pressing for payments months in arrears.

Stewart had already made certain sacrifices. He knew his wife would never let him sell their Rolls, so in the summer of 1985 he paid Robert Homick $200 to steal it from his garage. Before rolling it over a cliff below Mulholland Drive, Robert lifted Stewart's car phone.

The Rolls was a write-off, and the insurance company ponied up, including a thousand extra for the car phone.

Stewart, so very accomplished a liar, conveyed convincing outrage and indignation to Vincent Franzini, an old family friend. "My father is behind this," Stewart fulminated. "He knows how much I loved that car. I'm sure he did it, or paid someone to do it, it's exactly his style."

The brothers received still another insurance settlement, although they were less than happy about it. Their thoroughbred mare, Strange Ways, died of a freakish accident when the foal she was about to drop got tangled in her intestines. The insurance settlement was well into six figures, but that was only a fraction of what the horse and foal might have brought at auction if her foal had been born healthy.

It seemed like nothing had gone right for the Woodman brothers since their father had gambled and lost control of Manchester. Neil offered to generate some cash by having Steve steal Melody's jewelry. "There are very few things that would have made my wife go crazy," said Stewart. "Losing me wouldn't be one of them. Losing the jewelry would. I told Neil, 'Don't even think about it. I don't want them in my house. Let them into *your* house, why don't you?'"

"They can't rob my house again," said Neil. "My safe is now in the closet, underneath a wooden floor, a burglar would never know where to find it, the insurance company will never buy it."

But Yom Kippur, the Day of Atonement, the holiest day of the Jewish calendar, was approaching, and when it ended, the brothers knew, their family would gather. Gerry and Vera would almost certainly make the journey to Muriel Jackson's home in Bel Air for the break-the-fast dinner. They would be vulnerable, at long last, to Steve Homick's desperadoes.

It was that month, September 1985, when Robin Lewis, who had replaced Catherine Clemente as the executive receptionist at Manchester, answered a ring at the front door. A middle-aged man with feral eyes and a head of thick, snowy hair said his name was Anthony Majoy and asked to see Neil.

Earlier, watching Majoy's car pull into the lot, Neil had called Lewis to say, "I'm expecting this guy, let him in."

Lewis, assuming Majoy was there for a job, handed him an employment application. He took it and walked away with Neil.

But Steve and Robert Homick, who had been frequent visitors to Manchester, were strangely absent during the month of September. Both continued to phone Manchester, but Neil and Stewart, instead of taking these calls, usually told their secretary to take a callback number.

Oddly, the fourth digit of these callbacks was always a nine.

Even more oddly, the brothers did not return these calls from their office. Instead, one or the other left the factory for a short time, usually returning in half an hour or less.

When Stewart married Melody and moved out of his parents' home, Vera did nothing whatever to his room. She neither disconnected nor changed the listing for Stewart's telephone. It remained as it was until the house was sold to satisfy creditors in 1983.

Among Stewart's prized personal possessions was a scrapbook of his bar mitzvah, which along with almost every other childhood keepsake remained in his former room. When Gerry and Vera sought the protection of bankruptcy court, this bar mitzvah book, among other personal items, was added to the inventory to be sold in the satisfaction of creditors' claims.

In 1984, a bankruptcy attorney contacted Stewart and asked if he wanted to bid on anything in the inventory. Stewart, who even before the final rupture with his parents had asked for the bar mitzvah book, now offered $500 for it. A document ordering Vera to surrender the book was conveyed to her in the form of a court order during the eight days of Passover.

Vera and her sister Sybil Michelson took this unfortunate timing as a calculated insult. Sybil, by now one of the few in the family still speaking to Stewart, telephoned. "She was hysterical," said Stewart. "She cried, 'How can you do this to your mother on *Passover?*'"

In the end, Sybil brokered a barter between Stewart and Vera: if he would give his mother recent pictures of his own three children, she would give him the bar mitzvah book.

At Melody's suggestion, Stewart tried to get some of his other personal things back, but Gerry, through Sybil, refused.

Arrangements were made for the swap: Linda Rosine, Sybil's daughter, would deliver the bar mitzvah book and pick up the snapshots.

"In July of 1985 I met with Linda at her house," said Stewart. "She brings this box of stuff out, and there's my bar mitzvah book and pictures and—oh God, there were letters from girls I had dated, and all sorts of things that my mother dug up. Everything I had left was in there."

Linda, very emotional, started crying. "When can your mother get more pictures?" she sobbed.

"In a couple of months," said Stewart.

"She asked about my getting together with my mother. She wanted it in a restaurant, nobody had to know," added Stewart.

"She just wants to see you, to talk to you," said Linda Rosine.

Stewart said he'd think about it.

"But I never did. I just couldn't," said Stewart.

While talking to Linda, Stewart confirmed that, as usual, the family would be getting together at Yom Kippur.

"Linda wanted to know if there was any way I would go that year to Yom Kippur," said Stewart.

"No," he said.

"Well, we're all going to be at Muriel's, and we'd like you there with us," said Linda.

Stewart took the bar mitzvah book and his other things and left. He told Steve Homick that the family would be at Muriel Jackson's Moraga Lane home on September 25, Yom Kippur.

Not long after Stewart's meeting with Linda, Steve told Stewart not to call his home in Las Vegas because he was sure those lines were tapped. If Stewart had something for Steve, he could tell Robert. If it was an emergency, he could leave a message at a New Jersey area code number that Stewart thought belonged to one of Steve's girlfriends.

Two days before Yom Kippur, Stewart called Sybil and asked her to give a message to his mother. "Tell her that I love her, and she should have a good year," said Stewart.

"It would mean a lot to your mother if you called yourself," replied Sybil.

"I can't do it," said Stewart. "I'd be too emotional."

"At least send her a card," said Sybil. "I'm sure that would make her feel better."

"Well, I don't have her address," said Stewart.

"Send the card to me, I will give it to your mother," said Sybil.

"I will, Aunt Sybil. I'll do that right away."

"Couldn't you let your mother see her grandchildren again?"

"I don't know about that. I'll have to think about it."

"So think about it. But why punish the children because you're angry with your father?" asked Sybil.

"It's ... too complicated," returned Stewart. "I said I'd think about it, and I will. Uh, are you all getting together at Aunt Muriel's?"

"Yes, same as last year," said Sybil.

When the conversation was over, Sybil, very excited about the breakthrough, telephoned Vera to tell her the good news. A few minutes later, Sid Michelson arrived home to find Sybil crying.

"What's wrong?" asked Sid.

"Stewart ... loves his mother! He's going to mail a card to us to give to Vera," sobbed Sybil.

The card never came.

A few minutes after Stewart hung up from his call to Sybil, about four o'clock on the afternoon of September 23, Jesse Homick called him for the second time in half an hour. Stewart said, "They're going to be at the Jacksons', night after next."

"It'll be taken care of," said Jesse. Later that day, Stewart told Neil about both conversations. Then he said, "Let's see what horse-shit they come up with this time, because there is no question they're going to be at Muriel's."

Jewish holidays start at sundown. On Yom Kippur, a day of fasting, a big meal is traditionally consumed before going to synagogue for the evening Kol Nidre service that begins observance of this holiest day.

This year, Melody's family was invited to join her and Stewart. At six on the evening of September 24, with Melody's family due momentarily, Stewart called Jesse, got his answering machine, and left word about a bet on a particular game. Melody overheard—and blew her top. "Just one night a year, can't you stop with the betting?" she screamed.

Then the doorbell rang, and Melody put on her happy-family face.

It was Stewart's unfailing habit to leave his home about seven each morning and go to the factory. This Yom Kippur morning was no exception—there was mail to open, a task he and Neil allowed no one but themselves to perform.

The journey between Stewart's home on Hoback Glen and the freeway on-ramp was no more than ten minutes, and it took Stewart close to a mini-market and gas station. At 7:17 that morning, Robert Homick, standing at a coin telephone in his Sawtelle neighborhood, dialed the pay phone outside that mini-market. He charged this call to Manchester Products.

On Yom Kippur morning, Muriel's daughter, Fran Sanders, picked Vera up outside her Brentwood condominium at 10:15 and drove her to Temple Magen David, an Orthodox synagogue near Pico and Robertson, a few minutes from the Duxbury Circle home where the Woodmans had raised their children.

Gerry, who had driven himself over earlier, was already in the synagogue, praying, as was Muriel Jackson.

Rosh Hashanah is New Year's Day on the Hebrew calendar (literally, the head of the year). Yom Kippur is the Day of Atonement. In the ancient Jewish tradition, at the start of each year God writes out what the next twelve months will hold for all His creatures.

But this heavenly decree is not final. Prayer, penitence, and good deeds can annul the harshest decree. During the ten days between Rosh Hashanah and Yom Kippur, "the days of awe," Jews prepare themselves spiritually for the Day of Atonement, and on

Yom Kippur they fervently pray that their sins against God of the previous year will be forgiven, that they will be inscribed in the "Book of Life" for a good year, even though, being mortal, they may have sinned.

But Jews believe that sins against other people can only be forgiven by the offended person. It is the responsibility of each Jew to seek out those whom he or she has affronted and to beg their forgiveness. Traditionally, this is done in the month preceding Yom Kippur.

Yom Kippur is one of two days when, except for those sick or infirm, neither food nor drink may be taken between sunset and sunset. The purpose of the fast is to liberate one's thoughts from earthly concerns and thereby come closer to the Creator.

It is also a day of prayer and Torah. The *shofar*, a ram's horn, is blown, as it was in Biblical days, evoking the noble memory of Abraham's willingness to sacrifice in subservience to God.

On Yom Kippur, Jews pray to ask God to honor the covenant of Abraham, Isaac, and Jacob, despite their own sins. Torah readings recount arcane rituals of Moses' era, of Solomon's Temple, of a culture over 5,700 years old.

"We abuse, we betray, we are cruel," goes the litany. "We gossip, we hate, we insult. We jeer, we kill, we lie. We mock, we neglect, we oppress. We pervert, we quarrel, we rebel. We steal, we transgress, we are unkind. We are violent, we are wicked. . . . We yield to evil. . . . "

Rivers of tears flow as penitents seek forgiveness not only for their own sins, but solace for the martyrs of Warsaw, Auschwitz, and Buchenwald, of Babi Yar, Baghdad, and Hebron, of Masada, Jerusalem, Vilna, Usha, Kfar Etzion, and all the other places where, over the millennia, Jews have been butchered for their faith.

Gerry and Vera, remembering their English roots, always made mention of York, whose Jews all perished in 1190.

Vera, encouraged by the news from Sybil that her beloved Stewart had at last responded to his heart, that a reconciliation might be at hand, forgave her son for her own sufferings. After the *amidah*—silent meditation—when it is allowed, she made a special, personal prayer for God's forgiveness on her family. She prayed that her sons would be reunited with their father, that her home would once again be filled with the happy shrieks of her grandchildren.

Together, Vera and Gerry chanted "Our Father, our King *Avinu malkeinu*, inscribe us in the Book of Happiness. Inscribe us in the Book of Deliverance. Inscribe us in the Book of Prosperity. Inscribe us in the Book of Merit. Inscribe us in the Book of Forgiveness . . . act for Your sake if not for ours, answer us though we have no deeds to plead our cause, save us with mercy and loving kindness.

"On Rosh Hashanah it is written.

"And on Yom Kippur it is sealed.

"But penitence, prayer and good deeds can annul the severity of the decree."

The Day of Atonement ended at sunset with the blowing of the *shofar* and a heartfelt chant, *L'shanah ha-ba-ah bi-rusha-layim!* Next year in Jerusalem!

A few hours later, after a meal fit for royalty and an exchange of love and affection with their family, after watching the season premiere of "Dynasty" and a swift ride from Bel Air to Brentwood, Vera and Gerry Woodman were shot to death in the parking area beneath their rented condominium.

The murders were late in the news cycle and so missed the next day's early editions. The "Ninja" angle, however, insured big headlines in evening papers around the state, and all seven Los Angeles TV stations led with the Ninja story on their evening news broadcasts.

The murders were also big news in the United Kingdom. Ironically, the first to notify the brothers about the murders was one of Gerry's cousins, who telephoned from England to offer condolences. His call came at lunchtime on September 26, while the brothers, as was their habit, were lunching with their sales staff at Solley's, a Ventura Boulevard deli in Woodland Hills.

Robin Lewis took the message and immediately called the restaurant to have Neil paged.

"I've just received a phone call that your parents were found dead," she said.

Neil was quiet for a long moment, then asked if she had told anyone else.

"No," she answered.

"Write the message down and hand it to me when I come back, but don't give it to Stewart."

Neil returned to the factory, icy calm. When Robin put her arm on his shoulder to comfort him, he pushed her away.

"Don't do that," he said.

Neil brought Stewart into his office and without preamble said, "They both got killed. You're going to have to hold yourself together through this."

After giving Stewart the news, Neil called his uncle, Lou Jackson, at Angelette. "I just heard what happened to my parents—" he began, but Jackson cut him off.

"If it's the last thing I do, I'm going to make sure the truth comes out," screamed Jackson, then hung up.

"They *know* what happened," said Neil.

Stewart looked at Neil, his face a question. Neil answered it.

"Lou's going to be our problem," said Neil.

Stewart nodded.

"And you're going to be the weak link," continued Neil. "They're going to try to get to you, so you've got to pull yourself together."

"I will," said Stewart, unable to manage more. He went to his office and locked the door. During the next hour he tried to call Melody, but she was shopping with a neighbor. Eventually, Stewart got through to the neighbor's car phone. He told Melody to pick up their children from school and take them home, but refused to say why.

Too upset to drive, Stewart asked a friend, Peter Wolins, to take him home. He remained there two days, until Saturday. Stewart usually led the monthly sales meeting, but this time it was all he could do to attend and sit silent in a corner.

A few days after the murders, Robert called Stewart at his home. He said he was calling from jail and asked for a thousand dollars so he could make bail. Stewart told his wife about the request. "Just leave him alone and let him get his own money," said Melody.

Worried, Stewart called William "Moke" Homick in Las Vegas and asked, "Does this thing have to do with what's going on in L.A.?" William cut him off abruptly. "Nothing to do with anything in L.A. Don't worry about it."

William was telling the truth—Jesse had been arrested on fraud charges. He had collected County General Assistance—welfare— for years by pretending to be disabled.

The insurance on Vera's life, $506,000, including policy dividends, was paid in December. To keep Union Bank from getting any of it, the brothers deposited the check at First California Bank. Most of it went to placate Manchester's suppliers, but enough was left for Neil and Stewart each to buy a new Mercedes sedan, and for each to give his respective wife $30,000 in mad money.

Less than a month after the murders, Stewart's firstborn son, Ian, celebrated his thirteenth birthday and Jewish manhood with a Temple Judea bar mitzvah. Despite the recent deaths, Stewart dug deep into his pockets for a celebration.

"My bar mitzvah was a big deal," he recalled. "The party was at the Beverly Wilshire Hotel. This was right after my father had lost all his money—but he had to put this big show on. We reserved the Bellefontaine Room, and I remember my parents screaming and arguing about the bills. It cost ten thousand dollars. Today, that party would cost forty thousand dollars.

"But I didn't want a traditional party for Ian. You go to a bar mitzvah, you have the food, and people always bitch about it, then they dance, and that's the end of it. So I rented Malibu Grand Prix in Northridge for a whole night. We had three different caterers, all the food you could ever think of. Everything inside was on free play. The party started at seven o'clock and we stayed until four-thirty in the morning," added Stewart.

Over two hundred guests turned out. The party cost Stewart over $25,000. "I gave the guys that worked there a thousand dollars in tips. Money meant nothing. I didn't give a shit. It made no difference then," said Stewart.

In February 1986, when police hadn't been around for weeks and the brothers were certain that they were home free, Stewart hired a contractor to build an addition to his million-dollar home to harbor Melody's vast wardrobe. A special temperature-controlled cabinet, lined with fragrant cedar, would protect her eight fur coats. An automated overhead track, like those found in dry cleaning shops, would make it easier to retrieve things. Melody's "clothes closet" included a dressing area and dozens of double-hung drawers. It would require over 1400 square feet, roughly the size of a typical three-bedroom tract house in Southern California. The price tag: $68,000—$5,000 just for the plans. But Stewart thought of it as a smart investment: Melody owned a colossal quantity of designer clothes, dresses and other items, many valued at several thousand dollars each.

Melody's friends were a bit envious, but they were all well aware that the Woodmans *always* went first cabin.

Stewart and Neil were arrested on the morning of March 11, 1986. The wardrobe room was never built.

Arrests

Neil was in the plastics factory at seven when a squad of uniformed police and FBI agents, revolvers drawn and shotguns at the ready, burst into Manchester. He offered no resistance, said nothing except to confirm his name, and was unceremoniously stuffed into the back seat of a police cruiser that took him to the LAPD holding facilities at Van Nuys Civic Center. While Neil was en route, detectives with search warrants began going through the factory and offices.

At almost the same moment, Stewart, behind the wheel of his Bronco, rolled through the Hidden Hills security gate. He saw what looked like about thirty police and sheriff's patrol cars parked along the road leading to the Ventura Freeway.

Stewart stopped, rolled down a window, sniffed the fresh spring air, and addressed a policeman in a squad car.

"Something wrong?" asked Stewart, motioning toward the phalanx of lawmen.

"Nothing's wrong here," said the cop. "Just routine."

Stewart resumed his journey toward the freeway. He drove perhaps a tenth of a mile before a police cruiser screamed up behind him, lights flashing, siren blaring.

"Pull off the road," said a voice amplified by loudspeaker.

Stewart obediently stopped the Bronco.

Instantly, what seemed like fifty officers waving guns swarmed over his car. The door was wrenched open, Stewart was jerked out, his hands were handcuffed behind his broad back, and he was shoved facedown on the pavement.

Police officers know that being handcuffed can hurt. When the cuffs are put on tightly, wrists and hands swell painfully. And when the cuffs go on *behind*, arms and shoulders are cruelly wrenched. This is especially agonizing to heavy people with broad backs.

Some police relish the thought of this pain being inflicted on a vicious criminal, a small sample of the grief that is to follow, a down payment on justice.

Nattily clad in a stylish dark suit and monogrammed shirt, Detective Jack Holder savored the moment. He read the Miranda warning to Stewart's ample backside.

Holder gave Stewart a few minutes on the cold asphalt, until his shoulders and wrists began to ache and burn, until the reality of his predicament had sunk in. Then he had uniformed officers lift him to his feet and put him into the back seat of an unmarked car. Stewart was driven via traffic-laden rush-hour freeways to downtown Los Angeles and a holding cell at Parker Center.

At the same moment that Stewart and Neil were arrested, other LAPD squads arrested Robert "Jesse" Homick at his Corinth Avenue apartment. Allowed to use the telephone in the booking area at the West Los Angeles police station, Robert's first call was to Manchester Products—collect.

Steve Homick and Sonny Majoy were picked up at Majoy's Sherman Way apartment in Reseda, in the heart of the San Fernando Valley, and taken to the Van Nuys jail.

Majoy, however, was charged only with a weapons offense and released on bail.

Within seconds of the Los Angeles arrests, FBI/Las Vegas Metro squads in Las Vegas arrested Delores Homick, Steve's estranged wife, Charles Dietz, Ronald Bryl, and Lawrence Ettinger. Michael Dominguez, already in custody on a parole violation, was now charged with murder by Las Vegas Metro and with racketeering and interstate murder-for-hire by the FBI.

*   *   *

The day Stewart and Neil were arrested, Melody Woodman did two things. First, she searched Stewart's closets, looking for anything that might help exonerate—or incriminate—him. Beneath sweaters in Stewart's armoire, Melody found an I.O.U. from Jesse Homick for $15,000, money Stewart got from the Albaum insurance kickback and gave to Jesse as an expense advance for the hit. Robert had taken it upon himself to give Stewart the I.O.U. against the possibility that someone might later question *why* Stewart had given Jesse money.

But it also proved that Stewart *had* given money to Jesse. Creating a document linking Robert with Stewart and a chunk of money was the same kind of reasoning that had led the younger Homick to purposely ram another car in the alley near Brentwood Place on the day of the Woodman murders.

Melody, knowing neither the reasoning nor the reason but supposing that proof that Stewart had given money to a thug like Jesse Homick for *anything* was not likely to help her husband, tore up the I.O.U. and flushed it down a toilet.

The second thing Melody did was to tell Jay Jaffe, Stewart's attorney, about the secret meeting she'd had with Neil almost eighteen months earlier, when Neil had insisted that all of Stewart's family problems would "be handled."

Jaffe told Melody to say nothing about this meeting to anyone. He now decided that he could not represent both Woodman brothers, because it seemed likely that their interests conflicted: if what Melody said was true and could somehow be confirmed, then Stewart's defense might be that Neil, acting alone, was responsible for the murders.

Jay Jaffe had a peculiar relationship with Stewart. They were about the same age, and Jaffe had moved to a home on Duxbury Circle in 1964. But although only ten houses separated them, Jaffe barely knew Stewart then.

Jay, however, recalled Gerry Woodman very well: he was the foul-mouthed neighbor whose dog always crapped on the Jaffes' lawn, and who, whenever he saw young Jay, tried to kick his young tush in a way meant to convey Gerry's most tender affections. As a boy, Jay Jaffe had feared and hated Gerry Woodman.

Now he was about to defend one of his accused murderers.

What Stewart Woodman told Jay Jaffe in confidence is privileged information, protected by ethical canons and legal restrictions. But there can be no doubt that Stewart is a super salesman, a superb actor who helped build a $12-million-per-year business by convincing all manner of people that he was someone they should trust. And there is little doubt that Jay Jaffe absolutely believed in his client's innocence, and defended him to the limits of his considerable talents. He also made an emotional commitment to Stewart, a dangerous practice for those who choose to bear the burden of saving other people's freedom—or their lives.

Neil retained Gerald Chaleff, then forty-seven, a Santa Monica–based criminal defense specialist. Chaleff had spent two years in the Los Angeles D.A.'s office and eight years as a public defender before entering private practice in 1977.

Chaleff rose to prominence in 1979 when, along with Katherine Mader, he accepted a court appointment to defend Angelo Buono. Buono was one of the so-called Hillside Stranglers, who with cousin Kenneth Bianchi raped and murdered several young women and girls. Buono was convicted on nine counts of first-degree murder after an often bizarre two-year trial. Chaleff and Mader, however, saved Buono's life by convincing jurors not to issue the death penalty.

In criminal law's highest-stakes arena, where appellate and Supreme Court decisions and executive clemency have led to retrials and even occasionally freed convicted killers, anything short of the gas chamber qualifies as a victory.

After the Hillside Strangler case, Chaleff became one of a handful of high-profile Southern California attorneys who seem perpetually involved in the nastiest murder cases.

Two days before Neil and Stewart were taken into custody, Chaleff was quoted at length in a *Los Angeles Times* article about proposed changes in fee structures for court-appointed attorneys in capital cases. Chaleff, who got $75 an hour for defending Buono, argued that over half of that had gone for overhead expenses and that lower rates might discourage younger attorneys from accepting capital cases.

With Neil Woodman as a client, however, Chaleff would not worry about scraping by on what a judge decided was fair pay for defending an indigent. Neil lived in an expensive home in the "golden ghetto" of Encino and drove a Porsche and a big new Mercedes sedan. His wife dressed in one-of-a-kind designer frocks and all but dripped diamonds.

Legal fees for representing those accused of a crime punishable by death are entirely negotiable. In Southern California, that can range from a few tens of thousands of dollars to seven figures, depending on the assets of the accused—essentially, whatever the traffic will bear.

Jay Jaffe and Gerald Chaleff negotiated fees of $300,000 from each of the Woodman brothers.

Because even acquittal after a jury trial subjects defendants to enormous stress and deprives them of liberty for a long time, the most desirable outcome for someone accused of murder is that authorities drop all charges without a trial. When such a dismissal occurs, however, clients sometimes balk at paying stiff fees to an attorney whose efforts seem limited to fleeting court appearances. So, with rare exceptions, attorneys in such cases demand their fee up front.

Stewart gave Jaffe a check for $10,000, a down payment.

It bounced.

For all the millions that had been skimmed from Manchester and passed through the Woodman brothers' hands on their way to jewelers, bookies, couturiers, casinos, furriers, racetracks, and auto dealers, Stewart and Neil raised the $600,000 required to front their attorneys' fees by selling their half-interest in Manchester's Prairie Avenue building.

One of Jaffe's first suggestions to Stewart was to transfer all his assets to Melody. Thus, explained the attorney, should the Federal government attempt to use its powers under racketeering statutes to seize Stewart's money and property, it would face the burden of proving that Melody, too, had engaged in racketeering. Like his late father before him, Stewart signed everything he owned over to his wife.

On March 20, 1986, Stewart and Neil were arraigned in Municipal Court on two counts each of murder and conspiracy. Each entered a plea of not guilty.

*   *   *

As a UCLA senior in 1977, Steve Strawn had majored in political science, minored in accounting, and toyed with the notion of going on to law school. Instead, he had dropped out. He joined Manchester in 1981 as credit manager, under Wayne Woodman's supervision.

Even before Wayne and Gerry were ousted, Strawn had been given authority to hire and fire, a perk that allowed him to fill the receptionist's position with whomever he was dating.

When Stewart and Neil took over the company, Strawn was elevated to controller and paid well over $40,000 a year. In 1984, when the company was unable to ship polycarbonate products but was sucking millions from Union Bank on unshipped invoices, Strawn personally went into Manchester's computer and changed the shipping document dates, an innovation in fraud for which an admiring Stewart Woodman gave Strawn full credit. Strawn's annual salary was over $50,000 by the time the Woodman brothers were arrested.

On March 6, 1986, Stewart told Strawn to write a check to National Collection Service, Robert Homick's sham company, for $735.00, inferring, however, that Robert had not actually collected anything. Strawn created a phony document naming a real customer in Mississippi, then cut a check for Robert.

"I inquired why we were paying him," said Strawn, "and was basically told that it was simply good to have someone like him around, that this was, in essence, a 'retainer.'" Strawn understood that this would be a regular monthly transaction.

Five days later, Strawn found LAPD detectives searching his place as his employers were led away in handcuffs. About ten-thirty that morning, Neil telephoned Strawn from a pay phone in the holding area of the Van Nuys jail. His voice was quiet, lacking its usual bluster. He sounded like a frightened, beaten man.

"Steve, where are you?" asked Neil.

"In my office," answered Strawn.

"You alone?"

"Yeah."

"Cops still there?"

"Not now."

"I want you to do something for me," said Neil. "Go into my

office and get behind my desk. Lift the desk leg closest to your right, next to the chair. You'll find some papers."

"Okay," said Strawn, as though this was the sort of thing he did every day.

"Burn those papers. Don't look at them, just burn them. Flush the ashes down a toilet."

When Strawn tugged the heavy oak desk away from its position, he found that its weight had pressed a deep hole in the pile carpet. At the bottom of the hole were two business cards folded into a sheet of paper. In what he would later describe as "a serious lapse of judgment," Strawn burned everything, then dropped the ashes down a toilet.

But before he did that, he looked at the cards. Both bore Steve Homick's name. The paper had telephone numbers written by hand. One of the numbers included a Nevada area code.

Unfortunately for Strawn, however, someone had overheard Neil's end of the telephone conversation.

Pay telephones available to inmates in Southern California jails are generally in exercise areas called "runways." Thus, unless precautions are taken, anyone listening nearby can hear what is said by one party.

Some inmates habitually loiter near these telephones, listening for anything—a scrap of conversation, a sentence, even a single word—that they can use to barter with police for consideration in sentencing ("work off a beef") or, for those beyond such redemption, for increased jail privileges.

These informants are usually called "snitches." By any name, career criminals and repeat offenders loathe snitches—and are well aware that most jails teem with them.

One such snitch was a petty thief named Sidney Storch. "Storch is arrested and thrown in a holding cell at Parker Center," said Jack Holder. "And, lo and behold, Stewart was in a cell across the way. Now, Stewart is—well, he called his *mother* on his honeymoon night! Now he's been arrested. He's got to be scared, if not actually crapping in his pants.

"So right away he's on the phone. We never could put together *who* he spoke to, but Storch says he heard him say something about how twenty-five thousand dollars ought to be enough to keep somebody quiet. Now, I have talked to Storch on a number of occasions and 99.9 percent of the time I don't believe him. But in this case," continued Holder, "I *do* believe him, only because we have this pilgrim who's never been through the system and doesn't understand that the walls have ears."

To Holder, the $25,000 Storch reported meant payment for the murders. "I was not privy to that conversation. But I *think* that whoever he's talking to asked him, 'Do you think the Homicks will talk?' And he answers, 'No, twenty-five thousand ought to keep them quiet,' " said Holder.

After arraignment, Neil, Stewart, and the Homick brothers, Steve and Robert, were all transferred to pretrial custody at the Los Angeles County Jail, where an entirely new set of snitches were in residence.

In Las Vegas, Jerry Daugherty, Tom Dillard, and Bob Leonard, with Rich Crotsley, decided that the key to unlocking Steve Homick's gang might be Baby A. "We brought Mike Dominguez in and sat him down," recalled Daugherty. "We told him, 'You're going to fry for the L.A. murders and the Tipton murders, and either you talk to your attorney and cooperate, or you're going to die.'

" 'You'll get the gas chamber for the Woodmans in L.A., and if by some miracle you don't, then you'll get lethal injection in Las Vegas for the Tipton thing,' " continued the FBI agent.

"And I said, 'If that doesn't work I'll come in with RICO and get you for interstate murder-for-hire. Whatever it takes, we'll nail you. It will happen unless you talk *now*.' "

Mike Dominguez said he wanted to think about it. A few hours later, he asked to speak with his attorney.

"At that time Dominguez was represented by Steve Stein, whom we knew personally," recalled Tom Dillard.

Stein had been hired by Dominguez's parents. When Dillard called the attorney, he laid out, with broad strokes, the evidence against Mike: hours of wiretapped conversations incriminating Dominguez; testimony from FBI informants Stewart Siegel and Art Taylor and witnesses who had seen him take money from Steve Homick; eyewitnesses who confirmed Dominguez as a passenger on P.S.A. flights to and from Los Angeles the days before and after the murders; and testimony from Richard Altman, who had seen Mike in another car after Jesse Homick's Buick had collided with Altman's car in the alley near Brentwood Place.

Stein convinced Baby A that his one chance to live was to spill his guts *now*. A plea bargain was arranged: Dominguez would plead guilty to all crimes he confessed, he would testify against Steve and Robert Homick, and he would be sentenced to life, *with* the possibility of parole.

It was a *very* good deal for Dominguez; at the time, all the investigators and prosecutors involved felt that Mike's testimony would be necessary to convict the Homick brothers.

Dominguez also agreed to give a videotaped statement.

"We got Jack and Rich up here," said Tom Dillard. "They, Bob Leonard, and I and Jerry Daugherty sat in the room, and Mike went through his criminal life history. He wanted to tell us everything that he could remember. You have to remember that Mike is not real smart," added Dillard.

Among themselves, the lawmen decided that LAPD would lead off, because as far as they knew, the Woodman murders had happened first. Dillard and Leonard from Las Vegas Metro would go next, followed by the FBI. The interview, with only brief pauses for trips to the bathroom and to eat, took eight hours. It was the most astonishing confession any of the law enforcement officials present had ever heard. At least twenty policemen, FBI agents, and prosecutors from two states and the Federal government crowded into a Las Vegas Metro conference room, spellbound by Dominguez's matter-of-fact chronicle of mayhem and murder.

Speaking in an incongruously high voice that reminded listeners of heavyweight boxer Mike Tyson, Dominguez began by confessing his role as an armed lookout in the Woodman murders. He readily implicated Steve and Robert Homick, but said he knew nothing about who had hired them. He'd seen Sonny Majoy at a distance, didn't have his name, but picked him out of a photo lineup. "Then [Tom] Dillard and [Bob] Leonard took their turn, and Mike says, 'Once Steve told me about putting a live grenade in this guy's pickup truck,' " recounted Daugherty.

"We confirmed that. Metro reports show that when the driver

started the car, something fell on the ground. The guy saw it was a live grenade and called the fire department.

"Mike says, 'Many times Steve had us go out and break some-one's legs. Once, when he was trying to stop the culinary workers at a downtown casino from going with a union, we went to this guy's house and when he answered the door we hit him with pipes and broke his knees.'

"Mike just kept going on with these, one crime after another. 'Another time Steve came by and we did this and that.' Tom and Bob wanted to get to the Tipton murders. They said, 'Okay, now tell us about Mrs. Tipton.'

"Mike said, 'Can I tell you one more thing?'"

Dillard and Leonard sighed, but nodded yes. To their astonish-ment, Dominguez then confessed to murdering, with Steve, Ray-mond Godfrey, the elderly man they had beaten, tortured, and drowned in search of cash that he had never had. This was Metro's first inkling of who had killed Godfrey, or why.

Dominguez went on to confess his role in the arson fire at Lawrence Ettinger's Maui boardinghouse and the attempted mur-der of Ettinger's ex-wife and her fiancé, Craig Maraldo. Baby A confirmed that Steve Homick hired him for both jobs.

When it came to the Tipton murders, however, all Mike could say was that he had seen a .38 like that used to kill all three victims in Steve's car on the morning of the murders.

Based on Mike Dominguez's identification of Sonny Majoy and the LAPD's previous surveillance of Steve Homick, which con-firmed the link between the two first established by Art Taylor's reports, Holder and Crotsley rearrested Majoy on April 23 and charged him with murder.

On May 9, a Clark County grand jury indicted Steve Homick for burglary, robbery, and three counts of murder in the Tipton case.

But Baby A wasn't the only one singing to police. Ronald Bryl, an unemployed cabinetmaker who let his old friend Steve store the Tipton jewelry and an arsenal of handguns at his house, made a full confession. Over the ten years he'd known Homick he'd been involved in fencing stolen jewelry and had bought and sold nar-cotics.

Bryl explained that before learning that the Tipton jewelry was mostly high-class fakes, Steve asked him to remove identifying inscriptions and marks with a miniature grinder.

After Bryl made a deal—probation in exchange for what he knew about Steve Homick's criminal pursuits—and was released, William "Moke" Homick dragged a clothes trunk onto the driveway of Bryl's home. Bryl called the Bomb Squad, but the trunk was empty. That was enough to get Moke arrested for attempting to intimidate a witness. Bail was set at $5,000, but Moke was broke.

Aside from Dominguez rolling over on Steve Homick, the biggest break in the case came from Steve's diaries, which were seized by search warrant from Homick's garage.

"Steve kept a journal of his daily activity," said Holder. "We recovered more than five years of these journals." When Holder and Crotsley got back to Los Angeles, they spent hours poring through these diaries, all written in Steve's bizarre code. Eventually, they were turned over to Jim Daloisio, a recent law school graduate then clerking in the L.A. District Attorney's office. Because the diaries were filled with obscure references to movies and television shows, Daloisio took them to the University of Southern California's School of Film, and availed himself of their unequaled library.

"Daloisio broke a lot of the codes," said Holder. "For example, Steve Homick always referred to somebody as 'Kookie.' Then we learned that Gerald Woodman habitually carried a comb in his pocket—so, bingo, Daloisio finds that in the sixties there was a TV series, '77 Sunset Strip,' where one of the characters, 'Kookie,' always carries a comb.

"Okay, that's easy. But another character on the series was a bookmaker, 'Roscoe.' When Steve made that entry, Gerry and Vera lived on Roscomare Road, so Steve, in his wisdom, calls it 'Roscoe's Mare.' There's bunches of stuff in his notebooks like that. We brought in the curator of the USC Film Library, an expert on cinema, to tell us what these things meant in relation to various films and television series," said Holder.

"We actually thought about having Edd Byrnes, the actor who played 'Kookie,' testify about Steve's notations and what they meant, but it was decided that this would be a little too sensational," added Holder.

*   *   *

After his arrest, Neil became increasingly nervous about $28,000 he had wired to Robert Homick after the murders. Stewart, however, didn't know about the wire transfer; he had assumed that Neil had sent cash or a check. Not until both brothers went to a holding area while waiting to speak with their lawyers did Neil share this information with Stewart.

"Neil was petrified about the money," said Stewart. "But he said [the authorities] would never find it because it was wire transferred. But every time we went into the attorney's room, he'd bring it up. He'd look at the ceiling, like, you can't talk in here, and he'd start screaming, 'Don't talk about it, you can't, because they're listening.'"

A few days after the arrest, Melody, in Jaffe's presence, told Stewart about her meeting with Neil in the spring of 1984. Stewart seemed astonished to learn that two years earlier, Neil had boasted that Gerry would be "taken care of." Jaffe told Stewart that if Neil could be induced to confirm what he had said to Melody, it would strongly underpin Stewart's defense.

"I was pissed," said Stewart. "Really mad—I was upset."

Undoubtedly, Stewart was all these things. But he was also shrewd and cunning, and now he had both a chance to save his own neck and a reason to do so at his brother's expense.

"I wanted Neil to explain why the hell he had met with my wife behind my back and told her what was going on with the murder," said Stewart.

The brothers were in the same cell block, separated by two cells. They could speak to each other without shouting, so just minutes after he met with Jaffe, Stewart said to Neil, "Melody is in the attorney's room, she's hysterical, something about a meeting with you at El Caballero."

"I didn't do anything—I'll tell you all about it," replied Neil.

To foil anyone listening, Neil sent a note, passed to Stewart's cell in an empty candy box.

"The first note said that he'd just talked about my weight, the food, all that crap," said Stewart.

"Neil, it had to be something else because she's hysterical," said Stewart aloud. "Whatever it was, she's going to tell everything to Jay [Jaffe] tomorrow."

"Just hold on a minute," said Neil. He wrote a second note.

"That one was about Woodman Industries," said Stewart. "He said that his discussion with Melody was about dealing with the strain caused by my father's new company. But Dad had already gone bankrupt *before* that meeting. That's what I told Neil. And I said, 'Tell me the truth, tell me what you really said to her.' I knew what it was, because she had told me, but I wanted it from him, in writing.

"Neil fully believed that Melody would have gone to Jay and told him everything," explained Stewart. "His fear was that Jay would then tell Gerald Chaleff [Neil's attorney] and then Chaleff would no longer believe what Neil had been telling him. At that point, Neil thought Chaleff was God; if he said something, that's what it was going to be."

Manipulated by this fear, Neil then wrote a third note implicating himself—but not Stewart—in the plan to kill their parents.

Stewart made a show of flushing the notes down a toilet in his cell—but instead he palmed them and flushed blank crumpled paper. He now had Neil by the short hairs, but his brother remained unaware of what Stewart had done.

"Neil never had any idea I kept those notes," said Stewart.

After working with Crotsley for several months on the Ninja Murders, the thing that Jack Holder came to admire most about his partner was his work ethic, his single-minded, bulldog approach to the hardest part of the detective's job: meticulously building an unshakable case by assembling legions of damning details.

"If I asked him to do something, he did it," said Holder. "He goes straight down that line, he doesn't go to the right or to the left, he goes to the objective and he completes it."

Crotsley had also proven himself to Holder in another important way: no task was too dirty, too ugly, too intimidating for him. "I don't want to say I gave Richie assignments," said Holder. "We didn't have a partnership like that. We worked together, and I did certain things, and he did others. But when I asked him to do something, he did it. If it took a week or a month it would get done," said Holder.

As an investigator, Holder's strength was interviewing witnesses. He could be a hardass, even a badass, if that's what it took. But that wasn't his strongest suit. Holder was masterful at getting witnesses to trust him, to tell him everything they knew, even when it was the sort of things that might make them look foolish, or stupid—or even criminal. Jack brought to his work an innate sympathy; he felt that the friends and family of those murdered are also victims, that bringing baddies to justice was necessary for the survivors to begin healing. He was good at putting people at ease, and encouraged witnesses to call him by his first name.

"Every case I've ever done, I get very close to the people that are involved in it," said Holder. "Because I need them, and I can't be standoffish. I don't coach them and tell them what I want them to say, but like the old saying, you catch a lot more flies with honey than you do with vinegar.

"Defense attorneys make a big deal out of this," continued Holder. "They say, 'Oh, you call him *Jack*?' and they try to make the jury think there's something wrong about that."

Not every witness brings to Holder the empathy that allows him to enter into a first-name relationship. And, even in a murder case, not every potential witness comes forward of his or her own volition. Accordingly, following the arrests, Holder and Crotsley went out to the Chatsworth factory to interview Manchester's employees, among them Steve Strawn.

"Strawn and Rick Wilson, they're right out of the same mold," said Holder. "Assholes. I don't think they knew that the Woodmans were going to be murdered, but they did know about the Homicks. After we did the search warrant, we got information from somebody that Strawn had removed evidence from underneath Neil's desk and destroyed it.

"This evidence was Steve Homick's business cards. We talk to Strawn—and a cadet at the Academy could have got the information out of them, that's how easy it was. It's not that we *got* the information, but the fact that we had to *ask* because he didn't volunteer," explained Holder.

"I mean, he picked up an eight-hundred-pound oak desk with Steve Homick's business cards underneath it, and here's Homick in jail for murder, and he doesn't call the police, he throws the cards away," said Holder.

Holder delivered an impromptu lecture on penalties associated with California obstruction of justice statutes, and Strawn agreed to testify about what he had found under Neil's desk, and about Neil's request that he destroy this evidence.

Among the items recovered from Robert Homick's apartment was a pair of bolt cutters. The LAPD Crime Lab confirmed that they had been used to cut the links in the bicycle chain securing gates at Brentwood Place, the murder site.

But juries are odd creatures, and good defense attorneys are expert at planting the seeds of doubt. If only one juror could be convinced that these bolt cutters *might* have belonged to someone else, then it was a short leap to the possibility that Robert wasn't involved in the murders—and a hung jury.

So Holder set out to tighten the noose. "A lot of people think that finding out where Robert bought the bolt cutters was a great piece of investigation," said Holder. "But I knew Robert was *lazy*. He was not going to do anything that took effort. Where's the closest hardware store? On Santa Monica Boulevard, two blocks from his apartment. I walked down there and said, 'Do you sell cutters like this?'

"They said, 'Yes, we do.'

" 'Have you ever seen this man?'

" 'Yes, I have.'

" 'Do you remember him buying these cutters?'

" 'Yes, he did.'

"No big deal."

Also found in Robert's apartment was the mobile telephone from Stewart's Rolls-Royce, not a link to the murder but a connection to Stewart.

"The phone has a serial number and we ran it," said Crotsley. "When Stewart reported his Rolls stolen he reported his telephone stolen, because it was in his car. So then we go to the phone company and say, 'What car did you install this in?' and they say, 'Here's our records, we put it in Stewart Woodman's Rolls-Royce.' And one of the installers remembered that Rolls because it was almost an antique."

Beyond the limited physical evidence tying the Homicks to the

Woodmans, witnesses and documents established motives for the murders: insurance money and hatred. But prosecutors also needed to show a jury not only that the Woodmans knew the Homicks, but that they had been in communication among themselves just before the murders.

That made Holder's and Crotsley's expeditions to locate pay phones, a big investment in time, gasoline, and shoe leather, one of the more important elements of their investigation.

The partners had driven and walked around Chatsworth to find all the pay phones near Manchester Products. They had canvassed Sawtelle for a few blocks around Robert Homick's apartment. Then Crotsley plotted all pay phone locations and numbers on a map.

Records of all calls from these coin telephones during the months before and after the murders were subpoenaed. Search warrants yielded phone bills from Manchester and from Stewart's and Neil's home phones. Holder and Crotsley had asked the California Attorney General's Office to keyboard these forty-one thousand call records into their computer, then sort and print them out to illuminate any patterns that emerged.

In this way, Holder and Crotsley found a small group of calls between pay phones near Robert Homick's apartment and other pay phones in gas stations, convenience stores, and donut shops within a few miles of Manchester Products.

They found another group of calls from Sawtelle-area pay phones to pay phones near Steve Homick's home and Art Taylor's CB shop. And they found calls from Las Vegas pay phones to the same pay phones near Manchester.

And all this because the FBI wiretaps had Steve, William, and Robert Homick repeatedly using the phrase "box to box," which meant from one pay phone to another.

"This thing comes down to about three days of phone calls," said Holder. "The computer told us stuff like, 'Phone number 123 called phone number 456 twenty-seven times during the time period.'"

This information was broken out in several different ways that could be presented to a jury, different ways of looking at facts that essentially confirmed the detectives' working hypothesis: in the days before the murders, Woodmans were talking to Homicks several times a day. "The Woodmans used pay phones near their business, and the Homicks used other pay phones," explained Holder. "Robert used phones along Santa Monica Boulevard near his apartment. He took calls there from the Woodmans, and he made calls there to his brother in Vegas."

The printouts also suggested that during the days before the Yom Kippur murders, Robert several times called Manchester from a pay phone. His calls were short, less than a minute. About thirty minutes later, more or less, one of the Woodmans called him back from a pay phone near their factory.

From subpoenaed telephone records came another fact: Steve had regularly made calls from Las Vegas and elsewhere to various Los Angeles pay phones and billed them to Manchester. "The printout told us the number of times Steve called Robert and charged it to Manchester, and the number of times he called Manchester from Vegas and reversed the charges," said Crotsley.

The wheels of justice, by Los Angeles standards, ground quickly onward. On May 9, 1986, Dominguez pleaded guilty to being the lookout during the murder of Gerry and Vera Woodman.

Three days later, Neil and Stewart Woodman, Steve and Robert Homick, and Sonny Majoy all entered not guilty pleas to Municipal Court Judge Sandy Kriegler at a preliminary hearing. Since the sole purpose of a prelim is to allow a judge to determine if there is sufficient evidence to *try* an accused, defense attorneys do not put on witnesses or offer evidence.

First to testify was Jean Scherrer, who said that Steve Homick had offered to kill Vera and Gerry if it was necessary to prevent them from attending Neil's son Paul's bar mitzvah, and that Neil had told him and O'Grady to use their guns if they had to to keep his parents away from the bar mitzvah.

CHAPTER Twenty-four

Trials

Ex parte is Latin for "from one side only." In California's courts, an *ex parte* proceeding is generally held in judge's chambers with lawyers and/or witnesses from either the prosecution or defense—but not from both.

Such hearings are common and quite legal, so long as certain rules are observed. One of these is that in capital cases, the entire proceeding *must* be on the record, so that in the event of an appeal, appellate judges will be able to review every ruling and the facts and circumstances supporting it. Prosecutors rarely initiate *ex parte* proceedings, and even more rarely during preliminary hearings. But when they do, they often ask the judge to seal the record to protect ongoing investigations. Defense motions in opposition to such sealings are common, but judges often rule against them.

When the Woodmans, the Homicks, and Sonny Majoy came before Judge Sandy Kriegler for their preliminary hearing, Deputy D.A. John Krayniak's second witness was the Professor, Stewart Siegel. The defense, which suspected that Siegel had a history as a snitch, challenged Siegel's admissibility as a witness. So Krayniak, a former Pasadena policeman, asked for an *ex parte* hearing.

Jack Holder accompanied Krayniak, Siegel, and a court reporter to the judge's chambers.

According to Holder, "The judge said to the famous Stewart Siegel, 'Have you ever told anything to any other agency other than what you've told the LAPD?'

"Well, of course he had," said Holder. "Who knows what he's told the FBI, and we'll never know what he's told other agencies. But the FBI told him, 'Under no circumstances ever tell anybody that you're our snitch, or what you've told us.'"

So Siegel remained silent.

"Have you ever told anything about this case to anybody else?" asked Judge Kriegler.

"Your Honor, I can't answer that until I ask you a question," replied Siegel.

"Okay," said the judge, "we'll go off the record."

The court reporter lifted her fingers from the keyboard.

"I told the FBI certain things, but they told me not to tell anybody. So, do I have to tell you?"

Judge Kriegler asked Siegel to say what the FBI had warned him never to divulge—that he had been a paid FBI informant who had taken money in exchange for information provided to the New Jersey Gaming Commission. But the judge kept Siegel's testimony off the record. Kriegler did this, he would later announce to the news media, because to do otherwise "would constitute a clear danger to Mr. Siegel's well-being."

Later, in open court, Siegel testified that he'd known Steve Homick for several years, and that Steve had told him the previous September that "Neil and Stewart were having some financial difficulties and he was employed to kill two people" for $20,000. "I didn't believe it," said Siegel. "It went in one ear and out the other. I knew Mr. Homick and I didn't think he was capable of it."

But the next time Siegel saw Homick, Steve told him that "We put five in them." The Professor also testified that in September 1985 he'd loaned Steve four two-way radios and a lapel microphone for what Homick said was "surveillance." Siegel added that Steve had also questioned him about the meaning of Yom Kippur and what activities Jews customarily engage in on that day.

On cross-examination, Siegel admitted that he hoped to get a lighter sentence for grand theft charges he faced in connection with the bingo scam. But the Professor, mindful of heavyweight thugs still doing hard time because of what he had secretly told the FBI and the New Jersey Gaming Commission, denied ever having been a paid government informant.

Judge Kriegler knew this was perjury, but he said nothing at the time.

Next, Steve Strawn testified about Neil's postarrest request to destroy papers hidden under his desk, and about the check he'd prepared for Stewart to give to Robert Homick.

Mike Dominguez took the stand to describe lookout duty. He said that when he saw Gerry driving home on Yom Kippur night, he radioed ahead with a walkie-talkie. "I told them, 'They're coming, they're on the way.' I knew what was going to happen," said Mike. "They would be killed."

Dominguez also confessed to several other crimes, including the Godfrey murder. He said that Homick had paid him $7,000 to torch the Maui boardinghouse and another home in Texas.

Anthony Majoy did not testify at the prelim, but Krayniak played a tape recording of an interview he had given to police after his first arrest. On that tape, Majoy said that Steve had told him, "We picked this day [Yom Kippur] for access."

"That was a holiday," said Majoy. "They would be together."

On the tape, Majoy denied having any role in the shootings. "I knew they [the Homick brothers and Dominguez] were planning to bring harm to somebody, but all I know is that I wasn't there," said Majoy. "I have no idea why Dominguez is putting me at the scene of the crime."

Majoy acknowledged that he had received $20,000 from Robert Homick in early 1986. He said it was a loan from the Woodman brothers to start a video business.

Sybil Michelson testified that Stewart had called her two days before the murders to ask about the traditional break-the-fast gathering. Krayniak introduced telephone records to show that Robert Homick called Manchester one minute before Stewart called Sybil. Five minutes after Stewart's call to his aunt, Robert called Stewart again. Both calls were from pay phones.

After hearing these witnesses, Judge Kriegler ruled that all defendants would stand trial on murder and conspiracy charges. "Based on the evidence, it is obvious to the court that there was a conspiracy to murder" Gerry and Vera, said Kriegler. "Why would people with no independent motive become involved in the execution-style murder of Gerald and Vera Woodman? That, to me, is the crux of why the focus shifts to Neil and Stewart Woodman," he added.

Stewart was stunned by the ruling. He stared blankly at Melody, who burst into tears. Soon Maxine, Neil's wife, and Majoy's two daughters joined her.

Gerald Chaleff, looking professorial with his neat salt-and-pepper beard, dark-rimmed spectacles, and a brown double-breasted suit, handled the hallway press conference masterfully. He told reporters that the case against Neil was "long in motives and short in facts. If this is the evidence they present at the trial, there will not be a conviction."

Jay Jaffe told the media that the evidence against Stewart "doesn't even rise to the level of a suspicion."

While they awaited trial, Rabbi Stephen Reuben, then of Temple Judea, visited the brothers in the county jail. His conversations with them revolved around the strain that their arrests had put on their families. They said, "What do we tell our kids about the justice system, about America?"

"They felt it was unjust, they imagined what their families were being put through by police coming in and ransacking their home and terrifying their families," said Reuben.

"I kept telling them not to worry. They said, 'We haven't done anything, it'll be okay, justice will prevail and we'll be out of here.'"

Neil and Stewart told Reuben the *only* reason they were in jail was "because their sisters were out to get them and had made big contributions to [D.A.] Ira Reiner's campaign," said Reuben. "If that's true or not I have no idea."

As is standard in capital cases, bail for all five accused killers was denied.

While cooling his heels in the VIP wing of the Los Angeles County Jail, Neil came to believe that there was a way to beat the murder charges by explaining away his and Stewart's connections with the Homicks. This, however, depended on Stewart's cooperation, and that of Steve Homick. To bring his brother aboard, Neil begged a yellow legal pad from Gerald Chaleff and, during a few minutes when he was waiting alone in the attorney's visiting area, wrote Stewart a two-page letter, printing his words in neat capital letters between the green–ruled lines:

JERRY TOLD ME THE JUDGE TOLD HIM THAT HE (THE JUDGE) WOULD NOT LIKE TO BE THE D.A. TRYING TO CONVICT YOU & ME! JERRY SAID THAT THAT MEANS WE HAVE A GREAT CHANCE AT COMPLETE SUCCESS! I AM NOT JUST SAYING THAT & NOR WAS JERRY!

MAX SAYS THAT SOME OF OUR FRIENDS WANT TO HOLD A BIG FUND RAISER FOR US & IF DONE RIGHT COULD ALSO MAKE THE PAPERS & MEDIA (THEY ARE SOME OF OUR FRIENDS). ARNE LATKIN THINKS WE SHOULD HIRE AN AGENT TO GET US POSITIVE NEWS IN THE PAPER & TV. SHE IS GOING TO TALK TO JERRY IF WE SAY TO—I THINK WE HAVE SAT LONG ENOUGH—SILENT—WHAT DO YOU THINK?

THE THING WITH MR. "S" IS ONLY "IN CASE" WE HAVE TO THINK OF A WAY IT COULD BE DONE WHERE HE CAN SAVE HIS BROTHER—OTHERWISE IT WON'T WORK. IT MAY TAKE ME A FEW WEEKS, BUT, I AM CONVINCED HE WOULD DO IT IF IT WAS A FOOLPROOF WAY TO SAVE US & BROTHER—EVEN IF HE HAS TO TAKE MAJOY WITH HIM. NEVER TALK TO "S" OR BROTHER ONLY ME (ABOUT THIS)—I HAVE BROTHER WORKING ON REASONS FOR HIM TO HAVE BEEN THERE THAT DAMN NIGHT & BEFORE ON JUNE 22—IF WE COULD DO THAT HE ("S") WOULD I'M SURE SAY IT WAS HIM AND DOM & MAYBE MAJOY & THE ONLY CATCH IS THAT IT IS VERIFIABLE AND BELIEVABLE & TRY TO THINK OF ANGLES & AND WE CAN DISCUSS THEM ON VISITS ETC.—NEVER PASS A NOTE ABOUT THIS SUBJECT! ABOUT THE JUDGES—MAURY'S—1 WORKS NOW AND 2 OTHERS ARE ELECTED & START IN NOVEMBER—HIS FRIEND OWNS THEM—AS AN OUTSIDE CHANCE—IF THINGS AREN'T GOING AS WE WANT—WE COULD DELAY IF WE THOUGHT WE HAD A VERY GOOD CHANCE OF GETTING THEM! I KNOW IT SEEMS A LONG TIME—BUT IF IT WOULD MAKE THE DIFF'S WHO CARES? (I THINK WE WON'T NEED TO WAIT THOUGH.)

THe ONLY THING ABOUT THE TRIAL THAT BOTHERS JERRY IS THAT AS YOU KNOW SOME "EVIDENCE" POINTS TO ME & SOME AT YOU (ALTHOUGH HE SAYS IT ALL ADDS UP TO DOG SHIT) & IN COURT CAN BE VERY UPSETTING WHEN JERRY & JAY START MAKING IT LOOK LIKE THAT

YOU ARE POINTING AT ME AND VISA [sic] VERSA! HE KNOWS IT WILL BE
VERY UPSETTING FOR BOTH OF US—THAT IS WHAT HE MEANS WHEN HE
SAYS HE IS WORRIED. EXCEPT JAY WOULD HAVE TO SAY THE $$$ (IF IT
COMES OUT) CAME FROM MY ACCOUNT—JERRY WOULD HAVE TO BRING
OUT YOUR PHONE CALLS—I SAID IT CAN ALL BE EXPLAINED, ETC.—I
WOULD NEVER LET JERRY DO ANYTHING TO "POINT A FINGER"—I
ASSUME YOU WOULD [sic] EITHER—SO—ALL WE HAVE TO DO IS EXPLAIN
JUNE 22 (JERRY IS WORKING ON THAT) & IRON GATES—JERRY IS CON-
VINCED THAT IS <u>EASY</u>! & WE WILL DO IT—DON'T WORRY—JERRY SAID HE
WILL GET ME (MEANING US) OFF & HE THINKS JAY (LIKE YOU) WAS JUST
VERY DEPRESSED & TALKED TO YOU TOO SOON—HE DOESN'T FEEL THE
ASSOCIATION WITH "S" IS TOO HARD TO GET OVER!! PLEASE THINK
ABOUT THOSE PARTS THAT I TOLD YOU TO—I NEED YOUR HELP—WE
ONLY DISCUSS—FACE TO FACE OR WHEN YOU OR I CAN HAND THE
NOTE PERSONALLY—LOVE YOU.

Stewart secreted the note among his personal belongings. Some-
day it might be useful, he thought, especially if the time came when
he might need some leverage on Neil. Indeed, ultimately the letter
would find its way onto the prosecution's list of potential witnesses.

Neil and Stewart filed into Superior Court on July 16 to enter
pleas of not guilty. Judge Ernest Hirashige set July 24 as the open-
ing day of the trial, when pretrial motions would be argued.

Just as jury selection was about to begin, everything was put on
hold. When they learned of the few moments that Judge Kriegler
had allowed the Professor's *ex parte* examination to go off the
record, defense counsels for all the accused appealed the prelimi-
nary hearing. All asserted that the judge had knowingly allowed
Siegel to perjure himself in open court about being a paid govern-
ment informant. And, they argued, by denying them access to the
ex parte transcript for months, they were illegally denied informa-
tion needed to discredit Siegel in cross-examination.

The D.A.'s answering brief argued that despite the perjured tes-
timony, Judge Kriegler was not deceived about Siegel's true motiva-
tions, and that the defendants' attorneys had eventually received
transcripts of the *ex parte* hearing.

While these arguments were considered by the Court of Appeals,
the Superior Court proceedings were suspended.

In a few months four of the five defendants got *pro forma* notice that their appeals were rejected. The Court of Appeals, however, agreed to consider Neil Woodman's appeal.

Following their arrests early in 1986, the Woodman brothers, the Homick brothers, and Sonny Majoy were detained in the Los Angeles County Jail, where except for very occasional court appearances and conferences with their attorneys, they had little to do all day but talk and dream.

And scheme.

While they awaited trial, the Woodmans and the Homicks ran into a County Jail inmate named John Di Angelo, a cat burglar who specialized in major-score hotel robberies. Di Angelo also dabbled in con games, which was what had brought him to the County Jail on this occasion.

"Di Angelo tells the Woodmans and Steve Homick that he's got access to a guy with stolen Mexican gold coins—and the guy will turn them over for five thousand dollars," said Holder. "The whole thing is a scam. Now, here's Neil, a guy accused of murdering his parents, claiming he's innocent, and he gets his wife to borrow five thousand dollars from her father and bring it down to the County Jail and give it to this con man for hot gold. This is the kind of mind that Neil Woodman has.

"I understand Chaleff went through the ceiling when he heard about that," chuckled Holder. "Because that was five thousand *he* didn't get."

Di Angelo wanted Neil's $5,000 because he was due to get out of jail soon. He arranged for the money to be paid to an outside confederate, and told Neil that as soon as he was out he'd pick up the coins and give them to Neil's wife, Maxine. Of course, he never did. And he's now serving a sentence in a Federal pen.

While the "Ninja" murder defendants awaited their day in a Los Angeles court, Nevada went forward with its prosecution of Steve Homick. He was extradited to Las Vegas on September 14, 1987, to begin the process leading to his trial for the Tipton murders. But that trial was also delayed.

*   *   *

On Tuesday, April 12, 1988, the California Court of Appeals ruled on Neil Woodman's appeal. Writing for the two-to-one majority, Justice Leon Thompson said Judge Kriegler had erred in meeting privately with Stewart Siegel because he had thereby deprived the defendants of their right to effective counsel, and because this had infringed on their rights to due process of law.

Murder charges against Neil and Stewart Woodman, Robert and Steve Homick, and Anthony Majoy were dismissed.

Jack Holder was outraged.

"Majoy and the Homicks sent up their appeal. They got a post-card denial, which is normal. Neil sends his up on the same issues and they throw the prelim out? Give me a break. It leads you to wonder," said Holder.

No matter how it happened, the score was now Gerald Chaleff, one, L.A. County District Attorney, zero.

The "Ninja" murders and the investigation that followed came at a time when Los Angeles County District Attorney Ira Reiner was coming under repeated and highly publicized criticism for his office's performance in several other high-profile cases.

One was the so-called "Twilight Zone" case, where a helicopter crash on a movie set killed two child actors and veteran actor Vic Morrow. Five high-profile movie executives, including director John Landis, were indicted on charges of criminal negligence, but a jury cleared them all.

Another case constantly in the news was the McMartin Pre-school case. Hundreds of counts of child molesting were brought against members of a family that ran a popular preschool. The media was full of allegations about satanic rituals. Several family members were charged initially—one, Raymond Buckey, shared a cell with the Woodman brothers for a time—but none were convicted.

Because of these and other failed prosecutions, those who ran the D.A.'s office sometimes appeared stupid, misguided, or ineffec-tual. By 1986, the D.A.'s office had adopted a siege mentality. So it was not surprising that when the Court of Appeals threw out the prelims for the Ninja Murder suspects, D.A. Reiner's office announced that rather than simply refiling charges, he would ask the Second District Court of Appeals to retry the issue before dif-ferent appellate jurists.

On May 24, the Second District ruled against L.A. County.

Chaleff, two, L.A. District Attorney, zero.

The D.A. appealed to the California Supreme Court, asking that august body to reinstitute murder charges.

Just before its 1988 summer recess, the state Supreme Court announced that it would not hear the case.

Chaleff, three, L.A. District Attorney, zero.

So Reiner refiled all charges, and the process began again. Except, by this time, the only attorneys whose calendars would allow them to defend a murder trial were those representing Stewart Woodman and Sonny Majoy.

Their cases were separated from those of the Homick brothers and Neil Woodman. Early in 1989, after an uneventful arraignment and preliminary hearing, jury selection began.

By this time John Krayniak, who was widely if erroneously perceived as the goat in the *ex parte* fiasco, had moved on.

The new prosecution team was headed by Patrick R. Dixon, and seconded by John M. Zajec. Their offices, on the eighteenth floor of the Criminal Courts Building in downtown Los Angeles, were a far cry from the opulence of Jaffe's Century City suite and the charming seaside cottage where Chaleff hangs his hat. Dixon's office, shared with another deputy D.A., was grimly functional, jammed with law books and case files. It had scuffed tile floors and faded travel posters on the walls. Zajec was forced to work out of a windowless, stifling cubbyhole that doubled as a storage closet.

But these men did not practice law for the satisfaction of spending their time among fine furnishings.

Dixon was in his late thirties, six feet tall, blond and slim, with the musculature and shoulders of a swimmer. Always exceptionally well-dressed and groomed, in a courtroom he conquered his inherent shyness. Though Dixon sometimes seemed slightly stiff, his well-spoken phrases could rise to eloquence. An alumnus of the University of Southern California (USC), he was active in the local Bar Association and a Lincoln Club (an old, monied Establishment group) Republican. "Pat Dixon could be a U.S. senator if he wanted to," said Holder. "He could be a judge tomorrow, if he wanted it."

Indeed, more Southern California judges are USC alumni than

those of any other university, and most were appointed by other USC grads.

Many colleagues and defense attorneys know, however, that Dixon has a hair-trigger temper. If he rarely displays it to judges, more than one lawyer has felt Dixon's sudden, inexplicable wrath. "You could ask him the time of day, and if he didn't like your tone of voice he'd jump down your throat," said Malcolm Funderburke, who spent nearly twenty years in the D.A.'s office before returning to private practice.

John Zajec was almost Dixon's exact opposite. Dark haired and soft-spoken, a rumpled, beardless but decidedly Lincolnesque presence, he was bulldog methodical.

"He's the one that took this entire case and put it in a computer," explained Holder. "He handles bank records and all like that. That's his bailiwick. Zajec is even more straight arrow than Dixon—as straight as they come. They complement each other a great deal."

Because of the immense publicity surrounding the Ninja Murders case, jury selection was exceptionally difficult. It took more than six months to seat a panel; testimony in the trial did not begin until August 1989.

By that time, a Las Vegas jury had convicted Steve Homick on three counts of murder and sentenced him to die by lethal injection. While Stewart's trial was in progress, Steve was on death row in a Carson City prison, awaiting the outcome of his appeal of both convictions and sentence.

Whenever a major case is brought to trial, prosecutors must convince the jury that the accused is/are responsible. This requires development of a theory that answers the questions *why* was this crime committed, *how* did it happen—and therefore, *who* did it.

The prosecution's theory of the case was that the brothers killed their mother in order to collect $506,000 in insurance. They killed their father "out of pure hatred." Pat Dixon told jurors that Stewart was a "linchpin" in the plot.

The defense counsel's task is to develop a *different* theory to explain the case. The successful hypothesis explains how the crime was committed by someone other than the defendant.

Once Jay Jaffe had the three notes that Neil had written in jail and passed to Stewart, he had the basis for a case theory that shifted all blame away from his client. In his opening statement, Jaffe made his theory quite plain: Neil Woodman, and Neil alone, had ordered the murders of Gerry and Vera Woodman *out of love for his brother.*

"Neil Woodman, from the time they were children, was an overprotective brother," Jaffe told the jury. "He saw the stress that his brother was going through and this interpersonal conflict that Stewart had [with his parents]."

Knowing of Stewart's poor health, including his heart problems and gout, "the last thing [Neil] wanted to do was involve his brother in a conspiracy," said Jaffe.

During a recess, Jaffe told reporters: "To the extent that either of the Woodmans was involved, the evidence will clearly indicate that it was Neil and not Stewart." While his client, Neil, was not on trial here, Gerald Chaleff nevertheless felt moved to offer a different theory to the media mob that clustered in courthouse corridors: Steve Homick and Mike Dominguez had intended to *rob* the senior Woodmans, but wound up killing them instead.

"Neil Woodman had nothing to do with the murder of his parents. Period," said Chaleff.

In his opening statement, Jaffe agreed that the brothers were deeply in debt at the time of the murders. But, he insisted, the case had little to do with insurance money; the payoff represented only 11 percent of what they owed.

If unflattering information is to be introduced by prosecutors, a skilled defense counsel will attempt to defuse its effect by volunteering potentially damaging facts first.

Thus Jaffe was quick to acknowledge that Stewart was a gambler who spent money "foolishly." He also conceded that after Vera sided with Gerry in the struggle to control Manchester, Stewart had told people, "I hate them. I wish they were dead."

"He was a bigmouth and a big shot, but deep down he knew better," Jaffe asserted.

As for the Homicks, Jaffe had hoped to show that Steve had acted as a "modern-day Robin Hood" when he murdered the elder Woodmans. To prove this, Jaffe tried to introduce evidence suggesting that Steve had acted on his own initiative in the slaying of

Raymond Godfrey, in the three Tipton murders, and in three other serious crimes for which he had been convicted.

"I wanted to proceed by way of the theory that Steve did things on his own, and then looked at the five different cases where this occurred," explained Jaffe. "The Woodman case was just one of them, and if we had gotten that in I think it would have given the jury another option to consider."

Judge Candace Cooper excluded all this evidence, saying it was inconclusive and would unnecessarily lengthen the trial.

Because witnesses are excluded from the courtroom except when they are themselves testifying, Jack Holder did not testify at Stewart's trial. Instead he sat with Dixon and Zajec at the prosecutor's table. Holder held the entire case in his mind, reams of minutiae that the lawyers could tap instantly. He also worked with individual witnesses, bringing them into court and helping to prepare them to testify.

Holder's role left Rich Crotsley free to testify about the crime scene and about evidence from the police investigation.

To sketch the story behind the lawsuit that led to the family breakup, Dixon put several members of the Covel clan on the witness stand, including Muriel and Lou Jackson, Sybil and Sid Michelson, Gloria Karns, and siblings Maxine and Wayne.

Steve Strawn and Rick Wilson described their own actions in falsifying documents to siphon millions from Union Bank.

Several other Manchester employees, including Vicky Wayne, Richard Nuckles, Nancy Housel—an office worker who had defected to Woodman Industries—Fred Woodard, Robin Lewis, and Catherine Clemente, testified about the strange working environment at the plastics company, and about the Woodman clan's feud.

Jack Swartz and his daughter Tracy recounted their dispute with Stewart Woodman and Robert Homick's attempt to intimidate them into a financial settlement.

Union Bank officials, including Diane Eng and Jon Strayer, testified about Manchester's mounting debt crisis. A C.P.A. named Stanley Levine testified that $3.6 million Manchester owed Union Bank was unaccounted for.

Dominguez, who after his confession in Las Vegas had led

Holder and Crotsley on a tour of every place he visited on his excursion to murder Vera and Gerry, testified about his role as a lookout in the Woodman murders.

Crotsley took the stand to present the damning pattern of pay telephone calls between the Woodmans and the Homicks. "This was very damaging," explained Holder. "The jury could see how and when they were talking to each other just before the murders, and just before the earlier attempt on June 22, Gerry's and Vera's wedding anniversary."

Other prosecution witnesses described how Robert Homick had parked across the street from Brentwood Place almost all day on June 22, 1985, and how Homick had cased Brentwood Place by feigning interest in buying one of the building's units. Betty Saul described seeing Robert near the Fine Affair Restaurant on Moraga Drive early on the evening of the murders. Richard Altman described the hit-and-run accident in the alley behind the murder scene.

Norma Drinkern, a True Value Hardware clerk, identified Robert as the purchaser of a set of bolt cutters like those found in his apartment. A police forensic expert described the perfect match between striations on the bolt cutter's blades and marks on the chain-link halves found near the gate.

Insurance agent Harold Albaum testified about the insurance on Vera's life, and about Vera's and Muriel's attempts to have it canceled. Officials from the California Department of Insurance took the stand to describe the letters that Vera and Albaum had sent in an effort to cancel the policy.

Stewart Siegel did not testify. "He was seriously ill with cancer at a medical facility—if you can believe it—the Mayo Clinic," said Holder. "Only the best for our prisoners. The judge authorized Richie and me to charter a Learjet air ambulance with two pilots, a doctor and a nurse, fly to Minnesota, pick him up, bring him out here. After he testified, we were going to fly him back. It was only going to cost the taxpayers fifty thousand dollars to bring out this con man. The night before we were to leave, I got a call from Rochester," added Holder. "The son-of-a-bitch died on me."

So the prosecutors played the videotape Siegel had made as part of his plea bargain.

Melody Woodman came to court virtually every day for nearly six months of jury selection and never wore the same dress twice. Shortly before testimony began, when it was revealed that she would be a defense witness, however, Melody was barred from the courtroom.

One evening when court was out of session, Stewart was beaten up by a fellow inmate. He claims this assault was ordered by Steve Homick and Neil to discourage him from testifying against them.

Holder pooh-poohs this: "He used to take the phone all night. He'd call and talk to his bookies—just monopolized the phone. If there's only one phone and you want to use it and you're a big, bad thug and you've got this pussy standing there, you thump him, and that's what happened to Stewart."

In all criminal proceedings, the prosecution is obliged to turn over copies of all evidence to the defense, a process known as "discovery." (Because the Fifth Amendment guarantees protection against self-incrimination, however, the defense is not required to share evidence with the prosecution.) So, well before trial, Dixon and Zajec provided all defense attorneys, including Jaffe, with evidence, including copies of Steve Homick's diaries and the forty-one thousand numbers (on a computer printout) that came from subpoenaed telephone records.

It was an enormous volume of information.

One of the most damning facts came from one of Steve's diaries: the number of a pay telephone at a mini-market very near Stewart's Hidden Hills home. Steve Homick called the number at 7:17 on the morning of September 25, 1985. He made that call from another pay phone, and he had charged it to Manchester.

As part of discovery, Jaffe had been given the diary page—among hundreds of others—that held this number. He had also been given a printout documenting forty-one thousand telephone calls. Unlike the police, however, he hadn't made the connection. He was surprised when this evidence was offered to the jury.

"That was one that got by," said Jaffe. "There must have been a million facts I knew, and the million-and-one they get."

When Pat Dixon made his presentation, he suggested that this particular telephone call, coming as it did on the morning of the murders, gave the lie to the defense theory that Neil, and Neil alone, had plotted the murders.

It was a devastating blow to the defense.

When the prosecution had rested its case, Jay Jaffe put Melody on the stand to testify about her strange meeting with Neil at El Caballero in the spring of 1984. And he entered into evidence the damning notes that Stewart had manipulated from Neil in jail.

Jay Jaffe had planned to make Stewart his last witness. "I expected Stewart would testify—until the last couple weeks of the trial," said Jaffe. "[Then] I sat down with Stewart, Melody, and [co-counsel] David Wesley and we all agreed that he shouldn't. But obviously, if Stewart had insisted on testifying, that would have been his decision."

Stewart would later remember things very differently.

"We had Stewart's testimony all mapped out," continued Jaffe. "But toward the end we thought the prosecution's case could only be strengthened if Stewart testified. They would have been able to fill in blanks where otherwise they could not have done so.

"For example: there were a lot of phone records, calls placed from gas stations near Manchester Products. But no one ever saw Stewart use those phones. Had Stewart testified, the D.A. would have had an opportunity on cross-examination to ask about every one of those phone calls," said Jaffe.

"Stewart couldn't very well deny it, because we all knew that he made the phone calls," added Jaffe. "He might have come up with an explanation like, 'We used those phone booths to make bets for gambling.' That's kind of a flimsy excuse."

Jaffe anticipated that once Stewart was on the witness stand, forced to offer explanations to certain things which police could not themselves explain, it would have strengthened the prosecution's case immeasurably.

"I didn't think the prosecution had enough to convict him," said Jaffe. "I didn't want to give them more than they had."

Had Stewart taken the stand, prosecutors would have the opportunity on cross-examination to go through their entire case a second time. "They could have asked Stewart about his relationship with every one of the witnesses. They might have asked, 'Stewart, did you tell this witness that? Did you ever say this? Did you ever say you hated your father?'

"It would have compounded the prosecution's case," added Jaffe. "The jury would have been reminded again and again, ad nauseam, of everything that they heard in the trial."

Stewart, who had been looking forward to the opportunity to tell his version of events since the day he was arrested, was disappointed. At the time, however, he didn't fault Jaffe's reasoning.

Pat Dixon was elated. "I was prepared to cross-examine Stewart," said Dixon. "But this guy is a terrific salesman. Look at all he did to build that company. Maybe he could have sold himself to the jury. Maybe."

During the year-long trial, Stewart often expressed confidence that he would not be found guilty. "He felt good the whole time," said Rabbi Reuben. "He'd say, 'Oh, we wiped them out here and there. They have no evidence. They have nothing. It's circumstantial—I *knew* this person, I *talked* to that one. They're building their case out of that I knew the people that allegedly murdered my parents, and they'd done money transfers and so on, but it's all circumstantial.'"

The jury took only a few hours to find Stewart Woodman and Anthony Majoy guilty of murder in the first degree.

"Like the infamous Professor Siegel said, if the Homicks had just kept a roll of quarters in their pocket they'd have all been home free," said an elated Jack Holder.

"Stewart was feeling very good, and all of a sudden *boom*, he's convicted of murder. He never expected that," said Didi Reuben, wife of Rabbi Stephen Reuben.

Stewart was in shock. So was Jaffe, who had been confident that with only circumstantial evidence against his client, the jury would believe that Neil alone was responsible.

In California, sentencing in felony cases is delayed for thirty days following conviction to allow time for preparation of a probation report. In a murder case where there are "special circumstances," which include murder for financial gain and laying in wait for a victim, a jury decides if the convicted should get life without the possibility of parole, or death by asphyxiation in the gas chamber.

A death penalty hearing is like a miniature trial, with both sides allowed to introduce evidence and call witnesses. A jury is asked to decide whether the convicted is to live or die.

No lawyer likes to lose, and capital cases are always emotion-laden. But after Stewart's conviction, Jaffe was devastated. "We became very, very close. I got very personally involved in the case," said Jaffe. "I honestly did believe that he was innocent. That was what caused me to devote four years of my life to his case. I couldn't imagine he'd be found guilty."

A few weeks after the verdict, Jaffe was devastated again. Stewart telephoned, asking him to come to the jail. In the attorney's room, he hunched forward and quietly told Jaffe that he was, in fact, guilty.

"Now," said Stewart, "go talk to Dixon. Tell him I'll testify against Neil and the Homicks. Make me a deal.

"You've got to save my life."

CHAPTER Twenty-five

Confessions

In April 1990, after an extended death-penalty hearing, the same jury that had convicted Stewart and Sonny Majoy found Majoy guilty of "special circumstances," and Judge Candace Cooper sentenced Majoy to die in the gas chamber at San Quentin Prison.

Stewart's sentencing, however, was deferred.

Jay Jaffe, emotionally shattered by Stewart's confession, could hardly trust himself to speak to his client. Jaffe turned the delicate negotiations to save Stewart's life over to his able co-counsel, David Wesley.

Dixon was open to the possibility of a deal. He knew that Chaleff, representing Neil, was a formidable opponent who, within the limits of the legal system, would go to almost any length to prolong a trial, badger a witness, confuse a jury—whatever it took to sow doubt in even one juror's mind.

And the evidence against Neil was, as it had been against Stewart, largely circumstantial. No one had seen Neil use pay phones to call the Homicks. One jury had found the prosecution's case sufficiently compelling to vote for conviction—but another might not.

If Stewart, however, removed the veils shrouding his clan's Byzantine relationships, if he painted in the details of Manchester's financial plight and revealed the depth and nature of Neil's relationship with the Homicks, it would give the prosecution a far stronger case, especially against the Homicks.

The Woodman case had attracted enormous publicity for several years and Pat Dixon had a hard sell. But in the end he convinced District Attorney Ira Reiner's top deputies to let him offer Stewart a chance to live.

"I wasn't privy to the negotiations," said Holder. "But I'm sure Dixon says, 'Here's what we'll give him: life without parole. In return, Stewart testifies at our trial and also at the Federal trial.'"

And if Stewart balked at testifying against his brother?

"We couldn't compel him to say anything," said Holder. "But we could say, 'Either you testify from now until everything is over, until your brother and the Homicks start sucking wind, or we choose a new jury and we have a death-penalty hearing.' So if Stewart pisses backward on us, he goes right back into the courtroom, we pick a new jury, and we let them decide whether Stewart goes to the little green room or not."

Stewart Woodman signed the agreement and agreed to testify against his brother and the Homicks. In return, he extracted a few concessions: instead of being confined in a state prison, where he would be at the mercy of brutal, nothing-to-lose lifers, he would serve a life sentence, with no chance for parole, in a Federal penitentiary. Thus Stewart joined a distinctive class of felons: inmates given special living conditions and protection from any who might seek to harm them. The Witness Protection Program is not exactly El Caballero Country Club, but it is light-years better than Tehachapi, San Quentin, Soledad, Folsom, or any California prison to which Stewart was otherwise likely to be sent.

On Wednesday, March 21, 1990, Stewart sat down in front of a video camera and spilled his guts to Jack Holder, Rich Crotsley, Tom Dillard, Jerry Daugherty, Pat Dixon, John Zajec, and a dozen others, including Assistant U.S. Attorneys, Nevada prosecutors, and his own lawyers.

It was there and then that Stewart revealed the family's hoariest secret: how he and Neil, like their father and grandfather before them, had skimmed tax-free money from their business. Stewart described the slush-fund accounts, revealed the kickbacks from suppliers such as insurance agent Harold Albaum. Mostly, however, he talked about the impossible man Gerry had been to live and work with. Stewart supplied many details to police and prosecutors about the plot to kill his parents.

But while he took responsibility for hiring the hit men, Stewart's responses did not illuminate every facet of the intricate scheme that led to murder. And what he did reveal was not always the whole truth.

When Mike Dominguez "flipped" on Steve Homick he was almost impossible to shut up. But Stewart was smarter than Dominguez, far more calculating—and much more emotionally needy.

Stewart refused to sacrifice the love of his three children on the altar of truth—he never wanted his kids to know that he was capable of murdering his own mother for mere money.

And, while Gerry Woodman is dead and buried, his shade continues to haunt his son. Stewart cannot admit—perhaps not even to himself—that his father was right, that he and Neil *were* incapable of running the company by themselves. Nor that he, Stewart, who had believed that Vera loved him more than she did her unfaithful husband, had therefore failed the ultimate test and was unfit to succeed his mother's consort.

For these reasons, and perhaps others as well, Stewart in his two-day-long videotaped confession denied that Manchester was ever in financial jeopardy. He insisted that he and Neil could and would have paid off the millions owed Union Bank in three or four years—without altering their lifestyles.

Nor did Stewart ever concede that Vera was murdered for her insurance. Instead, he insisted that Gerry was the real target, and that Vera had to die only because everyone who knew Stewart knew how much he loved his mother—and would surely believe that he could not possibly have killed her.

But, as Holder and Crotsley have pointed out, if Gerry was the primary target of the murder plot, it could not have taken nearly two years to find a time and place to kill him. Gerry walked his dog virtually every night, an easy target for a hit-and-run driver, or a drive-by shooting—and there were hundreds of the latter in Southern California in 1985. Or Gerry might simply have been snatched from the street and killed elsewhere. There were many ways to dispatch him, each far more efficient than waiting for Gerry to drive into an underground garage.

But he was not killed in these other ways. "Vera was always the real target of the murder plot," said Holder. "If she hadn't been covered for half a million, I have a sneaking hunch that somehow Manchester Industries would have burned down from a mysterious fire in, maybe, the spring of 1986."

The U.S. Attorney in Las Vegas took Stewart's confession, plus the considerable evidence unearthed by the FBI/Las Vegas Metro operation, to a Federal grand jury. The Woodmans, Stewart and Neil, and the Homicks—Robert, Steve, and William—as well as Steve's estranged wife, Delores, and his pals Mike Dominguez and Charles Dietz were indicted on charges ranging from possession of narcotics to obstruction of justice, racketeering, and interstate murder-for-hire.

As he had previously agreed, Stewart pleaded guilty to Federal charges of racketeering and interstate murder-for-hire. Dominguez also pleaded guilty, and got twenty-five years to life in Federal prison. Both testified against the other defendants.

The Federal trial, which began in Las Vegas on November 5, 1990, was in many respects a replay of Stewart's trial. In Las Vegas, however, additional witnesses testified against Steve Homick, including attempted-murder victims Craig Maraldo and Cheryl McDowell, FBI informant Art Taylor, Ronald Bryl, plus the FBI's Jerry Daugherty and Metro detective Tom Dillard.

Physical evidence included transcripts from the 450 reels of tape from the FBI/Las Vegas Metro wiretaps.

Holder had intended to alternate weeks in Las Vegas with Crotsley, sharing the job of testifying and working with the "Yom Kippur" witnesses whom he now knew almost as family. Suddenly, however, he was fighting for his life.

"On my first week up there I got a phone message from June, my wife. It said, 'Call your skin doctor,'" said Holder. "I had this little spot on my chest," he continued. "I'm talking not the *head* of a pin but the *tip* of a pin. Tiny as can be.

"June had said, 'You ought to go in and have that looked at.'

For once in my life I listened to her. The doctor said, 'I think this is nothing, but we're going to biopsy it.'

"So I'm up in Las Vegas and I call the doctor and she says, 'I don't want to frighten you, but that thing is a malignant melanoma,'" recalled Holder.

"I don't know what a malignant melanoma is. I thought she was talking about a basal carcinoma, which everybody gets. They burn them off and it's no big deal. So I thought, Okay, I've got a little skin cancer. No wonder. I used to lay out on the beach for hours and just bake."

But melanoma is one of the most deadly cancers of all. It kills many victims before they know there is a problem.

Holder came out of the operation with a scar eight inches long and an inch wide on his chest. Months of follow-up treatment kept him from participating in the Las Vegas RICO trial. So Crotsley took over, and testified about the LAPD's investigation into the Woodman murders.

During this trial, Neil Woodman was afflicted with shingles, a painful, stress-aggravated condition that caused him to grimace frequently. Through court-appointed attorney Ron Dalrymple (Gerald Chaleff's fee did not include a defense on the Federal charges, and Neil was broke), Neil asked Judge Lloyd George to tell the jury about his condition so that they would not draw false assumptions from his facial expressions. Over the objections of prosecutors, Judge George allowed Dalrymple to so inform the jury.

Robert Homick, suffering from a neck condition, wore a cumbersome brace during the trial.

Because of the complexities of this case and the use of many esoteric terms, Judge George, in a rare break with judicial tradition, allowed jurors to submit questions to him about testimony or evidence—in notes passed through a bailiff—during the trial.

About the time the Federal trial ended—with convictions for all defendants, including all three Homick brothers and Neil Woodman—Holder's doctors said he was probably cured. To be certain, however, he has to make monthly follow-up visits to an oncologist for five years.

Confronted both with evidence of his mortality and a lull in the frenetic routine of a homicide investigator, Holder took stock of his life.

"I've got nearly twenty-six years on the job, and now I'm thinking, I don't really need this shit," he said. "I've been driving fifty-one miles—two hours—to work every morning for thirteen years. And every night, two hours back home to Orange County."

Holder had wanted to stay with the LAPD until every "Yom Kippur Murders" defendant was tried and convicted. "I owed it to Vera," he said. "Gerald may have been an asshole, but even he didn't deserve to die that way. And Vera didn't need to be killed— I've never met anybody who ever said anything bad about Vera Woodman."

But before Neil Woodman and Steve and Robert Homick could come to trial in Los Angeles, Holder got a new boss.

"Usually, when you get a new lieutenant in Major Crimes, he's just passing through, getting his ticket punched—and he's a dickhead," said Holder. "You just put up with him and listen to his shit for a while. I developed an attitude a long time ago. They tell me to do something and I say, 'Yessir, I'll be happy to do it for you, sir,' and then I go do whatever I want to do.

"But I was tired, I'd just gone through this cancer," continued Holder. "Then I got this new lieutenant. And he was just too much to put up with. So I said, 'Time for me to go.'"

Holder retired from the LAPD with twenty-seven years service in January 1992.

Neil Woodman and the Homick brothers finally came to trial in September 1992, before Judge Florence-Marie Cooper (no relation to Judge Candace Cooper, who had presided over Stewart and Sonny Majoy's trial).

"There's no doubt in my mind that Richie is capable and could have handled the third trial without me—but it's too much for one man," explained Holder. "And a new guy couldn't get up to speed. You had to live this case to understand it, almost. There were over one hundred and fifty witnesses and tens of thousands of pages of discovery. And by necessity, not everything was written down."

Pat Dixon saw things that way as well. He arranged for Holder to be hired by the District Attorney's office as a consultant. His duties were virtually identical with those he had performed in the

trial of Stewart Woodman and Sonny Majoy: in court he sat with
the prosecutors, for whom he served as a human encyclopedia of
witnesses and evidence. Outside the courtroom, he worked with
witnesses to make their testimony as effective and painless as possible.

Just before testimony in Neil's trial was to begin, Stewart gave
Pat Dixon the note his brother had sent him after the first preliminary hearing. The deputy D.A. saw immediately that it could be
very incriminating to its author, Neil, and offered it as evidence.
But Judge Cooper ruled in favor of the defense motion that the letter was prejudicial to the other defendants—the Homick brothers—and excluded the letter. The jury never saw it.

Rich Crotsley, still with the LAPD, testified as he had in Las
Vegas and in the previous Los Angeles trial. Other prosecution witnesses were identical to those in Stewart's trial. With one exception, their testimony was the same in all essentials. Only Mike
Dominguez, for reasons known best to himself, decided to be difficult.

"We had nine days of Dominguez," explained Holder. "Some
days he wouldn't speak at all, much less testify. Other days he got
on the witness stand and ranted and raved."

Dominguez began baiting Judge Cooper. He bragged of murdering Kelly Danielson, his one-time burglary partner, a death that
police knew was a boating accident. Facing two counts of contempt
of court in a Federal case—each of which could cost him seventeen
years of prison—Dominguez scoffed at Cooper's threats to hold
him in contempt and jail him for five days.

Instead, Dominguez sat mute at the trial while prosecutors,
over continuing defense objections, asked him questions, then read
aloud his answers to the same queries from previous proceedings.

According to prosecutors, Dominguez's performance was an
attempt to renege on his plea-bargain.

"Dominguez is as dumb as dirt," said Holder. "He pleaded
guilty and got twenty-five to life. He would have been eligible for
parole in maybe twelve years. Now, for some reason he wants to
withdraw the guilty plea and go to trial. If so, all bets are off, we
start over. The D.A. will file this as 'murder under special circumstances' so he has a chance at the gas chamber. But I don't think

Mike's appeal will ever get him a trial. I think what he's really doing is building a case where the parole board will never let him out."

After Dominguez, the pace of the trial resumed. Stewart Woodman was the last prosecution witness, in January 1993.

Gerald Chaleff, Neil's attorney, told the jury—and the media—that his client was completely innocent, that Stewart was lying about everything that implicated Neil, and doing it to save his own life after he was convicted.

"Stewart decided that he only had one way out, and that was to blame his brother—which he had done all along—and so he made a deal to be spared the death penalty," said Chaleff.

Steve Homick's lawyers introduced a novel theory: with Dominguez's testimony about Kelly Danielson on record, they suggested that Dominguez and Danielson had killed the Woodmans, and that Dominguez had later murdered Danielson to silence him. Homick also called an alibi witness who swore that on the night of September 25, 1985, Steve was in Las Vegas.

After closing arguments that consumed nearly a week—each of the three defendants' attorneys spoke at length, as did Pat Dixon for the prosecution—the case went to the jury on Friday, April 2, 1993. For three days the jury deliberated—and on the fourth day, they sent a note to the judge. It said that they were deadlocked eleven to one for convictions on all counts. The lone holdout, however, insisted that all defendants were *not* guilty on all counts—but refused to discuss his reasons or to say anything beyond "not guilty." This holdout was the foreman, a middle-aged Latino who had volunteered for that task.

Judge Florence-Marie Cooper, after conferring with the presiding judge of the Superior Court, scheduled a hearing on April 6. The juror would be instructed on his duty to deliberate in good faith, questioned about his failure to do so, and, if necessary, replaced by one of the three alternates. During a brief recess in this proceeding, however, the juror, who had yet to utter a word of explanation for his bizarre conduct, left the courthouse and vanished. Judge Cooper issued a bench warrant for his arrest. She then replaced him with an alternate, who had sat through the entire trial, and instructed the panel to begin deliberations again.

Three mornings later, Jack Holder, jogging on an Orange

County beach near his home, saw the missing juror strolling near the water. "I realized that the most important thing was the verdict of the jury, not this missing juror," said Holder. "So I just kept running. I didn't want any contact with a juror whatsoever."

After ten days of deliberation, the jury found Steve Homick guilty of conspiracy to commit murder, two counts of murder, and three of "special circumstances" (lying in wait, murder for financial gain, and multiple murders). Since any "special circumstances" finding allows a judge to impose the death penalty, a penalty hearing was scheduled for May 6. After hearing prosecutors describe in detail Steve Homick's life of crime, including his cruel murder of Raymond Godfrey and his three victims in the Tipton murders, the jury recommended the death penalty.

The jury also found Robert "Jesse" Homick guilty on two counts of murder, but deadlocked eleven to one for conviction on the conspiracy charge and ten to two for special circumstances. Judge Cooper dismissed these charges. After a probation report was prepared for the judge's consideration, she sentenced Robert Homick to life in prison without parole.

"Steve Homick could have taken Gerry and Vera hostage when they got home, got them upstairs to the apartment and killed them both. He could have then ransacked the apartment," said Holder. "If he'd made this look like a burglary that went sideways, West L.A. Homicide would have gone in and said, 'Jeez, we've got a burglary that went sideways,' and they'd have done their sixty-day investigation and that would have been it. Muriel Jackson would have raised hell and they would have said, 'Good theory, lady, but this is a burglary that went sour.' And then the kids, Neil and Stewart, would have made out.

"But instead he makes it look like a Mafia-type thing, and so it goes downtown, and then Richie and me get into it."

Before the curious and unprecedented (in Los Angeles County) departure of their first foreman, the jury had voted eleven to one for Neil's conviction on all charges. With an alternate sitting in the departed juror's place, however, the jury, after seven additional days of deliberations, remained deadlocked, seven to five, for Neil's conviction. When Judge Cooper decided that this jury would never resolve their differences over Neil's guilt, she declared a mistrial.

Maxine Woodman, who had kept her silence during more than seven years of her husband's confinement, told reporters she felt "a little confused" by the jury's failure to bring in a verdict. "We've waited around all these years for a decision," she said, as Gerry Chaleff put his arm around her in comfort. "I truly believed [the jury] was going to come back [and find Neil] totally innocent on everything . . . but I'm relieved that there are people who believe in his innocence."

Pat Dixon, exuding optimism, said that he would recommend a new trial for Neil. "That's a little unsettling," admitted Maxine. "But I'll be there. He'd be there for me and I'm there for him. I believe in him . . . I believe that once a good man, always a good man."

Anthropologists and biologists agree that all species evolve, in part, by protecting the lives of their closest kin. And so, venerating human life, our species reveres its own family above all others. So the peculiar horror of parricide lies not in the deadly force itself, but in the shattering of a taboo more primal even than incest. It is difficult for most people to wrap their minds around the idea that anyone—especially someone they know—could snuff out the life of a parent, the very person who gave *them* life itself.

And so a few people refused to accept that Stewart and Neil are murderers. Among their unwavering supporters are Don Hymanson, a former uncle by marriage; Lynda Beaumont, Jack Covel's last sweetheart; Rabbi Stephen Reuben, formerly of Temple Judea; and his wife, Didi.

Warm, sensitive people, the Reubens' lives revolved around child-rearing and the familial and spiritual needs of their congregation. They sought the good in people. Both were convinced that neither Neil nor Stewart was guilty.

"My number-one reason is my reading of human beings, my intuition, my relationship with the Woodmans," said Rabbi Reuben. "Given my conversations with them, seeing them with their families and how important family was to them, it's beyond my ability to imagine Neil or Stewart arranging to have his parents murdered.

"And, their fight was with their father," continued Reuben. "Whatever the arguments were, no matter how horrible, it was with the father. So they're going to arrange to have their mother blown away? For the insurance? With the kind of money they had, the kind of money their business could get with a loan in a minute? They're going to arrange to have their parents killed for half a million dollars? To me it's a joke."

Reuben, drawing on his pastoral experience, also pooh-poohed rage as a motive. "I *can* imagine one person being so outraged that they'd kill a parent," he said. "I *can* imagine somebody believing he's got to kill his parents for whatever reason. But *two* brothers, both of whom calmly and dispassionately, over a period of years, planned the murder of their parents—that stretches my ability to imagine."

The rabbi also felt that even if the brothers had plotted to murder their parents, they would not have killed them on that particular day because it was not only Yom Kippur, but also the birthday of Stewart's only daughter, Jaycy.

"So then Stewart decides, 'Not only am I going to kill my parents, but I'll scar my daughter emotionally for life, because every birthday she'll remember that her grandparents were killed?'" said Reuben. "That I cannot believe."

The rabbi also felt that the brothers, who profess fierce Jewish identities and were regular synagogue-goers, could never kill anyone on the holiest day of the Jewish calendar.

Reuben's final reason for believing in the brothers' innocence was that their quarrel with Gerry was so widely known that they, of all people, dared not kill him. "This was the most public, vituperative fight on the face of the earth," said Reuben. "Everybody knew that the Woodman sons and their father were at each other's throats. So who are the police going to assume is behind it if all of a sudden these people get bumped off? Neil and Stewart. It's insane. Are they so stupid that they would think no one will suspect them?

"The only other possibility is that they're sociopaths, out of touch with reality," said Reuben. "But I've talked to them for hundreds of hours. I don't buy them being out of touch with reality that much, I don't buy them being whatever it would take to kill their parents."

Despite his conviction, his subsequent confession to police and Federal authorities, and his guilty plea to RICO charges, Stewart continues to maintain his innocence to the Reubens.

With others he is merely circumspect, saying only that he must live up to his bargain with prosecutors or face the gas chamber, and refusing to discuss his role in the murders.

"The Reubens would think I'm innocent no matter what I told them," said Stewart, neatly sidestepping the question.

And, true enough, to the Reubens, Stewart *is* an innocent man. "There wasn't one piece of hard evidence against them in the entire trial," said Didi Reuben. "Stewart was convicted solely on circumstantial evidence. So until I see some hard proof, I won't believe it.

"I know he confessed," said Didi. "But that doesn't mean anything. If you knew the conditions under which he confessed, then you'd understand the confession.

"Everybody reacts to things differently," she continued. "There are some macho men and women who walk around and under no circumstances would they ever do what Stewart did. Stewart is an interesting kind of guy. He's a scared rabbit. Stewart's like a baby. He's very immature. He's a complainer, always kvetching. And Neil is a macho man. No matter what, he never waivers. Neil is always, 'I'm fine, everything is great, don't worry.' "

Didi says that Stewart told her that prosecutors approached *him* after his conviction, and offered him a deal.

In fact, it was the other way around. By all accounts except his own statements to the Reubens, Stewart sought the deal.

"Stewart said he was petrified when they told him he was going to get the death penalty, which of course was not true, but he believed them," Didi continued. "He was freaked. He was beyond rational. Then they came to him in that vulnerable state and said, 'You're dead, buddy, and you'll never see your kids again. You want to do something, you sign this thing and point to your brother and you confess and you won't get the death penalty. You'll go to the cushy place, you'll see your kids grow up. Obviously Neil's going to get convicted, if you got convicted, but he won't get the death penalty.' "

Actually, prosecutors made no promises about Neil's sentencing. But this is not what Stewart wants his last friends to think.

Neil's wife, Maxine, was left almost penniless by her husband's legal expenses. The family had almost no savings. After their house was sold to satisfy Union Bank's lien, she and her two children moved into her parents' home.

"Maxine has been an incredible rock of support and love," said Didi Reuben. "Maxine and Neil had a wonderful, loving relationship, and Maxine has stuck by him from day one.

"They had to sell everything," she explained. "Maxine was the kind of person who could ask Raffles, the most expensive boutique on earth, to bring in racks of clothing that she could buy in her home—and [after Neil's arrest] they went downtown to sell her jewelry and everything she ever owned," added Didi.

Maxine took a job selling designer dresses in one of the exorbitant boutiques she had once patronized. To make ends meet, she also worked part-time at El Caballero as a waitress.

"I couldn't believe that she had the strength and willpower to do something like this, to really lower herself," said Didi. "Maxine used to go to the manicurist every week. She had long, gorgeous nails. She had to cut those nails off—you can't serve people like that. And there she is in a *fercokte schmatte* [messy rag] walking around with a tray, serving her peers. Last week they were her peers. Now they're all looking down their noses at her because she's the wife of a murderer. What Maxine went through and put up with—and still held her head up with dignity—is unbelievable. It's inspirational.

"I was called in a lot at the beginning to talk to her kids, who went to school and heard, 'Your father's a murderer.' It was humiliating and scary, their whole lives were overturned, and the father they looked up to and loved is suddenly in jail.

"Neil has always been positive and up," added Didi. "Every time I've talked to him he's been worried about Maxine, his kids. Never about himself. He manages. He gets along with people. People like him. He does whatever he needs to do. He's said that he couldn't believe that Stewart would testify against him, and that under no circumstances would *he* ever do that; no matter what, he would never turn on his brother."

After Stewart's arrest in March 1986, Melody and her children were without the river of cash Stewart had brought home for so many years. When their $1.2 million Hidden Hills home was sold,

Melody realized almost nothing, because Union Bank held a second mortgage securing Manchester's debt.

According to Stewart, Melody was far from broke: she had, by his accounting, about $350,000 in cash, some stock options, plus costly fur coats and jewelry for which Stewart had paid upward of $750,000.

Stewart had many wealthy friends. He claims that one, whom he will not name, made Melody's $10,000 monthly mortgage payments for six months. Others, said Stewart, put her on their respective company payrolls, in some cases for over a year, or gave her the use of credit cards.

But Stewart does not mention that Melody was forced to sell almost everything to meet the demands of creditors. She took bankruptcy in 1987, long before Stewart's trial began. Following Stewart's conviction in 1990, Melody filed for divorce. Melody was so broke that she could not even afford a lawyer when Stewart began hassling her about getting telephone visiting rights with their children. She represented herself in court.

By this time she was living with Jerry Lesser. "Jerry was our jeweler before I got arrested," said Stewart. "He never had a chance. Melody came to see me in the county jail with Jay Jaffe and said, 'I'm going to go work for Jerry.'

"I said, 'Why would you work there? It's thirty miles away and you don't need it right now.'"

She said, "I'm going to, no matter what you say.'

"So I knew then. I told Jay, 'Two months, his marriage will be broken up and she'll be living with him.' I was wrong. It was four months," said Stewart.

After Melody and Lesser broke up, Lesser reestablished his relationship with Stewart. "The quirky part of the whole thing is that Jerry and I remained very good friends. And he's helped my kids out—he's been a gentleman," said Stewart.

About two weeks before Stewart was scheduled to testify in his own trial, Jaffe, after discussions with co-counsel David Wesley and Melody, decided not to have Stewart testify—unless he insisted. Stewart understood Jaffe's reasoning and did not challenge his decision.

But speaking to the Reubens, Stewart remembered the events

surrounding this decision quite differently. "I was scheduled to take the stand, to explain in detail what happened with the three notes from Neil," he said. "I'm ready to testify and Jaffe says, 'I've discussed it with Melody and you're not taking the stand.'

"I've not been allowed to say one word through this whole trial. Jerry [Lesser] later told me Melody came home on a Sunday night and she had been with Jaffe, who he was jealous of, and she says, 'I've talked Jay into not putting Stewart on the stand. I hope the son of a bitch never gets out.'"

After Lesser broke up with Melody, he told Stewart that she had enjoyed an amorous relationship with Jaffe. Stewart began telling anyone who would listen, including the judge who presided over his trial in Los Angeles—and the Reubens—that he believed that Melody seduced Jaffe *during* his trial to prevent Stewart from testifying.

Stewart has asserted that because of Melody's lifestyle, if he had been free he would have divorced her and used her behavior to convince a custody court that *he* should get the children.

And this, asserted Stewart, was why Melody wanted to make sure he was convicted of murder.

To support these assertions, Stewart claimed that he had pages from Melody's diary documenting her romance with Jaffe. "It's got names of restaurants and times," he said. "It's got a hotel [name] and a time, there's a heart around one of the times. They met twice a week almost since my arrest, late at night, places like Giaconno's and The Bistro. Those aren't restaurants where you discuss cases. At a dance club, TGI Friday's, the notations said, 'Danced all night.'"

Stewart claimed that his children kept him informed about Melody's affairs, including a purported tryst with Jaffe in the front seat of a moving limo while his daughter, Jaycy, and her young girl-friends were in the passenger compartment.

Melody vehemently denies she ever had an affair with Jaffe. "That's absolutely false," she said. "I can't believe he is still saying that. I wish there was a way I could sue him. Jay and I believed in Stewart's innocence for so long. We worked very closely together, and Jay was so hung up on this case, so emotionally involved in this case.

"He's a family man, very happily married to his high school

sweetheart," she adds. "Jay and I shook hands—that was about it. Not even a kiss on the cheek. I swear, it just aggravates me no end that he would still be saying that."

Melody acknowledged that she had an intimate relationship with Lesser, but denies that she had other affairs.

"That's nuts," said Melody. "I had one boyfriend and he was with me for two and a half years—that was it. I don't know why Stewart wants to trash me. I don't deserve that—I'm a victim. So are my children. I'm a survivor."

Jaffe was shocked and hurt by Stewart's assertions of an affair with Melody, which he ardently denies. He was also angry that Stewart has alleged he didn't do everything in his power to win Stewart's acquittal.

"It's a sore subject—the mere fact that there's a rumor and I have to say anything about it gives it some credence," he said. "It's like trying to unring a bell. Melody and I were very, very dear friends. Obviously, she was my most important witness. I'd call her, she'd call me—but only because we knocked ideas off each other's heads.

"I'm sure Stewart knows it wasn't true. But he thought that starting that rumor might somehow help him," added Jaffe. "So he turned against me—as he turned against everybody he was ever close to. That's his *modus operandi*.

"The shame of it is, if he had not turned against me I still would have been a very good friend to him," said Jaffe.

In support of his assertions about Melody's motives for ensuring his conviction, Stewart told the Reubens and others that she was a poor mother. "My daughter Jaycy walked out of the house," said Stewart.

"She couldn't stand it anymore—the guys coming into the house, the drinking."

Stewart also said that Melody threatened to commit suicide if her children didn't stop talking to him.

"My youngest boy was hysterical," said Stewart. "She kicked my oldest boy out of the house. She said, 'Go talk to your father at the jail. If he doesn't sign everything over to me in the divorce you're not living here anymore.'"

While acknowledging that Jaycy at age fifteen did move in with a boyfriend before returning to Melody's household, Melody angrily denies that these other incidents happened.

"Stewart is very bitter. During the divorce he threatened to take me through the courts if he didn't get to see the kids. And he's still hassling me. He's got attorneys calling to threaten me. I don't have the money, or the time, to go through all that again," she said.

The older Woodman children are now adults. Each could live on their own if they so chose. Yet they continue to live with Melody while they attend school. Jaycy, eighteen, has been to see Stewart twice since he became a Federally protected witness, and Ian, twenty, has visited three times.

"I have no objection to them visiting their father," said Melody. "And I never really say anything bad about him to my children. That's why I can't believe he keeps trying to trash my character.

"I think it must be all he's got—he has nothing else to do but think up this stuff," added Melody.

The Reubens have been very useful to Stewart in his battles with Melody.

Didi enlisted the help of one attorney friend to help Stewart get visitation rights with his youngest son, Morgan, and another to represent Stewart *pro bono* in his attempt to get Judge Candace Cooper to declare a mistrial and set aside his conviction. The basis for the mistrial is Stewart's allegation about his counsel's misconduct in having an affair with Melody. But so far, no mistrial motion has been filed.

"Stewart says, 'My confession will be null and void once all this stuff about Melody and Jay comes out,' " said Didi.

"Stewart has a wonderful capacity for believing things that he wants to believe are true," said Jay Jaffe.

Epilogue

Hassan Abdullah, Robert Homick's former roommate, still lives in his Corinth Avenue apartment.

Lynda Beaumont lives in the Pasadena area and recently retired from a twenty-year career in real estate.

Jerry Chaleff, who continues to practice criminal law, was elected president of the Los Angeles County Bar Association in 1993.

Amy Hearn, Gerry's out-of-wedlock daughter, recently married.

Muriel and Lou Jackson continue to operate their shoe importing business while living in Bel Air.

Gloria Karns runs a matchmaking service for Jewish singles on Los Angeles's West Side. She remains unmarried.

Sybil and Sid Michelson have retired to Palm Desert.

John O'Grady got half of the $50,000 reward posted by the children and grandchildren of Jack Covel. The Big O died of cancer in 1988.

Rabbi Stephen Reuben is now the spiritual leader of Congregation Kehillath Israel in Pacific Palisades, California. He and his wife, **Didi**, continue to passionately believe in Neil and Stewart's innocence. They claim that anti-Semitism played a significant role in the brothers' convictions and in their treatment while in custody.

Jean Scherrer got half of the $50,000 reward. He is retired and on many an evening may still be found at the Sportsman's Lodge, sharing recollections of his thirty-year police career with his friends and admirers.

Stewart "Professor" Siegel died of colon cancer in 1989.

Steve Strawn is president of Manchester Plastics. The company was purchased from receivers appointed by Union Bank by Steve Sachs, a close friend of Stewart Woodman.

Vicky Wayne lives in Phoenix. She collected the $7,500 Manchester owed her from the company's new owners.

Rick Wilson owns and operates a marketing company and a limousine service in Glendale, Arizona.

Fred Woodard now lives in Carson City, Nevada.

The curse of compulsive gambling that has bedeviled Woodmans since at least Izzy, Gerry's father, has penetrated to the youngest generation. Unlike his forebears, however, **Ian Woodman,** who learned poker at his father Stewart's knee, and who was encouraged to feed coins to Las Vegas slot machines long before he could shave, has sought professional help to deal with his gambling problem.

Maxine Woodman still believes that her husband, Neil, is innocent. She lives with her parents and two children, and works three jobs to make ends meet.

Melody Woodman lives with her mother and her three children, and makes a living selling Cadillacs at a Southern California dealership.

Ronald Bryl pleaded guilty to possession of narcotics and received probation.

Charles Dietz pleaded guilty to obstruction of justice and received a suspended sentence.

Mike Dominguez is serving twenty-five years to life in a Federal prison. He has appealed his guilty pleas in both Nevada and Federal courts.

Delores "Dee" Homick received a suspended sentence on Federal racketeering charges.

Robert "Jesse" Homick is serving a life sentence without parole.

Steve Homick is on death row in Carson City, Nevada. He has appealed his sentence of death by lethal injection in the Tipton and Godfrey murders. Should he succeed, he may still face the gas chamber in California, and should that somehow be overturned on appeal, a life sentence without parole in a Federal prison. According to Las Vegas Metro Detectives Dillard and Leonard, besides his victims in the Tipton, Woodman, and Godfrey murders, Homick may be responsible for three other murders, including a Russian businessman in Las Vegas and a former neighbor in his hometown of Steubenville, Ohio.

William "Moke" Homick is serving Federal time for racketeering and narcotics offenses.

Neil Woodman remains in the Los Angeles County Jail awaiting a second trial for two counts of murder.

Stewart Woodman, serving life without parole in a Federal penitentiary, continues to hope that he will somehow magically win his freedom. Prison doctors, however, diagnosed a sheath of muscle growing around his heart—an irreversible and inevitably fatal condition known as "hardening of the heart." Suffering from diabetes, he has lost most of his vision.

Rich Crotsley expects to join Jack Holder's investigations agency after he retires from the LAPD in 1993 or 1994.

Jerry Daugherty is head of training for all local police officers and FBI agents in Nevada.

Tom Dillard and **Bob Leonard** remain partners in Las Vegas Metro. Thanks to the lessons learned from the Homick investigation, Metro now has its own state-of-the-art wiretap equipment, and Dillard and Leonard recently completed two similar criminal operations. Dillard and Leonard have also remained close friends with Jerry Daugherty and Jack Holder.

Jack Holder segued into a new career as a private investigator in Orange County, California.

The **fourteen-inch bolt cutters** police recovered from **Robert Homick's** apartment, used only to cut two chains at Brentwood Place, and the severed chain-link pairs recovered by **Holder** and **Crotsley** from the ivy surrounding the building are on display at LAPD's Police Academy. Instructors use these items to show how the striations on the cutters match the marks on the chains—a classic example of forensic evidence used to help convict a killer.

Acknowledgments

Researching and writing this book would have been impossible without the help of many people. We gratefully acknowledge the invaluable support and many insights provided by Los Angeles Police Department Detectives Jack Holder (retired) and Richard Crotsley. Deputy Los Angeles County District Attorney Patrick Dixon displayed great patience and good humor in helping us to understand some of the myriad nuances of California criminal law as they unfolded in this case. Deputy D.A. John Zajec was obliging and considerate in advising us about the scheduling of witnesses and other trial events.

Detectives Tom Dillard and Bob Leonard of the Las Vegas Metropolitan Police Department generously shared their time and expertise in explaining events in Las Vegas, as did Special Agent Jerry Daugherty of the FBI.

Agent Michael Hamilburg, one of our earliest and most fervent supporters, offered encouragement and direction in fine-tuning a proposal.

Editor Craig Nelson nursed the project through years of research with patience and good-humored insight, and became its staunchest advocate at HarperCollins. Editor Lauren Marino managed the preproduction process, and copyeditor Pamela LaBarbiera saved us from innumerable crimes against the language.

Victoria Branch cheerfully line-edited first-draft copy and offered countless cogent suggestions on style and usage.

Julie Wheelock rendered invaluable assistance in organizing research material.

We are indebted to many individual employees of the Los Angeles Country District Attorney's Office, the Los Angeles Police Department, the Superior Court of the County of Los Angeles, the Los Angeles County Records Repository, and the Los Angeles County Law Library. Their courtesy greatly facilitated our search for information.

Thanks also to Mead Data Central, whose on-line database service, Nexis, proved invaluable in our search for published accounts.

Some who shared their insights and recollections with us, and some about whom we felt obliged to write, are best served by not making their real names public.

Lynda Beaumont, Anne Beaumont, "Michael," Susan Rosen, Amy Hearn, Malcolm Funderburke, Richard Nuckles, Vicky Wayne, and Gary Henry are real people, but we have changed their names in this account.